UTOPIAN
COMMUNITIES
IN AMERICA
1680–1880

UTOPIAN COMMUNITIES IN AMERICA
1680–1880

Formerly titled: *Heavens on Earth*

MARK
HOLLOWAY

Second Edition

DOVER PUBLICATIONS, INC.
Mineola, New York

Bibliographical Note

This Dover edition, first published in 1966, is a revised edition of the work
first published by Turnstile Press, Ltd., in 1951 under the title and subtitle
Heavens on Earth: Utopian Communities in America, 1680–1880.

International Standard Book Number
ISBN-13: 978-0-486-21593-8
ISBN-10: 0-486-21593-8

Printed in Canada
21593821   2024
www.doverpublications.com

This revised edition
is dedicated
with much affection
to
ALYSE GREGORY

PREFACE TO THE DOVER EDITION

This book was first published early in 1951, having been commissioned by its publishers. The material to hand in England was mostly secondary, and Professor Arthur E. Bestor's *Backwoods Utopias*, the most authoritative general work on American communities in the period ending about 1830, did not reach me until my own book had gone to press. As might have been expected, this scholarly work revealed some errors of fact in my own book. Although the latter was not intended to be a work of scholarship, I do not like inaccuracy if it can be avoided, and I am therefore grateful for the opportunity afforded by this new edition of correcting parts of the text. I am indebted to Professor Alice Felt Tyler for pointing out several mistakes; and to Professor Bestor for his kind reception of *Utopian Communities in America, 1680–1880,* and for his own book, which has enabled me to make extensive revisions in my chapter on New Harmony.

Utopian Communities in America, 1680–1880 was pleasingly received on both sides of the Atlantic, recommended by the Book Society in England and generally regarded as a stylish, entertaining and well-balanced account of the serious endeavours it describes. It is still, I believe, the only book on the subject which attempts to show the American phase of communitarian societies as part of a tradition stretching from Plato and the Essenes to the Kibbutzim, while trying to assign to each community its relative importance within the movement as a whole. From one point of view, I wish it performed these functions more fully. I would like to add a good deal of material relating these societies to the general social, political and economic history of the period and to similar communities contemporary with these in other countries. But I know that this would upset the balance of the book and diffuse the impact made by the communities themselves, thus leading to an entirely different kind of approach.

v

In this book I am concerned above all with the human interest which inevitably belongs to all those individuals who are brave enough to disregard conventional patterns of behaviour and willingly face hardship and criticism for the sake of ideas and ideals which they believe to be right. When, as in the present instance, these beliefs are in conflict with most of the assumptions on which our civilisation rests, the human interest is intensified. Although a more sociological approach might be of equal interest, I do not think it could be grafted onto this book in its present form. It seems best, therefore, not to meddle with this one in that way, and to leave the other project aside as a possibility for the future.

I would like to thank all those correspondents in the United States who responded so generously to my appeal for illustrative material for the original edition, and who so often went to much trouble to supply further information. I am now collecting material for at least one further book on communities, to cover the period from 1880 to the present day in all countries, and I would be grateful for any information, however trivial it may seem, which anyone may care to send. I would particularly like to hear from existing or recently-formed communities.

Finally, I would like to thank the present publishers for generously allowing me the space for a serviceable bibliography, a useful adjunct which was severely restricted in the original edition.

Sussex, England
July, 1965

MARK HOLLOWAY

CONTENTS

vii

LIST OF ILLUSTRATIONS

And the multitude of them that believed were of one heart and one soul: neither said any of them that ought of the things which he possessed was his own; but they had all things common. . . . Neither was there any among them that lacked: for as many as were possessors of lands or houses, sold them, and brought the prices of the things that were sold, and laid them down at the apostles' feet: and distribution was made unto every man according as he had need.

Acts iv. 32–5.

Plodding on their weary march of life, Association rises before them like the *mirage* of the desert. They see in the vague distance magnificent palaces, green fields, golden harvests, sparkling fountains, abundance of rest and romance; in one word HOME—which is also HEAVEN.

John Humphrey Noyes.

L'homme n'est ni ange, ni bête; et le malheur veut que qui veut faire l'ange fait la bête.

Pascal.

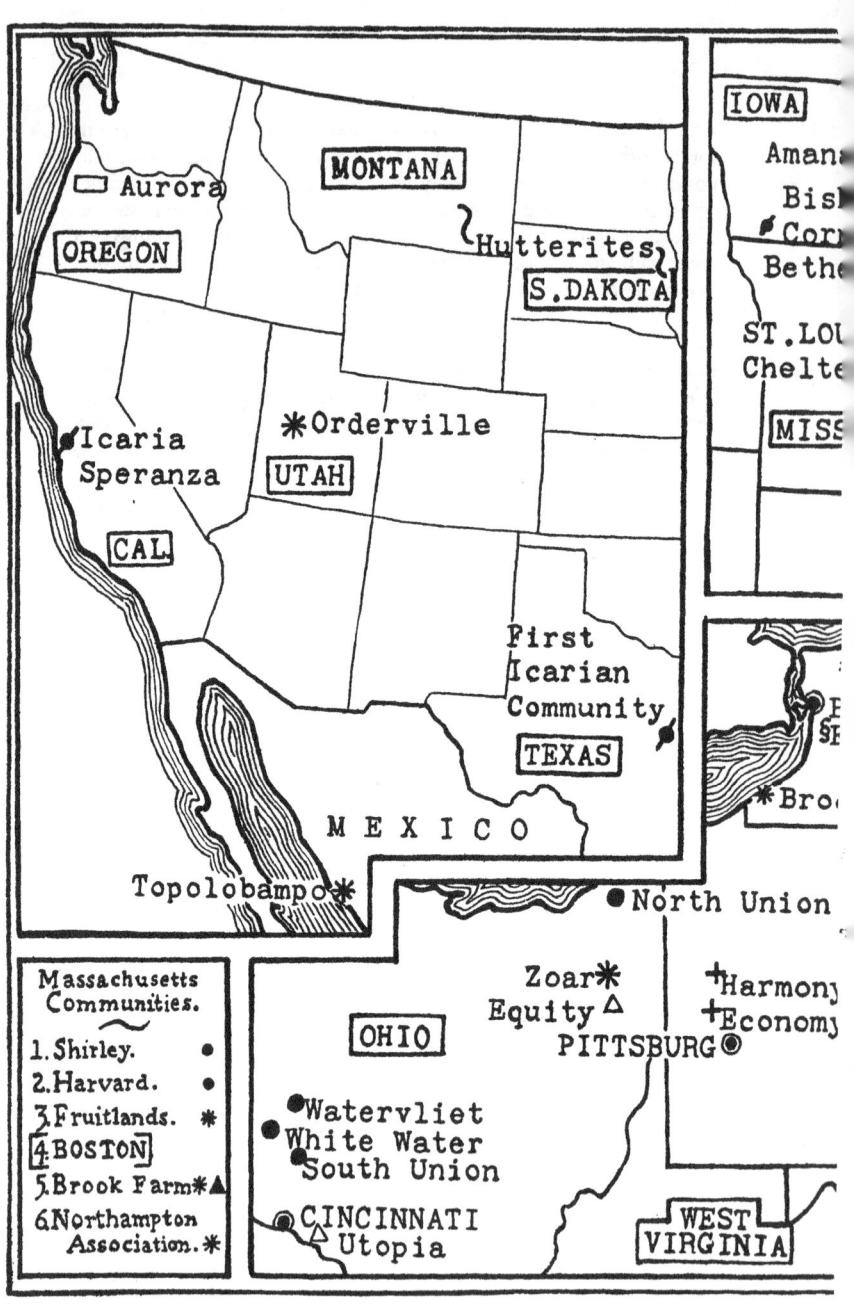

MAP SHOWING LOCATION

(*N.B. Only the three most important*

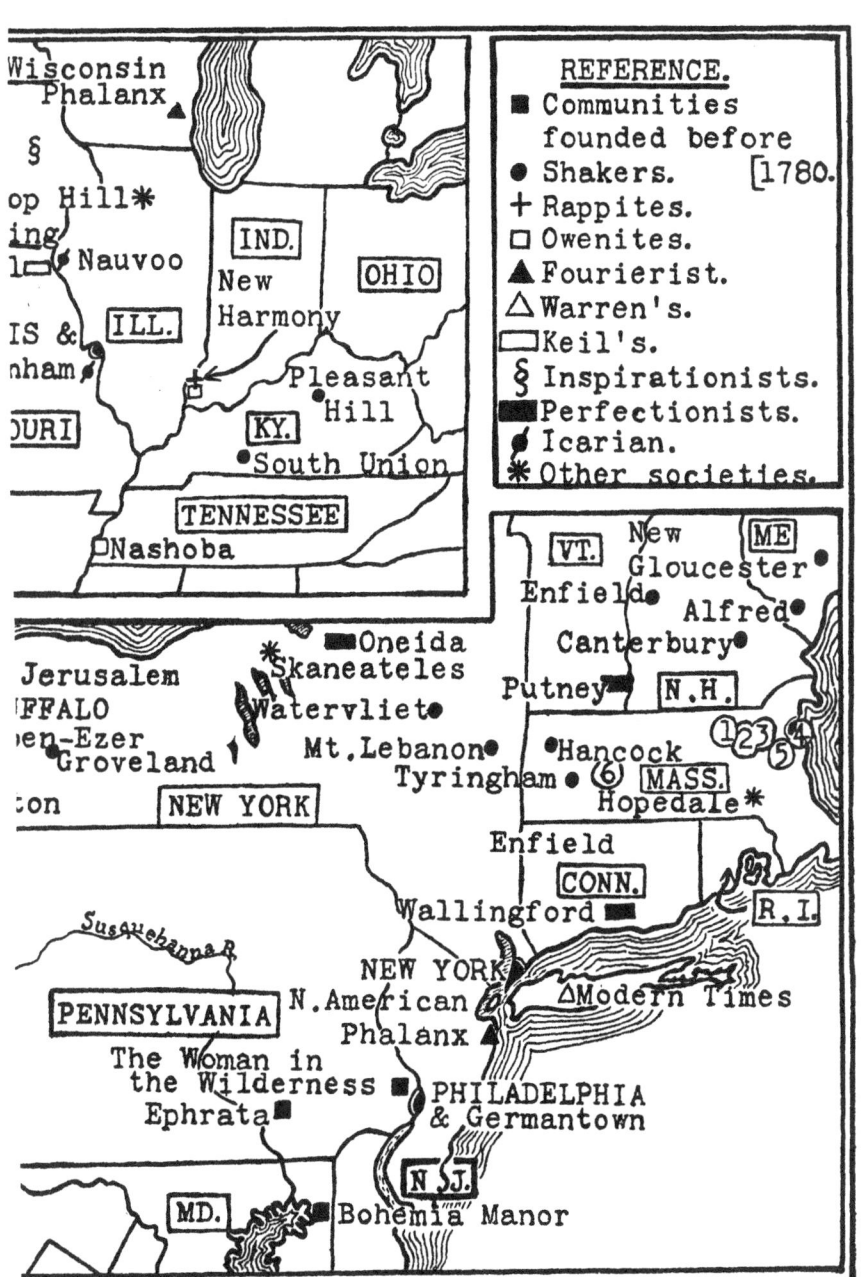

OF COMMUNITIES

Fourierist Phalanxes are shown)

INTRODUCTION

(i)

THERE is little to choose between heavens above and heavens on earth. Both are intended to compensate the weak and oppressed for their present trials; and the one heaven is as elusive as the other. The meek, who are blessed, 'for they shall inherit the earth', will also sit on the right hand of God in heaven above. Thus they may dream of having the best of both worlds, while slaving in the only one we know. And what can heaven above be like, we wonder, if it has room for those who have denied their earthly bodies and for those who have persecuted and slaughtered their fellow men in the name of God?

Utopia, that invention of a Christian saint, is no more attractive. It is true that we shall all share alike in that imaginary country: no one will be master; and the streets if we wish it shall be paved with gold. But the more ideal the picture, the greater the opportunity for boredom. Devoid of humour and those human peccadilloes that make life worth living, Utopia is a correct, systematised, priggish place, usually completely static—a secular heaven, in fact.

Like its ecclesiastical parent, utopian heaven has also been the cause of bitter strife on earth. In 1798 and 1917 the humble and oppressed overthrew the rich and the powerful, and stormed their way towards heaven on earth. They sought Liberty, Equality, and Brotherhood over the dead bodies of their brothers. Escaping from the bondage of King and Czar, they bound themselves anew to Napoleon and (eventually) to Stalin. Their ancestors, seeking a celestial paradise, had made the same mistake. Escaping from Pope and Inquisition, they rushed into the arms of Luther and Zwingli. These perversions of Christ's teaching and of the ideal Utopias have proved highly popular with mankind. Where wholesale

slaughter is involved, in the name of universal love and brotherhood, there is never a lack of volunteers.

Some men, however, have chosen another path. They too have
pursued the mirage of heavenly bliss, but quietly, even surrep-
titiously. For nearly two thousand years men and women of the
Christian heretical sects have attempted to live according to the
precepts of the Sermon on the Mount. Many of them, especially
during the last three centuries, have set up small societies of a
communistic nature, based upon the supposed practice of the
Apostolic Church, as described in Acts iv. Seventeenth-century
Europe was full of such sects. Persecution, however severe, did
nothing to diminish their fervour. And when America had been
colonised, vast numbers of them emigrated in search of religious
liberty.

By the nineteenth century they were firmly established. Heaven
had come down to earth—very much down to earth—in the
Shaker Societies and other communities; and where heaven led,
Utopia followed. Fleeing from the industrial problems of Europe,
utopian socialists tried to solve them by setting up model societies
in America. Thus it came about that the nineteenth century in
that country was the golden age of community experiments.

Over a hundred communities, with a total membership of more
than one hundred thousand men, women, and children, were
tried out in the course of the century. Some features of these
experiments, whether they were sectarian or not, were more
revolutionary than those of the much larger democratic and
working-class movements in Europe, from which they differed
fundamentally in that they attempted to dissociate themselves
completely from established society. Instead of trying to change
society from within, by parliamentary reform or by violent revolution, they tried to set up models of ideal commonwealths, thus
providing examples which (in some cases) they hoped the world
would follow. The ideals they sought, and often succeeded in
achieving, included equality of sex, nationality, and colour; the
abolition of private property; the abolition of property in people,

either by slavery or through the institutions of monogamy and the family; the practice of non-resistance; and the establishment of a reputation for fair-dealing, scrupulous craftsmanship, and respect for their neighbours.

The history of these experiments is one of few successes, many failures, and constantly renewed endeavour. Only three or four communities have lasted longer than a hundred years. Many vanished within a few months of their foundation. But all have contributed something of value, not only to the fund of experience upon which succeeding experiments of the same kind have relied, but also to the history of American society. When they failed, going down before the advance of large-scale industry and 'scientific' socialism, one of the most valuable qualities of revolutionary man suffered an eclipse from which it has not yet emerged. Socialists would be unwise to spurn the idealism with which these utopians were endowed, for although it led them up strange backwaters and provided them with fantastic hallucinations, the heart of socialism lies in it. It is better, perhaps, to be slightly mad with a sound heart, than to be sane without one.

Slightly mad, indeed, some of them were. From the emaciated Kelpius, who searched the heavens night after night for a portent of the Millennium, to Fourier, who thought that the sea would turn into lemonade; from the two Shaker girls who were ordered to whip one another for watching 'the amour of two flies in the window', to Bronson Alcott, who refused to 'enslave' animals by using them on his farm—from first to last, as was inevitable in a movement that tested the validity of almost every belief and almost every convention, there was a large number of cranks and a high proportion of fanatics. Emerson was certainly thinking of some of them when he wrote to Carlyle in 1840: 'We are all a little wild here with numberless projects of social reform. Not a reading man but has a draft of a new community in his waistcoat pocket. . . . One man renounces the use of animal food; and another of coin; and another of domestic hired service; and another of the State. . . .'

Surrounded by such men, it is not surprising that Emerson wrote as he did, for 1840 was to initiate the busiest decade in community history. The well-established Shakers, Rappites, and Zoarites were still flourishing and were to be joined by half a dozen new religious communities—Hopedale, Bethel-Aurora, Bishop Hill, Amana, and Oneida. Brook Farm, almost on Emerson's doorstep; the ephemeral Fruitlands; and the numerous Fourierist Phalanxes that were to spring up like mushrooms from New York to Iowa, were all established in the 'forties. And, finally, at the end of the decade, the Icarians were to begin their long and persevering struggle against bitter odds.

But however many religious, vegetarian, socialist, or anarchist fanatics may have been included in these schemes, they were merely the by-products of some of the most searching social experiments in modern times—experiments which although they will provide a certain amount of incidental amusement, nevertheless deserve serious consideration.

'For the most part', writes Professor Charles Gide, 'these communistic experiments have been laughed at. . . . My attitude to these things is different, however. To me there is something touching and instructive in the spectacle of these colonies, for they embody an indefeasible ideal—a longing that is always being born afresh for a Promised Land, into which perhaps, like Moses, man will never be permitted to enter, but which gives rise to this heroic and never-ending adventure. . . .'

'Heroic' is too solemn an adjective; 'quixotic' would be more appropriate. This quixotic adventure, then, began ages ago in ancient Europe—perhaps even in prehistory.

(ii)

The Promised Land, the Golden Age, Heaven, and Utopia represent myths that are common to all mankind. Those peoples whom we suppose to have lived ideal lives compared with our own, themselves knew legends of better times, when all was ease and bliss. Similarly, each civilisation and each century has its comparative golden ages. What the eighteenth century is to the present, the Renaissance was to the eighteenth century; and if the humanist scholars of the Renaissance looked back to a silver Rome and a golden Greece, the finest achievements of the Greeks themselves were inspired by traditions of an heroic age in which gods and men were sometimes indistinguishable, and all was veiled in legend half-accepted as fact.

If golden ages of this sort, real or mythical, were merely comparative, all knowing warfare, theft, murder, and an intense clash of individual passions; if all were dominated by a Zeus, a king, or a theocracy, there may nevertheless have been a Golden Age common to all mankind, of a more ancient and peaceable nature —the original, perhaps, of all golden ages. It is placed by some archæologists and anthropologists in the Palæolithic Age. In those times, they say, war was unknown, men lived harmoniously with one another, and had achieved a sufficient mastery over their environment to enable them to spend their leisure inventing the decorative arts. The Magdalenians, who painted the galleried caves of Les Eyzies and Lascaux, were the greatest, even if they were the exceptional representatives of Palæolithic Man; and if such remarkable skill—the product of an especially favoured culture—is not found among contemporary primitive peoples, there are nevertheless said to be about thirty peoples in the world to-day who are truly representative of the average men of the Old Stone Age. Most of them are food-gatherers and food-hunters; they neither till the soil nor work metals; and many authorities have testified to the peaceful, anarchic society in which they live. They are almost invariably of an innocent and childlike disposition, naturally hospitable and good-natured, and spontaneously moral in a manner that would put our own ethics to shame. The Punan of Borneo, for instance, own neither property, nor crops, nor boats, nor buildings, nor domesticated animals. They are ignorant of war, murder, and theft. They have no formal authority, no social grades, and no burial rites. Yet they are said to be rich in imagination, and the possessors of a fine sense of pictorial art and craftsmanship.

Here, if anywhere, are the ideal prototypes of those 'noble savages'—though savage they were not—so beloved of Rousseau and his followers. From them and their like, had our eighteenth-century philosophers known of them, there might easily have been derived that concept of the natural man that was to play so important a part in the sociological theories upon which many communities were to be founded. It is also worth noting that so long as the same types of simple economy and strict morality that are displayed by these societies were observed by communities, so long were they successful. In these respects, no more ideal models could be found than these primitive peoples—the last survivors, perhaps, of that possible golden age which has entered into the mythologies of most civilised races.

Among such civilised peoples, the Greeks, if we are to believe Herodotus and Diodorus Siculus, told tales of fantastic far countries in which men lived peaceful and ideal lives. Such myths, however, did not constitute the commonly-accepted golden age of Greece. This the Greeks placed in turbulent times, represented by gods and heroes who were as proficient in the arts of war as they were generous in bearing to mankind the gifts of peace. Thus the Greeks of the fifth century looked back with admiration upon the legendary figure of Lycurgus, the law-giver of Sparta. Whether Lycurgus ever lived, or whether he was invented to explain the conditions that had arisen in Sparta, there can be no doubt that his State was a betrayal of all that ideal communism stands for.

Sparta, in the first place, was based upon the slavery of the Helots. It could only prosper—indeed, it could only exist—at their expense. With the presence of this potential enemy within the walls, let alone the enemies beyond, the State dared not tolerate individual liberty. Deviation from the adopted criteria of physical fitness and mental subservience to the interests of the State was vigorously suppressed. Birth itself was subject to these repressive measures; infanticide of the sickly, like the tests of physical endurance imposed upon the schoolchildren, was part of a deliberate policy in the rearing of military citizens. The common meals, so beloved by More and other utopian writers, and so faithfully adopted by many utopian communities, were another consequence of a State perpetually organised for war, and constantly disciplined against the individual. 'Like bees', writes Plutarch, 'they were to make themselves always integral parts of the whole community, clustering together about their leader, almost beside themselves with enthusiasm and noble ambition, and were to belong wholly to their country.' Such conditions were paralleled in Crete, under the legendary Minos, when the state was organised on a pseudo-communistic basis in the interests of war economy. Yet so powerful has been the legacy of a supposed golden age of Greek communism, that Mably and other eighteenth-century writers upheld it as an ideal towards which all those interested in the establishment of socialism should work.

If these states put into practice a perversion of the true communist state, thereby cutting a track that would be followed many centuries later by the corporate States of the twentieth century, the theoretical propositions of Plato, which have exerted an even more powerful influence, cannot be said to be much more satisfactory. The communism of Plato's *Republic* was applied only to the guardians and their auxiliaries, the soldiers. In order that these guardians should not abuse their powers at the expense of the other citizens, a form of disciplinary communism was proposed. The guardians were to be kept, by those whom they governed, in poverty and asceticism, owning no possessions, receiving the bare necessities of life, and living together like soldiers in camp. This proposal is one of the earliest examples of that type of communism which is instituted in order that its members may escape the entanglements of this world, and in this respect is an interesting precursor of many religious communities.

Here also, in the fifth book of the *Republic*, is the source of that ideal of community of wives, with which we shall meet later. This scheme was proposed in order that greater unity might be achieved, and greater efficiency be promoted. It was thought that if children were bred solely for the preservation of the species and not for individual pleasure, community of property and interest

would follow more easily. It is an idea which recurs in the writings
of the Christian Fathers—notably in St. Thomas Aquinas—and
persists in the nineteenth century in both religious and secular
communities.

The type of society represented by Sparta and outlined by
Plato, could be said to foreshadow National Socialism; whereas
Zeno, the founder of the Stoics, who also wrote a *Republic* (of
which Diogenes Laertius has left us record), was prepared to
abolish the State in order to achieve freedom. The essence of
Stoicism was the natural life, and the natural life was life conducted according to the dictates of reason. Here is the earliest
formulation of that simple creed which tells us that everything
will run smoothly if all men are reasonable. There will be no need
for such contracts as marriage, nor will law-courts and temples be
necessary; money, schools, and academies, and all forms of com-
pulsion are also inimical to the truly reasonable man; all these
institutions are therefore abolished in Zeno's *Republic*. Further-
more, where reason reigns, war and international bickering will
not exist, and men will consider themselves all members of one
community; thus the Stoics referred to themselves as citizens of
the world, thereby showing a breadth of vision that extended far
beyond those previous ideals which had limited themselves to the
boundaries of the city-state. Godwin, who lived two thousand
years after Zeno, had little to add to the theories of the Greek;
and various anarchistic communities were founded upon the basic
principles of both.

Greek influence—that of Plato—was almost entirely responsible for the proposals contained in St. Thomas More's *Utopia*.
Here we find the same communal life, based upon slavery, and
the same regimentation. What is the advantage, we wonder, of six
hours' work a day, when leisure is strictly regulated, when families are limited to so many per city, when the size of families is
restricted, and when no one may meet and discuss the running of
the State (except in the proper assemblies) without the risk of
incurring the death-penalty? Where fashions never change and
there is no privacy; where gold, regarded with hypocritical con-

tempt, is nevertheless used to buy mercenaries for the purposes of war; and where foreign criminals are redeemed for the same purpose, it is difficult to suggest that an ideal society is likely to flourish. There might be a greater chance for it to reveal itself in Tommaso Campanella's *City of the Sun*, for here at least slavery is abolished—and abolished with the greatest of ease, since all the inhabitants of that delightful city were fortunate enough to consider work ennobling. In fact, the more unpleasant the work, the nobler it became to do it—a foreshadowing of one of the Fourieristic principles—and such was the enthusiasm and industry of the people that their hours of work were reduced to four a day. Where schools did not exist, since all knowledge was inscribed on the city walls; where the chief prince and his three subordinates were always in agreement upon everything; where the magistrates were given such delightful names as Chastity, Sobriety, and Virtue; where community of wives caused no strife—in this city we can be sure that we are no longer in the realms of plausibility.

With Fénelon's *Télémaque* we reach the most idyllic and impossible of all Utopias. An ideal climate, perfect inhabitants, and absence of all strife, are the characteristics of La Bétique and Salente. One point—Fénelon's insistence on the importance of a return to the land—is of interest to the student of community life, but loses all relation to actuality when we realise that this ideal countryside knows none of the disasters of drought or flood, always faithfully bearing abundant and ever-sufficient fruit and crops. Fénelon, in fact, outdoes all other utopian writers by carrying perfection as far as it will go. He presents us with a race of beings whom we hardly recognise, since all the charactertistic failings of humanity are absent. He shows us perfection simply by dismissing with a wave of the pen all that stands in the way of achieving it. This easy escape is one that cannot be practised by those who attempt to live in utopian communities on the common earth, in the company of ordinary human beings.

(iii)

More, Campanella, and Fénelon—saint, Dominican friar, and archbishop—have all achieved fame. So have many other creators of imaginary societies, in spite of the fact that most of them place an unwarranted faith in the reasoning capacity of the human race. On the other hand, the early attempts that were made to set up practical working utopias were almost exclusively the efforts of men and women of humble origin, who are unremembered in the pages of history.

The earliest communistic society of which we have any record is that of the Essenes, who flourished in Palestinian Syria some time before the birth of Christ. These men, about 4,000 strong, were scattered in various towns and villages, and did not live in separate communal settlements, yet they kept to a most rigid communism of property, and to a meticulously strict set of religious observances. A league of virtuous celibates, they depended for the increase of their numbers upon the adoption of children and the accession of pious novices. They wore white robes, indulged in prophecy, eschewed oaths, took common meals, held many esoteric beliefs, showed vestiges of sun-worship, had a passion for the world of angels, were extremely frugal, very strict Sabbatarians—they would not even obey the calls of nature on the Sabbath—and lacked those nationalistic and Messianic hopes in which almost all other Hebrews indulged. We know little of the origins of these grave silent brethren; they arise from, and fade back into a mist of legend and surmise; but it is possible that they had connections with the Pythagorean and Orphic religions; and that together with their counterparts in Egypt, the Theraputae, they formed a link between the Indo-Persian religious ideas—which, unlike western ones, included asceticism— and the ideas which were later to develop into Gnosticism.

The interpretation of the socialist element in Christ's teaching, and the degree of communism which may be read into it, vary according to the prejudice of the reader, but we may take it that no practice in any way comparable with that of the Essenes was observed by the Apostolic Church, although there was undoubtedly a comradely display of mutual aid such as might be expected from any evangelical society in its formative stages. This, however, rapidly disappeared from orthodox Christianity, and by the time the Roman Church had set itself against all such inflammatory doctrines as that of the sharing of property, revolutionary Christianity—that of the Sermon on the Mount—was obliged to run underground. It did not emerge in force until the thirteenth century, when the first significant struggle with the Catholic Church took place.

The Cathars or Albigenses of eleventh-century France were steeped in Gnosticism brought back from the Bogomils of Bulgaria during the Crusades. They believed in the separation of Church and State, in the limitation of clerical power, and in the restriction of rites and ceremonial. They were opposed to war and to the taking of oaths. They denounced the worship of saints and relics. They used adult, and not infant baptism; and they did not believe in transubstantiation. Scattered far and wide over Europe by a devastating papal persecution in the thirteenth century, their beliefs took root in far places, and encouraged the formation of similar heresies.

By the twelfth century the Waldenses had established themselves so securely in the valleys of the Cottian Alps, and resisted persecution with such success, that their descendants are to be found there to-day. Living within a communistic economy and fortifying themselves with their own vernacular translations of the Bible, they built up a faith that was virile enough to spare dozens of missionaries who were sent into Germany and Moravia throughout the thirteenth and fourteenth centuries. It is estimated that there were 150,000 Waldenses in Europe by the end of the fifteenth century—men and women living as nearly as possible according to the precepts of the Sermon on the Mount.

A hundred years after the crusade against the Albigenses, John Wyclif was born. The social nature of his Lollard movement was evident in the Peasant Revolt of Wat Tyler, which was inspired largely by the teachings of John Ball, the Lollard priest. It was a dramatic, but ineffectual gesture on the part of the Church to order the disinterment, cremation, and casting into the River Swift of Wyclif's bones in 1428. The bones had done their damage fifty years earlier. Missionaries had been sent into Bohemia, Huss had died at the stake after rousing a national movement, and the Church was hard pressed in the Hussite wars that followed. When both parties had exhausted themselves in this conflict, a compromise was reached by which a Bohemian national Church was permitted under the nominal supervision of Rome. From the middle of the fifteenth century for about a hundred years, the Catholics and Protestants of Bohemia lived peacefully side by side—an example which the Moravian Brethren, who later emigrated to Pennsylvania, were not slow to advertise and copy.

Here, then, were the seeds of the Reformation, planted firmly among the lowest classes and nourished by such influential noblemen—the Counts of Toulouse, John of Gaunt, and the Bohemian aristocracy—as were jealous of the power of the Church. The faith which held them together, and to which certain scholastics like Duns Scotus and William of Ockham had contributed, was based upon a return to the literal teachings of Christ in the New Testament. It began to look as though Christianity, in its socialistic aspects, might triumph over the Roman Church. This possibility seemed even more likely in 1517, when Luther nailed his ninety-five theses on the church door at Wittenburg, for at that time he was as revolutionary as any of the leaders of the heretical sects already in existence. But within ten years his uncompromising dogmatism on the subject of transubstantiation put an end to the possibility of a widespread revolutionary movement with popular backing. Abandoned by Erasmus and Melancthon, and roused to furious denunciation of the peasant revolts of the sixteenth century as being the work of the Devil, Luther chose the support of the aristocracy, and built up the authoritarian state religion of Germany, which became as intolerant in its own way as the Babylonish Church against which he had struggled. Luther's path was followed by Zwingli with such vigour that in Zwingli's own city of Zurich greater penalties were laid upon the truly democratic sects than in most other places. By 1526, for instance, anyone who underwent the Anabaptist ceremony of adult baptism was liable to the penalty of death by drowning.

The Anabaptists were the spearhead of the democratic religious movement, and were ceaselessly persecuted, two thousand being executed before 1530. Yet they grew in strength, and managed to capture the town of Münster, where John of Leyden (who was perhaps the first leader of a Christian sect to institute polygamy) led them for over a year, until the besieged city was betrayed to the enemy. The remnants of the movement fled to Moravia, where they continued their teachings among the surviving Waldenses.

The Anabaptists were persecuted as much for their radicalism as for their religious ideals. Their advocacy of religious reform combined with social amelioration brought against them the united power of bourgeoisie and nobles, irrespective of whether the latter were adherents of Rome or Luther. After Münster, therefore, they abandoned the economic issue, and concentrated upon the development of esoteric religious doctrines. The Lutheran Anabaptists, the Mennonites, and the Schwenkfelders—all of whom later established colonies in Pennsylvania —began to call themselves Baptists, in order not to be identified with their violently revolutionary associates. Such sects as these, together with many others connected with them in central Europe and the Netherlands, composed the left wing of the Reformation; and those that emigrated to America, where some of them formed communities, were to play an important part in the founding of American democracy.

At the time of their departure, government by consent, either in religion or politics, had scarcely been attempted. There was no State in which the Church was disestablished; and freedom of conscience was tolerated only theoretically, even in Holland. Yet these ideals were to be realised, to some extent at least, in America. If Paradise was not regained and Utopia was not achieved, some men, in the communities which existed in the New World from the seventeenth to the nineteenth centuries, worked earnestly for nothing else, and founded small social systems that became the envy of their neighbours.

CHAPTER ONE

THE IMMIGRANTS ARRIVE

Think how your fathers left their native land—
Dear German-land! O sacred hearths and homes!—
And, where the wild beast roams
In patience planned
New forest-homes beyond the mighty sea,
There undisturbed and free
To live as brothers of one family.

J. G. Whittier: from the Latin of Francis Daniel Pastorius.

THE democratic sects of Europe were not the first to take advantage of the shelter which America offered to the persecuted. Captain John Smith's expedition to Virginia in 1605, and the landing of the *Mayflower* Pilgrims fifteen years later, are the historic landmarks in early colonisation. Smith at Jamestown, and the Pilgrims at Plymouth, both made temporary experiments with communism, for reasons of expediency; but in neither case did the settlers regard communism as a moral or an economic ideal. When the necessity for it had passed, 'that conceite of Platos and other ancients'—as Bradford called it—was abandoned with evident joy by the Pilgrims. By this time they had worked off their term of bondage to the Merchant Adventurers, and the remaining debt was placed in the hands of those eight leaders known as the Undertakers. The colony, however democratic in theory and intention, could not be expected to jeopardise the solidarity of its particular religious witness. Its ranks were closed against divergence of belief and dogma. The atmosphere was soon as illiberal as that from which the founders had fled.

As early as 1632 this Massachusetts theocracy had become intolerable to at least one true democrat. Roger Williams, hounded out of Massachusetts for his outspoken criticism, founded Providence, Rhode Island, in 1635. Here he was joined by Anne

Hutchinson, who had also been expelled by the Boston oligarchy after accusing its ministers of not abiding by the Covenant of Grace. Rhode Island was the first truly democratic colony in America: separation of Church and civil government, and freedom of conscience, were immediately established; and it was the only colony at that time which extended complete religious freedom to Jews, Catholics, and Quakers. Here the democracy and toleration that had been sought through centuries of European persecution, had at last found a foothold.

While the Undertakers in New England were burying democracy, and Roger Williams in Rhode Island was resurrecting it, an earnest young man was preaching Christian communism in Europe. Trained by the Jesuits, and successively a Catholic canon, a Huguenot professor at Montauban, and a pastor at Orange, Geneva, London, Middelburg, Amsterdam, Utrecht, Herford, Bremen, and Altona, Jean de Labadie was one of the most famous dissenting preachers of the seventeenth century. He was also luckier than many of his kind, having noble birth and mental brilliance to qualify him for the protection of one nobleman or noblewoman after another, from Cardinal Richelieu to the scholarly and saintly Anna Maria van Schurman of Utrecht.

De Labadie, in his portraits, has a sharp eye, an immense beak of a nose, and a mouth capable of either suavity or a piercing retort. There is a hint of wit, and at the same time, of melancholy, in the general expression. One would hardly suspect that a fanatical or even an earnest character was represented. Yet de Labadie —short of stature, frail of body, and nervous or even feverish by temperament—appears to have been intensely earnest when calm, and thoroughly fanatical when roused. It is certain that no one lacking fanaticism could have endured the persecution and revilement that followed the Separatist preachers. That a nobleman should have added to the usual Separatist tenets a belief in communism, thus identifying himself with the rabble, presupposes a fire and an earnestness of unusual degree.

De Labadie apparently possessed a magnificent voice, of such magnetic power that those who were drawn by it came in

JEAN DE LABADIE.

crowds that overflowed the churches in which he preached. He is credited with a following of 60,000, but this is almost certainly a generous estimate, for when the Labadist leaders were driven into exile by the Lutheran Rector of Utrecht, only a few score followed them to Herford. Here they were sheltered by Princess Elizabeth of Bohemia, who was a close friend of both Anna van Schurman and Descartes (who praised both these ladies for their wit and intelligence). Popular opinion, however, was too strong for the Princess, and the Labadists were obliged to move again, to Bremen, and then once more to Altona. They were then offered the Castle of Thetinga in West Friesland by the owner, Cornelis van Aerssens, Lord of Sommelsdijk, whose sisters were members of the Labadist community; but before the gift could take effect, de Labadie died, in 1674, at Altona.

Anna van Schurman now took over the leadership of the group —until succeeded, at her death in the following year, by Pierre Yvon—and three or four hundred Labadists moved into the Castle, where they settled down to a happy community life that lasted until about 1732. As the community increased in number, daughter churches were founded at Rotterdam, The Hague, and elsewhere. Thus consolidated, the Labadists began to make plans for colonies in the New World.

Surinam, the only remaining Dutch possession in America, was their first choice, since the governor of the colony was none other than their patron, van Sommelsdijk. Indeed, it seems likely, in view of their later experiences, that it was van Sommelsdijk who persuaded them to go to Surinam, by painting a very rosy picture of the colony he wished to see populated—a picture that bore no relation to the facts discovered by the Labadists who emigrated. They found a 'molten and morbific' climate, and houses infected with snakes and mosquitoes. Finally, in 1688 van Sommelsdijk was murdered by mutinous soldiers, and the Labadists abandoned all further interest in Surinam.

They had meanwhile turned their attention upon New York, to which two of their members, Jasper Danckaerts and Peter Sluyter, were sent in 1679. These prudent men travelled under aliases, since the governor of the state was a Roman Catholic. For the same reason they also restrained themselves from open evangelism. Nevertheless, they managed a conversion or two, for it was in New York that they received Ephraim Herrman into their faith. Herrman, on being informed that they were looking for land in which to establish a settlement, brought them to his father, who had recently been granted a large estate named, after the country of origin of its owner, Bohemia Manor.

Augustine Herrman was a full-blooded old adventurer who had been an agent for the West India Company. He was as ardent a lover of the material delights of life as his son was a lover of self-denial and spiritual exercises. It must have been galling for the old man, with his liveried servants, his fine horses, his hunting, and his cheerful dissipation at table or among women, to see his son go to the other extreme. It seems, however, that he was tolerant enough to receive Danckaerts and Sluyter amiably, and to promise them 3,750 acres of Bohemia Manor as a settlement. The prudent Danckaerts and the crafty Sluyter, with a written agreement in their pockets, then went away, and shortly afterwards embarked for the Netherlands. Meanwhile, old Herrman hoped that his son would realise his folly, and leave the movement. This the son did not do; and before long (in 1683) Dankaerts and Sluyter were back at Bohemia Manor, having brought over from the Netherlands the nucleus of a colony. Augustine Herrman, utterly vexed by his former imprudence, refused to allow the Labadists to set foot on his land; they had to take him to law and engage in prolonged litigation before they were finally able to establish themselves.

Perhaps the old man was merely relieving his feelings with regard to this matter when he told his son that he would never be able to endure the celibate life in the colony, and the separation from his wife. 'It'll drive you mad,' he prophesied. 'Within two years you'll be dead.' Whether the prediction was made lightly or in earnest, it was fulfilled. Suffering frightful remorse at having left his wife, Ephraim rejoined her. He was then tortured by having broken his allegiance to the Labadists. The conflict persisted, became acute, drove him insane, and caused his death within the two years predicted by his father.

With regard to marriage, the partial cause of Ephraim's agony, the Labadists were endogamous, allowing it within, but not outside, the group. It was also a belief with them, and a notable departure from the tenets of the Reformed Church, that as marriage took place only between the regenerate, their children were free from original sin. Sluyter told a visitor gruffly that ordinary marriage was a profanity: 'Hell,' he said, 'is full of *ordinary* marriages.'

The community, which began as a communistic settlement, was rapidly dominated by Sluyter, but for a brief period it showed many characteristics that were to be shared by the more successful of the later sectarian communities. Newcomers were obliged to put all their possessions and funds into the common stock, and when they left were required to surrender them. Their meals began with chanting and ended with silent and spontaneous prayer. Men and women ate apart from one another. Any dish that excited or delighted the palate was forbidden; and anyone who was so foolish as to admit distaste for a certain dish was forced to eat it until his penance was complete. Household economy was so strict and the check on all individuals so detailed that a record was kept of how many slices of bread and butter were consumed by each person at each meal.

Upwards of a hundred men, women, and children lived at the Manor. Absolute equality existed between men and women in all activities, both physical and spiritual. They manufactured linen from large plantations of flax, and had also a considerable acreage given over to corn, hemp, and tobacco. The parsimonious economy and the rigid discipline that regulated their meals were effective in every department of their activity; consequently, they soon became economically and financially successful, although, like most of their successors, they gained this material prosperity at the expense of comfort and individuality, both of which were sternly suppressed.

The severe rules imposed by the wily Sluyter were, however,

not observed by himself. It was noticed, for instance, that although he forbad fires, he always had a good one burning in his own quarters, and a shed full of wood into the bargain. His rigid prohibition of smoking and his acres of tobacco grown for sale made another discrepancy that caused a certain amount of heart-searching among members of the community; and when, finally, Sluyter took up slavery and became one of the most vicious slave-owners in the colony, it became obvious to everyone that Sluyer was, to put it mildly, permitting himself strange liberties. As early as 1698, he had persuaded the Labadists to divide the land under private ownership, and from that moment had given full rein to his own acquisitive talents. He died rich in 1722. Sluyter was one of the first religious racketeers—a crafty brotherhood that was to increase with the growth of America and find its greatest opportunities in the twentieth century. Five years after Sluyter's death, the colony was extinct.

At about the same time, the mother church at Thetinga also came to an end. Its members decided to return to the Reformed Church, in which their leavening influence was to make itself felt for several centuries. Thus the outstanding contribution of de Labadie was achieved in the Netherlands half a century after his death, when his followers succeeded in bringing about a revival in the Established Church. The American experiment might also have been successful but for the duplicity and avarice of Sluyter.

William Penn, who had met de Labadie in 1671 during a visit to the Netherlands and had found his views so sympathetic that he had invited the Labadists to join the Quakers, became proprietor, ten years later, of that large tract of country midway between the New England and Virginian plantations that was named, in honour of his father, Pennsylvania. Penn decided to convert the territory into a large Rhode Island, and, desiring settlers, invited the persecuted sects of northern Europe to emigrate to this new territory. Among those who gladly accepted the offer were the German Quakers, represented by the Frankfort

Land Company; they bought from Penn a tract of land north of the Schuylkill and Delaware rivers; and in 1683 Francis Daniel Pastorius led out the first emigrants—including some Welsh Quakers—and became the founder of Germantown. This remarkable man, who had attended Altdorf, Strasburg, Basel, and Jena Universities, who read and wrote seven languages and was versed in law, theology, science, medicine, agriculture, and history (as well as being the author of melodious German poems), was perhaps the most learned man in the English colonies in the seventeenth century. If his abilities were exceptional, they were closely approached by many other emigrants who followed him, though none, perhaps, combined such learning with such organisational ability and such lack of fanaticism.[1]

The contingent led by Pastorius was soon followed by Mennonite and other groups, all of whose members took up their lives as ordinary settlers, living in families, marrying, and producing children as had been their custom in Europe. Among them, however, was a sect of Pietists that had been founded by Johann Jacob Zimmermann, an ex-Lutheran preacher noted for his detestation and denunciation of all clergymen—a detestation that seems later to have embraced the larger part of humanity, when Zimmermann began to live as a hermit. Like many of his fellow Pietists he had supplemented his theological studies with a generous indulgence in what was then known as astronomy, but was, in fact, nine-tenths astrology. Being an enthusiastic mathematician and a millennialist by conviction, Zimmermann had determined by exact calculation that the world would come to an end in the autumn of 1694. For this reason he was most anxious to gather a group to go to America to await the advent of Christ in the virgin wilderness—for was it not written in Revelations that the true Church, symbolised by a woman, was

[1] It was Pastorius who drew up the first protest in a British colony, against the practice of keeping slaves. Signed by three other colonists, it was sent, in 1688, to the monthly meeting of Friends at Lower Dublin, where it caused so much embarrassment that it was quietly passed on to the quarterly meeting in Philadelphia. The equally embarrassed Philadelphians sent it on to the yearly meeting at Burlington—where it was quietly suppressed.

given 'two wings of a great eagle, that she might fly into the
wilderness, into her place, where she is nourished for a time, and
times, and half a time, from the face of the serpent'?

Closely associated with Zimmermann was a young man of
twenty-one, who was almost as learned as Pastorius. This was
Magister Johannes Kelpius, a graduate of Altdorf University,
master of five languages, and an adept in Rosicrucianism. He
had made a thorough study of Thales, Jacob Boehme, Eck, Tauler,
and Osiander; and was conversant with the works of such early
Christian fathers as Tertullian, Chrysostom, Ambrose, Augustine,
and Cyprian. It was natural, therefore, that when Zimmermann
died at Rotterdam on the very day before the small group was to
sail to America, Kelpius should assume the leadership of the
brethren. Passing through London, they exchanged experiences
with Jane Leade and the Philadelphian sect, and on 13th February
1694 set sail in the *Sarah Mariabonae Spei* on a voyage that was to
prove eventful, even for those days.

A first storm knocked a hole in the ship, but miraculously
caused no leak. A second storm, attempting to repair the omis-
sions of the first, drove them on to a sandbank, where the captain
immediately gave up hope and told his passengers: 'Commend
your souls to the Lord, for we shall go down.' Kelpius, however,
'upon a third inward prompting', informed the captain that he
was wrong, and that the Lord had promised deliverance. And so
it turned out, for Kelpius had hardly spoken before powerful
waves 'at the behest of the Creator, whom they obeyed, lifted the
ship and carried it over the bank into a safe depth'. After this
miraculous deliverance, nothing serious—apart from a testing
battle with three French frigates—interfered with their progress
towards the promised land. On June 19th, they dropped anchor
at the head of Chesapeake Bay, at Bohemia Landing, not far from
the site of Bohemia Manor. They then travelled across country
to Newcastle, and up the Delaware to Philadelphia, reaching
Germantown on June 24th.

Being a highly superstitious brotherhood, the group immediately celebrated the rites of St. John's Eve according to ancient

German practice. Building bonfires of shrubs and trees, they raised hallelujas, made ritual incantations, and called upon the heavenly powers to sanctify the site of their new home. The brethren at first lived among the colonists, and soon began to make great strides in a movement of revival, being shocked to discover that there was but one place of worship in the district. Their pious endeavours met with considerable success, and were so much appreciated by the colonists, that when the brethren announced their intention of retiring to the wilderness, they met with vehement and scornful opposition. They were told in straightforward terms that their work lay in the world and not out of it. However, in August they began the building of the Tabernacle on the Ridge above the Wissahickon. This building was of wood, and measured forty feet square, containing a meeting-house, a schoolroom, and forty cells for the forty brethren—forty being a number of great mystical significance. Over the entrance they mounted the Rosy Cross in iron; and on the roof their telescopes patiently awaited the heavenly signs that would herald the approach of Christ and the dawning of the Millennium. Kelpius, who was a hermit by nature, found, to his great delight, a natural cave a few hundred yards away, which was enlarged until it measured sixteen feet by nine, with a height of eight feet. Having furnished it with books and apparatus for physical and chemical experiments, he spent most of his days in it.

The brethren called their community 'The Contented of the God-loving Soul', but it soon became known among the other colonists as *Das Weib in der Wuste—The Woman in the Wilderness*.[1] The brotherhood was wholly communistic in its economy, and seems to have owed the smoothness of its working to a complete and voluntary submission of the individual will. In an order half monastic and half evangelistic, in which each celibate and teetotal member believed that his salvation was intimately connected with self-denial, communism of a kind was more or less implicit. Nevertheless, there was an occasional defection almost from the start, as when the eccentric Köster left to join the Keithian

---

[1] I.e. The Church in the Wilderness; see p. 37, line 31.

Quakers, and when Beidermann took a wife. Such apostasies, of course, destroyed the possibility of those magical benefits which the brethren had expected to accrue from their being forty in number; and as early as 1699 Daniel Falckner—who was later deposed so mysteriously from the bailiffship of Germantown—returned to Germany to try to recruit new members for the community which he himself was to leave on his return.

Whatever the reasons for the early decline of the community, it is most likely that the increasing tardiness of the Millennium was a potent one. To be told by someone whom you accept as your faithful leader, and with whom your entire philosophy and religion are intimately linked, that the world will come to an end on a certain date, and then to pass that date by some months, and then by a year, and another year, until ten have gone by, is an experience likely to cause misgivings in the most steadfast and fanatical of adherents. When, in addition, you scan the heavens every night for signs and portents, when you are thrilled by the sight of a comet or a meteor, and confidently await—day after day and month after month—the descent of the angel with the flaming sword, only to be cheated times without number, then doubt must begin to enter even those heads that are normally closed to all uncertainty. One experience, in particular, will illustrate the type of humiliating frustration to which the unfortunate brethren were subjected by an apparently capricious Deity. On the seventh anniversary of their landing, at the moment when they were about to light their St. John's Eve bonfire, 'a white, obscure, moving body in the air attracted their attention, which, as it approached, assumed the form and mien of an angel. It receded into the shadows of the forest, and appeared again immediately before them as the fairest of the lovely'. They at once fell upon their knees to offer prayers of thanksgiving for this sign, expecting to receive an announcement that the Day of Judgement, so long overdue, was about to dawn. In this expectation, however, they were premature, for even as they prayed—and this was the cruel blow—their angel vanished, without so much as a word of good cheer. As if this experience were an insufficiently bitter draught, the mischievous angel repeated the entire performance three days later. . . .

It is noteworthy that, with the exception of Kelpius, who lived alone in his cave as much as possible, all the defections were made by the most intelligent and scholarly members. When Kelpius and a few others rejected all worldly preoccupations, the majority of the learned brethren began to drift away from the community, for there was a great demand among the colonists for such capable men. Consequently, the nightly vigils were gradually abandoned, the devotional exercises in the Tabernacle became less strict and less frequent, the general discipline was relaxed, and those who were left, if experts in such matters, became absorbed in occult studies and researches, or if less intellectual, abandoned themselves to the luxuries of self-contemplation and mortification. The bitter enmity which developed between Pastorius and Daniel Falckner, over the questions of which was the true representative of the Frankfort Land Company, and which should be Bailiff of Germantown, also harmed the reputation of the community.

The religion of these men was a rich blend of Primitive Christianity, Theosophy, Rosicrucianism, and half pagan superstition. They believed in physical resurrection for everyone who led a virtuous life and adhered to the principles of Theosophy. From the Dark Ages they carried forward the mysteries of the Kabbalah, wore astrological amulets and talismans, practiced phlebotomy with incantations, and used much of the mumbo-jumbo of medieval medicine. Their lives were ordered according to a very simple routine. The usual and necessary drudgery of any poor but self-sufficient community occupied a large part of their days, while their evenings were given over to esoteric studies, and their nights—turn and turn about—were often spent at the telescope. Religious observances were, of course, frequent. Yet in spite of these activities the brethren found time for others. They went out among the German colonists on many evangelical missions and were also zealous educators who exerted a considerable influence on the general cultural advancement of the neighbourhood.[1] Reynier Jansen, at Philadelphia, printed the first volume of music to be published in America—a book of hymns collected by Kelpius, who contributed many of his own composition. In common with all the German Pietists, and unlike the English Dissenters, who regarded it as a diabolical art, the brethren were keen musicians. (Kelpius himself brought the first virginal, and possibly the first organ, to America.) They also made another contribution to early colonial culture by establishing friendly relations with the Indians and compiling a vocabulary of Indian words. This was the result of an attempt to spread the Pietistic faith among a people whom they believed—in common with many other Bible students of those days—were one of the lost tribes of Israel.

Whatever may be thought of this typically ascetic brotherhood, so tiny in comparison with the enormous congregations of the more worldly-minded sects, there is an almost poignant quality in the innocent obstinacy of these superstitious millennialists. When every sign—both worldly and heavenly—was against them, they persisted in the belief that they would never die. Kelpius, indeed, was so bold as to proclaim his immortality even while the seeds of death were implanted in him, and it was not until his 'heavy cold'—the last of a succession—obliged the brethren to carry him into Germantown, utterly exhausted by his labours, and miserably emaciated from fasting, and from tuberculosis—it was not until then that his faith in physical translation was shaken. His doubt, and perhaps his disappointment at the non-fulfilment of the Millennium, produced a kind of ecstatic despair to which he gave expression in a striking poem. Perhaps then, for the first time, this small, slight, nervous man with the paralysed eyelid, felt truly carefree, because utterly beyond all caring:

> Therefore kiss or correct, Come to me or Go
> Give Presents, or take them; bring Joy or bring Wo
> If I can but have thee, thy will may be so. . . .

[1] And, indeed, far beyond it: in 1703 the Rhode Island Sabbatarian Churches sent envoys to the *Woman in the Wilderness* in order to receive religious instruction that might be applied to the congregations on the island.

Within a month, at the age of thirty-five, he was dead. They buried him according to their rites, within a stone's-throw of the Tabernacle, filing out in the twilight and waiting beside the open grave until the sun had sunk low on the horizon. As the last rays were seen, Johannes Seelig—who succeeded Kelpius as head of the community—made a sign, whereupon the coffin was lowered into the grave and at the same instant a snow-white dove was released from a hamper, while the brethren, with uplifted hands, chanted thrice in succcession, 'God grant him a blessed resurrection'.

The departure of their immortal leader in the manner of any mortal was, no doubt, an inescapable testimony that the reality of death, which they had always denied, could no longer be avoided. Seelig himself set the future pattern of the already broken community by resigning his position in favour of a hermit's life; and when Conrad Matthaei (who appears to have been a man of greater realism) took over the position abandoned by Seelig, he found the brethren indulging in almost continuous self-contemplation, being solely concerned with preparing themselves for death. Perhaps they realised, at last, that the world could only be brought to that end so confidently predicted by Zimmermann, by the individual deaths of those who had for so long refused, in spite of all evidence to the contrary, to recognise its existence. A few of the brethren lingered on, nevertheless, until the death of Matthaei in 1748. The community then came to an end which it had virtually reached forty years earlier with the death of Kelpius.

As a result of the Collegiant and Pietistic movements in Germany, small independent Baptist sects began to appear. They were unconnected with the Mennonites or the Anabaptists, but like them, they emigrated to Pennsylvania. About twenty of these families arrived at Germantown in 1719, and three or four years later the first German Baptist Brotherhood was organised by Peter Becker. This consolidation of their faith in America brought over all the small Baptist congregations, together with their founder, Alexander Mack. They became known in the colony as the Dunkers or Dunkards (German *dunken*, to dip, i.e. baptism); and they brought with them their customs of the love-feast, of feet washing, and the kiss of charity.

In 1720 a few men had arrived in America from Germany, intending to join the *Woman in the Wilderness*, but, finding that it was virtually moribund, they stopped at a Dunker settlement, where the most remarkable man among them, Johann Konrad Beissel, was baptised in the Pequea Creek and became assistant to Peter Becker. Beissel, however, was a Seventh Day Baptist, and, being unable to convert Becker's Dunkers to his point of view, moved on, gathering about him a nucleus of followers. Having obtained a great deal of valuable advice from Matthaei, Beissel, in 1735, founded a new settlement on the Cocalico, to which he gave the name of Ephrata.[1]

Like the *Woman in the Wilderness* Ephrata was a celibate settlement, but unlike the earlier community it included women as well as men; it also acquired a large secular congregation, of Dunkers and others. The Brotherhood, like that of the *Woman in the Wilderness*, was forty in number, and constituted the Spiritual Order of the Solitary. Again, like their predecessors, the Ephratans were not bound by any written covenant; and although they required the surrender of all important properties, which might not be withdrawn upon the resignation of a member, they apparently did not extend this practice to include small personal possessions. They observed Saturday as the Sabbath and, pre-ferring the teaching of the Old Testament to that of the New, based many of their customs upon those of the Hebrews, even going so far as to observe the hours in Jewish fashion, by which our six o'clock becomes one o'clock. Their religion also forbade the use of medicines, since the hand of God must not be stayed— a practice which led them, on occasion, to a point of casuistry unrivalled by any Order save that of the Jesuits. When, for instance, they were afflicted by a serious skin disease, which had already lasted long enough to drive them nearly mad, they

[1] Alternative name for Bethlehem (see Mic. v. 2).

decided in solemn conclave that it was not a *bona-fide* disease at all, but was caused by 'a noxious animal which they might innocently destroy'. Whereupon, rising as it were from the conference table, they set about their destruction with such effect that the noxious animals were annihilated in record time.

The community started in a humble way with such accommodation as could be provided easily. A large communal building was then erected, with cells on the ground floor for the brethren, cells above for the Order of Spiritual Virgins, and a large hall for devotional purposes. This original building was soon outgrown, and many more arose, including separate houses for the two Orders, a church, and workshops. In none of these buildings was iron used; even the hinges of the doors were of wood; all the furniture was dowelled, the laths were fixed in slots, there were no metal plates or utensils, and the vessels of the Communion table were made without the *use* of metal tools, even the ironing or smoothing of the altar cloth being accomplished with a 'smoothing-iron' of wood. According to one writer, their mystical principles were also responsible for the fact that one of the stateliest of the buildings had doors that measured only 60 by 20 inches, for 'narrow is the way that leadeth unto life'. Similarly, in the brothers' and sisters' houses the passages were only 20 inches wide, and the cells 6 feet by 7 feet by 9 feet in height. Another explanation suggests that the dimensions and material of the buildings were based upon the Biblical description (1 Kings vi. 7) of Solomon's temple, where 'there was neither hammer, nor axe, nor any tool of iron, heard in the house while it was in building'. Their mysticism, however, which embraced millennial beliefs, did not make the mistake of Zimmermann in giving an actual date to the Millennium.[1] This they were content to envisage as an event that would occur in the vague and distant future. Thus,

[1] In spite of the incident, narrated by Phebe Earle Gibbons, concerning a certain period of intense millennial excitement, during which many of the faithful prepared ascension robes. 'One person whom I heard of', writes Miss Gibbons, 'went to the roof of his house, where, in his robe, he could look for the coming of Christ, and whence he was prepared immediately to ascend.'

although they were ever on the alert, scanning the skies for portents, much heart-sickness was avoided by their prudence in omitting to fix a definite millennial year.

The same austere life predominated at Ephrata as had been observed in the earlier community. Discomfort was regarded as a virtue. Mattresses and pillows in particular were regarded with especial loathing as instruments of the Tempter—in each cell was a plank bed with a lump of wood or stone for pillow. Brothers and sisters alike were dressed in coarse woollen habits like those of the Capuchins, with hood, veil, and apron, so that the sexes were more or less indistinguishable. They wore them, of course, next their skin, in order to suffer the irritation of the rough cloth. The women's hair was cut short, and their faces were made as plain and unattractive as possible. The men were tonsured by Beissel himself, and wore beards from ear to ear in imitation of the ancient Jewish patriarchs. The men took great pride in their beards, grasping one another by them in greeting, and swearing by them as by a binding oath.

They worked all day long except when eating. In the evening from seven to nine they wrote or studied. From nine to midnight they slept, and then rose to spend an hour at their devotions, to which they were summoned by Beissel, who pulled a rope that passed through his house and was linked to two bells, one in the brothers', and one in the sisters' house. (It seems that Beissel, in a capricious mood, would sometimes ring these bells during the hours of rest, when the brothers and sisters would have to tumble out of bed and make their way to the church.) Normally, they went back to sleep again at one in the morning and rose at five for a second morning service before going to work, which lasted until nine o'clock, when they breakfasted.

They lived on a very meagre diet, most meals consisting of gruel with dry bread; consequently, most of them looked appallingly emaciated. During the meals, which began with an appetising reading from the Bible, not a word was spoken. At the end of the meal, a second chapter was read from the Bible, which no doubt made up in spiritual fare what was lacking to the grosser appetite. At the beginning of the actual physical part of these meals there was a touching little ceremony when each brother and sister produced a small linen bag from which was extracted a bowl and spoon, and to which, at the end of the meal, after carefully licking the spoon clean, and polishing the bowl with a piece of bread, these indispensable articles were returned.

As if the hours they kept, the beds upon which they slept, and their scanty diet were not sufficiently galling to the flesh, they also washed one another's feet before taking the sacrament, and harnessed themselves to their own carts like willing horses, or humped heavy loads upon their thin backs like sickly mules. They treated themselves with severity, not only physically, but mentally and morally as well. Apart from the chastening experience by which each individual wrote a weekly paper confessing his sins—a paper that was read aloud by Beissel, and was afterwards discussed—the community as a whole refused the offer, made by Penn, of a further 5,000 acres of land, on the grounds that it would be injurious to their spiritual life to own so much property.

This form of communism was perfect of its kind, but, as we have already pointed out, somewhat limited in scope. If one is willing to abandon all but the last remnants of life itself, if one is united by a strong religious conviction, and if, at the same time, one's leader is not an opportunist of the Sluyter type, one can prosper materially as well as spiritually, since one's material demands are so few. But it is just at this point, when material prosperity is reached, that the Tempter is inclined to raise his ugly head; and the future of any religious community is always determined by its reaction to this crisis. The Ephratans, by 1745, had produced, mainly through the efforts of three brothers called Eckerling, a wonderfully flourishing industry. It was then that a struggle between the spiritual and material aspirations of the community, which had been developing along with the success of these industries, came to a head. The Eckerling brothers had concerned themselves with such mundane affairs as investments, property, and usury. They had even raised the question of

47

marriage, and had tried to suggest to Beissel (who was known as Father Friedsam Gottrecht) that it should be permitted. This was altogether too much. The brethren rose up on the side of Father Friedsam, burned the writings of Onesimus Eckerling, and expelled him and one of his brothers from the community. (The third brother, who could no longer hold up his head in Ephrata, left shortly afterwards.) Thus was solved, in an almost unique choice, the usual dilemma faced by many communities. Most of them, as we shall see, drifted into prosperity, and abandoned communism; but Ephrata abandoned prosperity and let its devilish mills and workshops become idle.

The austerity of their lives, however, in no way precluded an interest, and a high achievement, in cultural matters. In this respect, although living in plain and simple surroundings, without ornamentation or comfort of any sort, they did not make the mistake of some of the later religious communities in forbidding the use of books and music. The community began publishing almost as soon as it was founded, the first production being *Mystyrion Anomias*, a learned disquisition on the Sabbath. They then encouraged both Christopher Sauer (or Sower) and Benjamin Franklin to publish; and under the imprint of one or the other, many books were produced, ranging from hymnals and treatises on religion and theology, through the first Bible in a European language (German) to be published in America, to the enormous folio of the Mennonite Martyrology. Books on mysticism, and one on Plato's fanciful theory of the origin of the sexes, also appeared, while Beissel himself was the author of several works, including the *Godly Chants of Love and Praise* (1730), printed by Franklin, and the *Ninety-nine Mystical Sentences*, which was the first book published at Ephrata. The majority of these books were beautifully produced, the labour of craftsmen and devotees. Sower originally obtained his type from Frankfort, printed on paper watermarked 'Ephrata', and sent his sheets to the community for binding.

The music and singing of the Ephrata Cloister was of a high order in religious works. Many travellers and visitors have

'THE TEMPTATION OF EVE.' *A late eighteenth-century Ephratan wood-cut, with a descriptive hymn. The original was hand-coloured and used as a wall decoration.*

testified to the wonderful sweetness and purity of voice of the choir of Spiritual Virgins; and the collection of hymns and religious music—which has been preserved—forms one of the most remarkable evidences of cultural achievements in seventeenth- and eighteenth-century America. The Ephrata brethren were also renowned in the neighbourhood for their educational work, which drew pupils from a large area surrounding Philadelphia and Baltimore. In such ways, the community exerted a beneficial influence upon the outer world; and, like so many radical sectarian movements, the Ephratans set an example of resistance to authority in other ways. They refused to take part in war, yet cared for the wounded of both sides; and the brethren, some of whom were imprisoned for refusing to pay a tax levied upon bachelors, held out until a compromise was arrived at by which a tax was levied upon the group as a whole.

Like the Kelpius group, the Ephratans included among their number some individuals of outstanding talent. There was, for instance, Jacob Martin, who was said to be an alchemical genius who apparently numbered among his accomplishments the discovery of the philosopher's stone—which, unfortunately, in spite of every testimony to his abilities, he never produced. The reputation of Peter Müller rests upon firmer ground. As Prior of the community, he was not only a man of sound judgement, and an able organiser, but also a notable scholar who, at the request of Congress, translated the Declaration of Independence into seven languages.

Lastly, there was Beissel himself—a man who combined extraordinary physical energy and endurance with a tenacious will and great organisational ability. This son of a dipsomaniac baker is described, like de Labadie and Kelpius, as being of short stature, thin, wiry, and active. There can be no doubt that he was less neurotic than his predecessors, and it seems fairly conclusive from the evidence of Acrelius that he had a streak of the publicist in him. He also had a high opinion of himself, for when Count Zinzendorf, the famous Moravian who had attempted with the aid of Matthaei to unite the German sects of Pennsylvania, came to Ephrata on a visit, Beissel remained in his quarters. On being told that Zinzendorf would like to have a word with him, he announced that it was Zinzendorf's duty to come to him, and not his duty to go to Zinzendorf. The latter, being equally proud, refused to comply with this demand. Consequently, the two men never met.

Beissel, it appears, was so interested in the welfare of the Spiritual Virgins that he spent a considerable amount of time in their convent. This preoccupation of the good Father became so noticeable that Brother Conrad Weiser threatened to condemn him in public if he persisted in revealing such untiring solicitude for the Sisters. Whether this was a case of jealousy on the part of Brother Weiser or whether Weiser had good reason to suspect the motives of Father Friedsam we shall never know. Nor does the charge of whoremongering that was brought against Beissel illuminate the matter, for such charges were always being brought against certain members of any community in which men and women lived together in spiritual companionship. It is certain, however, that Beissel was particularly interested in the female population of Ephrata, and his diligence in seeking out new recruits, and in caring for them when they had joined the community frequently involved him in awkward situations. It even caused an estrangement between him and Christopher Sower. . . .

Maria Christina, Sower's wife, joined the community in 1730. At first, like many of the novices, she lived alone in the 'wilderness', where 'she showed by her example that a manly spirit can dwell in a female creature'. Under the influence of Beissel, however, she abandoned this hermit life—with which she might well have become so bored as to prefer returning to her husband—and was installed as sub-prioress of the convent. It was then that Sower, who had known Beissel since the early days in Germany, and had always respected him as a God-fearing man, began to suspect that the Father was becoming altogether too conceited and dictatorial. Therefore, when a book of hymns, most of which were composed by members of the community, was being set up in print by Sower, his suspicions were confirmed by a certain verse in a hymn composed by Beissel, which, Sower felt, could only be interpreted as meaning that Beissel thought of himself as a second Christ. Sower pointed this out and questioned its propriety, to the brother who was reading the proofs, whereupon that good man asked Sower whether he really believed that there was only one Christ. Sower, in whom all the indignation of a spiritual cuckold had now reached the limits of restraint, was angry enough to write to Beissel pointing out his spiritual pride. Whereupon Beissel, with the satisfaction of a man who already holds the better half of the enemy's possessions, replied in haughty vein, 'Answer not a fool according to his folly, lest thou also be like unto him', and continued, with even greater plainness of purpose: 'This may inform thee that hencforth I will have nothing to do with thy two-sided, double-hearthed, odious and half hypocritical pretensions of Godliness. . . .' Sower countered by distributing various writings against Beissel; and for a space of many years the two men engaged in an acrimonious battle of words. This only ended when Maria Christina, who had become too aged and infirm to bear the severity of the convent life, was induced by her son to return to Sower. From that time onwards, the relationship between Sower and the community was ideal, being sealed by many acts of mutual friendship and regard.

There was also the occasion when the wife of a lay member of the congregation, having visited Beissel so often as to arouse the intense jealousy of her husband, was pursued by that man, who came to Ephrata in a towering rage and attempted to assault Beissel. He was prevented from fulfilling this intention by members of the congregation, who had the good sense to forestall further visits from the irate husband by telling the woman not to come again to Ephrata until she was sent for. Beissel's own reaction to the episode was to retire precipitately into the woods with two sisters and a number of brothers—an action hardly calculated to discountenance the charges of immorality that had been brought against him. He was now regarded as having passed the whoremongering stage, and was accused of being a demon who fed his evil lusts upon rapine, foul seduction, and every lewd practice that the imaginations of the colonists could devise. A plot was made to set fire to the houses of the community, but, the plan being revealed, the action was frustrated. After this final defeat of its justifiably suspicious neighbours, Ephrata flourished in peace.

For three-quarters of a century, in fact, the community was so successful that several branches were established in other parts of America. Early in its history, fresh persecutions in Germany brought new recruits to Ephrata, who were eventually to form a new settlement on the Bermudan River in York County. Another group, which had a modest membership of forty in 1783, was started by an Englishman, Israel Seymour, in South Carolina. By 1786, however, Ephrata had abandoned its communistic principles, and the two regular Orders were rapidly dwindling—although its fame had spread so far that it found a place in Voltaire's *Dictionnaire Philosophique* (Amsterdam, 1789, Vol. IV, p. 81). The chief centre of the faith was then moved to Snow Hill. In 1814, the secular congregation became incorporated as the German Seventh Day Baptists, and the community, which had once contained 300 men and women, had only seventeen members in 1900, most of whom were married. The total number of Ephratans in America in 1920 was reported to be 194. Some of the ancient buildings, with their inherent symbolism of the faith they once housed, remain as a place of pilgrimage for the tourist, and as a monument to what is so far the longest-lived community in American history.

CHAPTER TWO

MOTHER ANN AND THE UNIVERSAL FRIEND

In the Church of Christ and Mother,
Carnal feelings have no place;
Here the simple love each other,
Free from ev'ry thing that's base.
Shaker song.

THE Ephratans, who celebrated the Love-Feast, with its ritual greeting of the holy kiss, were perpetuating a custom at least as old as Christianity, for in the earliest days of the Church, female ascetics, known as the Agapetæ or Virgines Subintroductæ, lived with male ascetics under a vow of celibacy. The custom may even have existed among the Theraputæ, and could have been a logical extension of communistic practices in a manner similar to that proposed by Plato when he suggested that wife and family were the most potent causes of attachment to private property, and should therefore be abolished in favour of a community of wives —the only difference being that the Christians proposed a community of brothers and sisters. Whatever its origin, the institution of spiritual wives was a custom approved by Tertullian and Origen; and it would seem, from that ambiguous allusion to a female travelling companion in the First Epistle to the Corinthians (ix. 5) that St. Paul and Barnabas may have had spiritual wives. Such, at any rate, is the opinion of St. Hilary, who describes the two apostles as being attended by rich women, whom they had converted, and whose duty it was to cook for them and comfort them, as well as to carry the gospel into harems and other places inaccessible to men.

The Agapetæ, beginning, no doubt, with the best intentions, speedily fell into disrepute. The Feasts of Love became orgies in which the pagan spirits of Bacchus and Aphrodite triumphed over the asceticism of the new faith. Even in the days of Paul, there are some sharp comments, in the Epistle to the Corinthians, upon the fornicators who turn the feasts at Corinth into libidinous festivals; and in the second century, despite Tertullian and Origen, Athenagoras finds it necessary to state that if anyone should give the holy kiss a second time, because he finds it pleasing, or if any impure thought should be in the heart while the lips meet, then the kiss is adulterous, and the soul is in peril of damnation. Finally, the custom was rigorously suppressed by the Church; and like so many customs that were suppressed, it found its way into the doctrines of the heretical sects.

Thus Christianity, which in its orthodox and established form had contributed to, and was to approve for several centuries, the domination of women by men, also contained some of the seeds of feminine emancipation. The perfect equality of men and women as servants of God was almost always acknowledged in the heretical sects: women often exerted as much influence in their leadership, as well as in their membership, as men. Anna van Schurman of Utrecht is a case in point; and Mrs. Jane Leade of London, the most notable figure of the Philadelphian group with which the German Pietists were closely connected, is another. The first, and perhaps the most important of all the women of this type in America, was Anne Hutchinson, who died in 1643, by which time the first stirrings of womanhood in the direction of emancipation from feudal bondage was plainly evident both within the Church and out of it. In 1641, for example, a Petition for the Redress of Grievances was presented to the Commons on behalf of the 'Gentlewomen, Tradesmen's London and the Suburbs thereof'—an indication of the desire of women in the rising bourgeois trades and professions to claim some degree of independent recognition.

In a limited sphere, of course, women had already proved

that they were capable of assuming responsible positions with as much success as men, for within the Catholic Church nuns and abbesses had left no doubt of their abilities. But it was only in the heretical and revolutionary sects that women were able to prove their organisational and intellectual capacity to the full. Their active participation in these groups is of particular interest, since the two communal experiments in America that next claim attention were both founded by women—by Ann Lee and Jemima Wilkinson.

Ann Lee, the most notable ornament of the United Society of Believers in Christ's Second Appearing—usually known as the Shakers—was born at Manchester on 29th February 1736. As a child she showed no desire to play, but was serious, thoughtful, and of a religious turn of mind. Soon, to her intense joy, she was favoured with heavenly visions, and became strongly impressed with a sense of the deep depravity of mankind. On reaching marriageable age, she began to express a particular hatred of the impure and indecent act of sexual union 'for mere gratification'. Whether or not this odious sin became known to her before or after her marriage to Mr. Abraham Standerin (known to Shakers as Stanley), we are not told; but if it became known to her afterwards we may assume that the birth of four children, all of whom died in infancy, contributed to her violent distaste for the pleasures of the bed. She had never wanted to marry, and had only been persuaded to do so by the earnest entreaties of her friends; and after her marriage she continued to live at her father's house. There, night and day, she prayed to God to show her some way of deliverance from the bondage of sin. She laboured so greatly, we are told, and mortified herself with such effect, that 'the flesh was consumed on her bones, and bloody sweat pressed through the pores of her skin'.

Meanwhile, when she was twenty-three years of age, her father, who, like her husband, was a blacksmith, joined a small group of people who had broken away from the Quakers, under

the leadership of Jane and James Wardley, to form their own
sect, being somewhat influenced in their religious attitude by the
example of the Camisards, or French Prophets.[1] The members of
the sect to which Mr. Lee brought his wife and children were
subject to those frenzied physical manifestations of religious zeal
that are characteristic of revivalists in general. At their religious
meetings they shook and trembled, whirled like dervishes, danced,
sang, and cried out in strange tongues derived from the spirit
world. These good people were derisively called the Shaking
Quakers, or Shakers.

Ann, with her visions and revelations, her deep sense of sin,
and her unremitting mortifications, enormously enhanced the
reputation of the Shakers among themselves. In the estimation
of the public, however, they were regarded as demented hooligans,
who communicated with spirits and broke the peace of the
Sabbath. For these reasons, they were frequently persecuted by
the mob and imprisoned by the authorities. If these persecutions
served no other purpose, they helped to prove the sanctity of Ann
in the sight of her followers; for it was noted with what remarkable felicity she was preserved from the fury of the mob. On one
occasion, for instance, when she was completely at their mercy,
a handsome, knightly stranger, a nobleman, was impelled by a
revelation to ride up to the very place at which Ann was held
captive, and although he had no idea what he was to do when he
came there, he rescued Ann and dispersed the mob. On another
occasion, while being vigorously stoned, Ann was surrounded by
the presence of God to such effect that she felt joy and comfort
while her unprotected enemies were utterly confused and distressed. These proofs of divine intervention on her behalf were
paltry compared with the judgement that befell a man who
started from Manchester to obtain a licence from the King to
banish the Shakers from the county, for this unfortunate individual never reached London. Being overtaken by the wrath of

[1] A Huguenot sect, the remnants of which escaped to England at the end
of the seventeenth century.

God, he suddenly dropped dead in mid-journey. . . .

It was while Ann Lee lay in Manchester Jail, on the usual conviction of Sabbath-breaking, that her prayers for deliverance from sin were miraculously answered. There, in 1770, after nine years of prayer and preparation, she was granted that astonishing vision of the Fall, in which Christ appeared to her in all his glory and showed her a 'full and clear view of the mystery of iniquity, of the root and foundation of human depravity, *and of the very act of transgression committed by the first man and woman in the garden of Eden'*. After this profoundly disturbing experience, Ann Lee told her adherents that they could not follow Christ while 'living in the works of natural generation'—they were all to become celibates. Whereupon, they hailed her as Mother in Christ and Bride of the Lamb; and she was known thereafter as Mother Ann or Ann the Word.

Her reputation and leadership were now secure; and when Mother Ann, accused of blasphemy, was examined by four scholars of the Established Church, whom she confounded by speaking in seventy-two distinct and separate tongues, it was plain that the Millennium had begun. As if to confirm this belief, Mother Ann received a vision of a large tree, every leaf of which shone with such brightness as made it appear like a burning torch. The tree told her to go to America, where the Church of Christ's Second Appearing would be founded. It was a discerning Providence that gave her this message at a time when one John Hocknell, a man of some wealth, had already joined the sect, for he was able and willing to provide the passage-money for his fellow believers.

In May 1774 Mother Ann, her husband, her brother William, her niece Nancy (also called Ann), her relative, James Whittaker, the Hocknells, father and son—and some few others—boarded the *Mariah* at Liverpool, and began a voyage which, like that of Kelpius, provided further evidence of the sanctity of the little band. They had not long been at sea when the captain, outraged by the method of worship in which the Shakers indulged, threat-

ened to throw them overboard if they should repeat the performance. They, of course, repeated it—on the following Sunday; and
the captain, knowing nothing of the odds against which he had
set himself, recklessly attempted to put his threat into execution.
Almost at once a storm of tremendous violence arose, and the
vessel, starting a plank, began to ship water. All hands were put
to the pumps, but they were unable to stem the fearful tide. The
wretched and despairing captain 'turned as pale as a corpse' and
announced that nothing could save ship, passengers, or crew—
all must perish before morning. Mother Ann, however, saw two
bright angels standing by the mast and told the captain that, on
the contrary, nothing could now prevent them arriving safely in
America; and scarcely had she spoken when a great wave—the
last of its size, perhaps, in the subsiding storm—knocked against
the side of the ship with such a well-directed thwack that the
loose plank was forced back into position, where it was secured
amid great rejoicing. After such a sharp lesson, it is not surprising
to learn that the captain allowed the Shakers to worship as they
pleased for the rest of the voyage.

They landed in New York in August, and while some of the
company went inland to seek agricultural employment, Mother
Ann stayed in the city, earning a living as laundress, and nursing
her husband, who had become seriously ill. (When he became
convalescent, he took to the bottle, and then to another woman,
with whom he eloped. Celibacy, no doubt, had imposed a great
strain upon his constitution.) In 1776, at the beginning of the
American Revolution, Mother Ann rejoined her adherents at
Niskeyuna (afterwards called Watervliet) in New York State.
Here the Shakers began to seek converts, and although at first
they met with little success, a revival in 1780 among the New Light
Baptist settlement nearby at New Lebanon doubled their numbers.

This accession to the Shaker faith brought new persecutions; for
the Shakers, refusing to fight or take sides in the War of Independence, and having so recently arrived from England, were
accused of anti-patriotic activities, and were required to take an
oath of allegiance; but since oath-taking was also against their

principles, ten leading Shakers were imprisoned. It would seem that the faithful must have conducted themselves with propriety, since many people were convinced of their sincerity, and public objections were made to the action of the authorities. This brought in more converts, and when, at the end of the year, Mother Ann and the other leaders had been set at liberty, a great missionary tour through the Eastern States began. Between 1781 and 1783 Mother Ann, accompanied by several elders, faced the bitterest opposition the Shakers had yet endured. However, they made many converts, and they were watched over by a farseeing Providence which, while it allowed them the honour of being whipped, beaten with clubs, stoned, kicked, dragged about by their legs and arms, and sometimes by their hair, did not allow their lives to be taken until they had completed the Lord's work on earth. Having fulfilled this task, Mother Ann died from the effects of her mission, at the age of forty-eight, in 1784. The Shakers were not yet, although they were about to become, a communitarian society.

Like many remarkable people, Ann Lee was not without imitators. One of them, Jemima Wilkinson, also founded a community.

Jemima was the eighth of ten children of Quaker parentage whose mother died, in bearing the last child, when Jemima was about ten years of age. It seems that owing to her attractiveness and precociousness, she was a spoilt child who managed to avoid both work on the parental farm and regular attendance at school. At this stage, unlike Ann Lee, she was frivolous enough to enjoy reading light romances and tales of adventure. When she was about sixteen, however, her religious emotions were awakened by the sermons of George Whitefield, and by the New Light Baptist movement. With the arrival of Ann Lee in 1774, Jemima, who was sixteen years younger than Mother Ann, was carried away by a desire to follow this illustrious example of feminine evangelism. The desire was no sooner born in her than the opportunity occurred of putting her strength to the test.

She shortly developed a fever, in the course of which she apparently fell into a coma, from which she emerged with the conviction that she had died. Her original soul, she declared, had ascended to heaven, and her body was now inhabited by the 'Spirit of Life', which came from God to warn a lost and guilty world to flee from the wrath to come. The doctor who had brought Jemima through her illness did not entirely agree with this explanation. Perhaps owing to a very natural pride in his own skill, he was unwilling that it should be ascribed to a supernatural agency; for he had the temerity to state quite bluntly that there was no evidence of Jemima having died. She, however, knew better. She had died—and risen again; and since this was an event that did not happen to everyone, nor, for that matter, with noticeable frequency, she felt an overwhelming desire to part with the information to whosoever would listen. It was not long before she was holding open-air meetings.

She had the advantage of Ann Lee in physical appearance, being tall and graceful, with lustrous dark hair and penetrating black eyes; and as if to emphasise the distinction between these attractions in a girl of twenty-three or so and those of her more matronly model, she assumed the curious title of the Public Universal Friend. This name was by no means inapposite, for, compared with Mother Ann, or Ann the Word, it conveys a feeling of less earnestness and less emotionalism—qualities indeed, that might even act as a screen to a certain degree of insincerity. . . .

With about twenty followers, the Universal Friend toured Rhode Island and Connecticut on horseback. Consciously or unconsciously, the little procession must have been a gracious sight, with the Friend, clothed in a long flowing robe that covered her habitual masculine attire seated upon a white horse, slightly in advance of the faithful disciples, who followed two by two in silence. There is an element of stage-management here that is æsthetically pleasing, although it contrasts unfavourably, as regards sincerity, with the rough-and-tumble methods that seem to have been usual among the Shakers. This picturesque graciousness was not adopted in vain, for since the Universal

Friend had no intention of wasting words upon those who could ill afford to repay her for the trouble of pronouncing them, she addressed herself, for the most part, to the educated and wealthy members of the countryside.

This selective planting of the gospel seed eventually bore rich fruit. By 1782 the Universal Friend had established three churches in these two states—a success, however, that was quite unimportant compared with the capture and enslavement of a wealthy and influential judge who built on to his mansion an annexe, the proportions and furnishing of which were luxurious enough not to disgrace a lady who had actually exchanged one soul for another in the mansions of heaven itself. Here the Universal Friend installed herself, and by various means—perhaps even by means that women have used who did not bother to insist upon their spirituality—she obtained almost complete control of the household and estate. What reward the good judge had looked for when he built a home for the Friend must surely have been an unearthly one; yet it is a curious coincidence—since husbands in those days exerted complete control over the estates of their wives—that as soon as the Friend had succeeded in separating the judge from the greater part of his worldly goods, the burden of which, to her immense credit, she took upon herself, she at once began to extol the virtues of celibacy. Had the good judge, one wonders, attempted to recoup the loss of his earthly possessions by a proposal of marriage? Or was Miss Wilkinson once again following the lead of Miss Lee? We shall never know.

Having obtained some power and some wealth, the Universal Friend began to adopt a more aggressive policy, calling upon men and women to leave their families and join her church, wherein, she insisted, their first duty lay. Now, the general run of mankind, which has little but home comforts to sustain it against a world that often fails to please, is extremely sensitive on this point. The average New England wife, hearing of the relationship between the judge and Miss Wilkinson, and noting the attractiveness of the latter, would sense an immediate danger in these incitements to the rupture of domestic life, and would not be slow to react to it. In no time at all, therefore, the Universal Friend became an almost sarcastically inappropriate title. 'Home-breaker' was the very mildest epithet with which she was greeted; and when her disciples attempted to stem this tide of abuse with the announcement that Miss Wilkinson was Jesus Christ—a device that, to us, is a somewhat tiresome cliché, but with which they, no doubt, hoped to stun their hearers—it only made matters worse. The Public Universal Friend was obliged to remove herself from the neighbourhood.

She went to Philadelphia. In the city of brotherly love, however, she met with no better reception. She so outraged the Philadelphians that not only the established churches, but also the tolerant Quakers turned against her. At one meeting she was even stoned. The Public Universal Friend was again obliged to remove herself from the neighbourhood.

Back in New England, she fared no better; but in 1788 she obtained a large tract of land near Seneca Lake in New York State, upon which she installed the vanguard of her faith. When they had prepared the ground, she, with the remainder, followed in 1790. Thus, following once again the example of the Shakers, whose first societies had been established a few years earlier, the community of *Jerusalem* was founded. It soon began to prosper. The land was fertile and yielded excellent harvests of wheat. A gristmill, a sawmill, and a school were built; and the numbers of adherents increased, until in 1800 there were about 250; but the prosperity of the community brought with it some unseemly dissensions. Judge Potter, whose patience had been strained for so long, lost it completely over the question of division of property among the Jerusalemites, and brought various lawsuits against the Friend. These he also lost, and then, the poorer by many thousands of dollars, withdrew from the community.

The Friend was now omnipotent, and it was observed that her little foibles were becoming more numerous. She had always shown a liking for personal gifts, and indeed for valuable acquisitions of any sort. She now began to demand them—not, of course, in any spirit of common rapacity, but for a higher purpose, which, if she did not trouble to divulge it, was amply excused, to her way of thinking, by the simple phrase, 'The Friend hath need of these things'. She was surprised when this ingenuous practice began to arouse resentment. She was also surprised when her innocent little punishments were criticised. It was surely unreasonable that a man who had been ordered to wear a black hood for a period of three months, as penance for some venial sin, should be regarded as the victim of injustice; or that another, who for the same type of offence, was obliged to carry a little bell sewn upon the skirt of his coat, should become an object of sympathy. What sort of religious adherents, she wondered, did her followers think they were, if they could not endure a few simple penances?

Secure in the costly house, amid 12,000 acres of land which she had kept for herself twenty miles from the centre of the settlement, the old lady pondered deeply upon these problems, reflecting as they did upon the weaknesses of human nature. Things were not what they had been.

Surrounded with the luxuries she had won by persistent effort and by a talent for exploiting every favourable opportunity, she was nauseated by the complaints and dissatisfactions of the men and women to whom, even if a chastening poverty were their present lot, she had brought the hope of riches in heaven. To make matters worse, she was afflicted with dropsy. Unable to move, and greatly disfigured, she remembered the vanished beauty of her youth, and became embittered. Now, instead of riding in a flowing robe at the head of a troop of disciples, visiting village after village, she was obliged to endure the visits of others —the visits of inquisitive strangers who wished only to stare at her as they might gape at some freak of nature. Life, indeed, was becoming intolerable. So much so, that when Death visited the old lady and removed her, for the last time, from the neighbourhood of men and women who, she felt, had never understood her, she was probably relieved.

She died in 1819, and *Jerusalem* rapidly disintegrated. After the death of Ann Lee, on the contrary, the Shakers were only beginning to take shape as a community.

CHAPTER THREE

SHAKER SOCIETIES

Whoever wants to be the highest
Must first come down to be the lowest;
And then ascend to be the highest
By keeping down to be the lowest.

Shaker song.

DURING the ministry of James Whittaker, who succeeded
Mother Ann, the first house for public worship was built, at
Watervliet, in 1785. Whittaker, who died two years later, was
succeeded by Joseph Meacham, whose gift for organisation
determined the future order of the Church. He it was who established the first eleven Shaker societies on a basis of independent
community of property. He also drew up the laws and principles
upon which they were to be governed by a central Ministry; and
he codified their theology.

Shaker theology is, I believe, unique. The Shakers believed in
the bisexuality of God, manifested in the creation of male and
female 'in our image', and duplicated throughout nature in the
vegetable as well as in the animal kingdom. All the angels and
spirits were imbued with a male and a female element. There
was, for instance, a Christ spirit, first clothed in the flesh of the
man Jesus, son of a carpenter; and, secondly, entering the body
of the girl, Ann Lee, daughter of a blacksmith. Similarly, the
John the Baptist spirit was first made manifest in the earthly
creature of that name, and later entered the body of Jane Wardley,
one of the two founders of the Shaker sect.

The Shakers thus made a great distinction between the Holy
Spirit and its temporary tabernacle of flesh, and for this reason
they looked upon Jesus and Mother Ann as Elder Brother and
Elder Sister in Christianity, whom they could love, but whom,

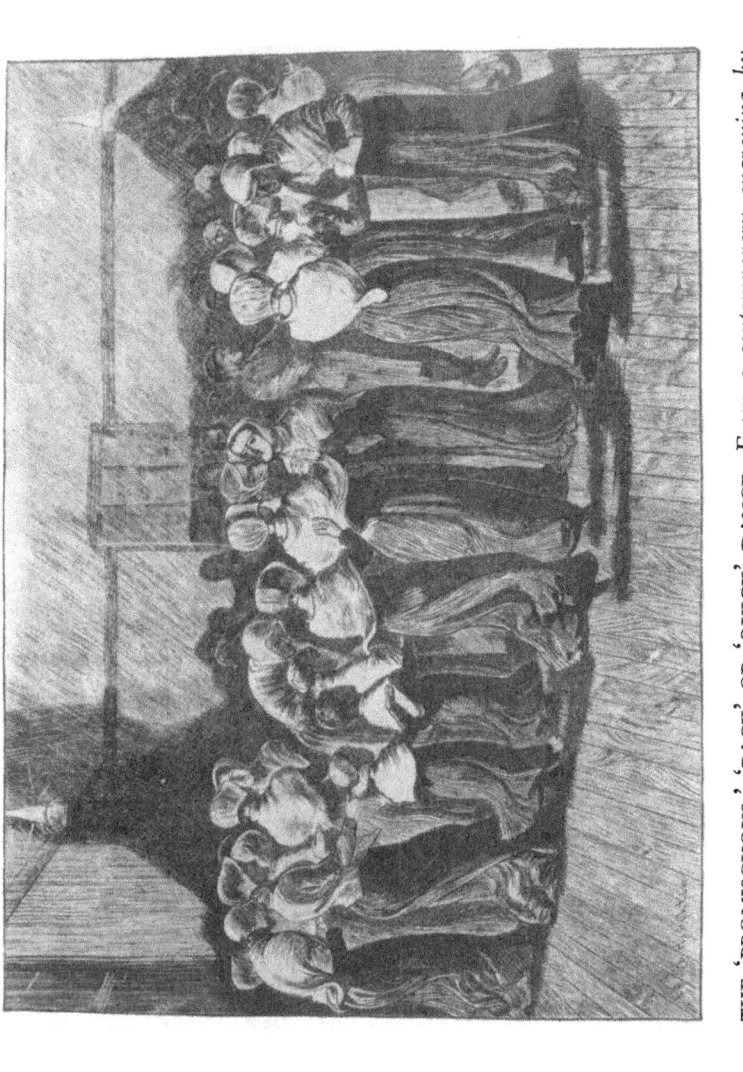

THE 'PROMISCUOUS,' 'BACK' OR 'QUICK' DANCE. *From a contemporary engraving by A. Boyd Houghton. A spontaneous Shaker dance surviving from 1788, before organised and pattern dances were introduced. It was often revived, especially for children.*

SHAKER MEETING HOUSE, NEW LEBANON. *Built early in the nineteenth century and typical of Shaker architecture. The building still stands.*

since they were mortal, they saw no reason to worship. They rejected the doctrine of the Trinity, and held physical resurrection to be 'utterly repugnant to both science, reason, and Scripture'. They acknowledged no death but the death-in-life that was bound to result from a fleshly state of mind—which state they constantly strove to avoid; and since the Day of Judgement had occurred at the foundation of their Church, they considered that they were living in the Resurrection Order, surrounded by, and in communion with, the spirits of the dead. They believed that numerous Shaker Churches had been established in the lower heavens, and they even went so far as to proclaim that 'all spiritual phenomena commonly occurring in "the world" had their inauguration among us'.

They drew much inspiration from the Primitive or Pentecostal Church, of which the five leading principles were common property, celibacy, non-resistance, separate government, and power over physical disease. They claimed that they had put all these principles into practice, with the exception of the last; and even in this they were partially successful, for Mother Ann had worked several miraculous cures, with and without 'the laying on of hands'. Christian communism, they held, could not be maintained without separation from the world, nor without acceptance of the Virgin Life of the Resurrection Order.[1] At the same time, their Church or Inner Order, was supported by, and had as its complement, the world, or Outer Order. Marriage and possession of property, therefore, were not regarded as crimes, but simply as symptoms of a lower order of society than their own.

They found many and various justifications for the celibate life that played so important a part in the practical application of their theology. 'We Shakers', they declared, 'are upstairs, above the rudimental state of men, which is the generative.' Christ's own example was, of course, of paramount importance, and they loved

---

[1] 'For in the resurrection, they neither marry, nor are given in marriage, but are as the angels of God in heaven.' Matt. xxii. 30.

to quote His statement that 'there be eunuchs which have made themselves eunuchs for the kingdom of heaven's sake'. But Christ's example alone might be regarded as a special case—in which event Nature could be invoked; for Nature, they maintained, has no law requiring the reproductive organs to be used 'simply because they exist'. The sacrifice of these organs to a higher use and a nobler purpose is, it would seem, *Nature's general law*. Moreover, if Christ and the general law of Nature were insufficient justifications for celibacy, one could always quote Mr. Malthus, whose appeal for a check to be made upon increased population could be answered in no better way than by an immediate cessation of sexual intercourse.

As to the world, let it solemnise its marriages and 'direct its churches to wink at the worse than brutish lusts exercised behind them, we nevertheless declare the flesh to be an abomination in the sight of God'. And in order to aid the practice of celibacy, the Shakers indulged in deliberate mortification of the flesh—a compensation very necessary to those who renounce the more ordinary pleasures of mankind. In the early days, especially, such mortifications were intense. Writing in 1812, Brown describes how 'imagination was exhausted by inventing, and nature tortured with executing, this arduous work. They often danced with vehemence through the greatest part of the night, and then instead of reposing their wearied bodies upon a bed, they would, by way of further penance, lie down upon the floor on chains, ropes, sticks, in every humiliating posture they could devise! This work continued with such unabated zeal that several . . . laboured into such a degree of mortification as to travail out of the flesh sure enough; the spirit took its departure out of its emaciated and ruined tabernacle—and being thus purged from carnal propensities, was consigned to the dark recesses of the silent tomb!'

Brown also recounts the last case of naked corporal punishment. This took place in 1793, when two young women were caught by an elderess in the act of amusing themselves 'by attending to the amour of two flies in the window'. For thus gratifying their carnal inclinations, they were ordered to strip themselves naked and whip each other. Brown's stories may not always be absolutely accurate, but his book was never repudiated by the Shakers; and other testimony would support the supposition that the Shakers of the early days were a wild crowd, among whom passion, when it broke loose, assumed violent forms. It is quite possible that the stripping and drunkenness attributed to Mother Ann herself and the quarrels which allegedly took place between her, James Whittaker, and her brother William on the question of her successor, may have some foundation in fact. On the other hand, it is probable, from the evidence available, that such orgiastic practices had ceased to be common by the turn of the century. By that time, highly ritualised dancing and singing, and regular participation in organised spiritual manifestations, had no doubt supplanted these earlier irregularities, by providing a more orderly method of sublimation.

It is odd that such enthusiastic celibates should have lived together in the same buildings in what were called, ironically enough, 'families'. One must presume that this proximity of the sexes, united yet scrupulously divided under one roof, was another delicious thorn in the hated flesh, a minor barb of mortification, a constant reminder that lust must be subdued by the most difficult, and never by the easiest methods. Such an arrangement of living gave rise to the most elaborate precautions. Brothers and sisters were not allowed to pass on the stairs or to shake hands with one another; they were not allowed to give each other presents; nor were they allowed to visit individuals of the opposite sex without being accompanied by companions of their own sex. The two sexes ate, worked, worshipped, and walked apart, and in all things maintained distance and reserve towards each other, in spite of the fact that, in their quarters, they were separated only by corridors and the common consent of both parties.

These families, four of which usually constituted a 'society', ranged in size from a mere handful to eighty or more persons of both sexes. Each family was administered by two elders and two elderesses, who formed the ministry responsible for both the temporal and the spiritual welfare of the societies. The first in the ministry was the leading elder of the society; and he it was who appointed all the other officers of the Church, including the temporal administrators—the deacons and deaconesses who were the household stewards, the 'care-folks' who acted as foremen and forewomen in the supervision of work, and the trustees who regulated the business affairs of the societies in relation to the outside world.

The authority of this self-perpetuating ministry was absolute, without appeal. It appointed its own successors, without election, and exacted implicit obedience. The leading elders, or 'leading characters' as they were sometimes called, heard all confessions, knew the whereabouts and occupations of every Shaker in their family, conducted the initiation of novices, controlled the movements of trustees in their dealings with the world, and exercised their power in numerous other ways. They indulged, for instance, in a teasing habit of 'testing' those whom they were about to elect to the ministry, 'crowding them down' by humiliation, and withdrawing patronage and attention from them in order that they might learn 'how it seems to be slighted and humiliated'.

In spite of their power, the elders appear, on the whole, to have been just and benevolent; and perhaps because they were so withdrawn from the world, they seem to have shown a real innocence, and not a hypocritical duplicity, towards the activities of some of their trustees, whose financial speculations in the world occasionally led to embarrassing defalcations during the great phase of Shaker prosperity. This innocence of the outside world, if innocence it was, was not a characteristic of the greatest Shakers such as Frederick Evans—but it must have been common among those who had been brought up from childhood in the seclusion of the Senior, or Church Order; for these people cut themselves off entirely from the world, making a solemn covenant to part absolutely with their property and dedicate themselves wholly to the service of the Shaker Church.

Aspirants to this Order were first of all, upon admission to the Shakers, placed in one of the two subsidiary orders, the Novitiate or the Junior; so that all Shaker societies were thus divided into three separate orders, as well as into families. The Novitiate Order was for those applicants who had been married, and the Junior was for those who had not been married. While in the Novitiate, the applicant lived separately from the family, but was admitted to its religious meetings, and was fully instructed, by the elders and elderesses, in the doctrines, practice, and requirements of the Shaker faith. Applicants were usually taken on trial for at least a year, and before admission were required to sever all matrimonial ties by common consent, and to settle all debts. They temporarily relinquished their property, but might at any time return to the world and resume it. If they brought children into the community, they were separated from them, and might only see them privately once a year, in the presence of an elder, for a very brief interview. In accordance with the practice of Mother Ann, the only question asked of those who sought admission to the society was, 'Are you sick of sin, and do you want salvation from it?'; and the first demand made of new members was a complete oral confession of the whole of their past lives to two elders of the same sex as the novice. It was emphasised, with the foresight born of long experience, that it often takes years for certain individuals to complete the confession of their sins—a statement with which psychoanalysts would certainly agree.

Converts to the Shaker faith were largely recruited from religious revivals—as, for instance, from that revival of unparalleled magnitude that began in Kentucky in 1800, and continued for several years, causing the most intense religious excitement ever known in America. The Shakers sent three missionaries 1,000 miles on foot to investigate this phenomenon. Their evangelism resulted in the foundation of five new Shaker societies in the states of Kentucky, Ohio, and Indiana. By 1830 the Shaker Church had reached its peak, upon which it rested during the whole of the second quarter of the century. At this time there were eighteen societies, comprising fifty-eight separate families, with a membership of over 5,000 souls.

The general aspect of a Shaker village has been described by Dixon: 'The streets are quiet; for here you have no grog shop, no beer house, no lock up, no pound; . . . and every building, whatever may be its use, has something of the air of a chapel. The paint is all fresh; the planks are clean bright; the windows are all clean. A sheen is on everything; a happy quiet reigns.' And Elkins, who was for fifteen years, from the age of fourteen, a member of the Senior Order, has left us a detailed description of the family mansion of that Order at Mount Lebanon.

This building was 100 feet long by 58 feet wide, with a basement and four stories. It was topped by a cupola, whose 'graceful symmetry' towered, 100 feet high, above every other object in the plain. The interior was lit by about 200 windows of twenty large panes of glass each. Within, the white pine woodwork, in which 'not a knot, blemish or nail head was anywhere visible even before painting', was finished in sky blue and white varnished paint that shone with the brilliancy of reflected light.

The ground floor contained two saloons 20 feet square, one for men and one for women; a dining-hall, 58 feet by 30 feet, with four white pillars on which were hung chandeliers; a white-walled kitchen with cupboards and closets painted sky-blue within; and a bakehouse, across a 10-foot wide corridor, painted entirely in sky-blue. On the first floor, above the dining-hall, was the sanctuary, in which not a post or support of any kind interrupted 'the felicity of space'. Two wide flights of stairs, and two doors, for brethren and sisters respectively, opened on this place of worship; and there was space enough, in the corners of this floor, for four large retiring-rooms, or dormitories, with clothes-rooms attached to each. The upper floors were divided by corridors 18 feet wide extending longitudinally through the whole length of the building. On each side of these corridors, which divided the sexes, were more dormitories 'of identical furniture and finish', with clothes-presses attached. The beds were painted apple-green, and were provided with coverlets of blue and white.

The furnishings were plain and simple. In each retiring-room one rocking-chair was permitted, but not encouraged; the remaining chairs were upright and easily portable. There might be one or two writing-desks or tables, an 'elegant but plain stove', two lamps, one candlestick, and two or three home-made rugs. A looking-glass 'not above eighteen inches in length', set in a plain frame, was permitted; and a book-shelf, containing Shaker-edited religious works, concordances, grammars, and dictionaries, was usually to be found over each desk or table. Images and portraits, shelf ornaments, and all superfluous decoration were forbidden; and clocks, if considered necessary, were to be stripped of decorative embellishments.

Not far from the mansion of the Church family described by Elkins, a large boiler-roofed church or meeting-house was built, and near it were various barns, workshops, machine-shops, laundries, and other buildings. A quarter of a mile separated the Church family from the rest of the village, but other communes of families were scattered along the way, each having its own interests, separately organised and forming a distinct community. The most striking feature of the main part of the village was the huge barn, nearly 300 feet long by 50 feet wide, and five stories high. 'Next to this', wrote Nordhoff in 1875, 'lies the sisters' shop three stories high, used for women's industries; and next, the family house, one hundred feet by forty, and five stories high. Behind these buildings is another set—an additional dwelling-house, in which are the visitors' rooms and several rooms where applicants for admission remain while they are on trial; near this an enormous woodshed, three stories high; below, a carriage-house, wagon sheds, the brothers' shop, where different industries are carried on, such as broom-making and putting up garden seeds; and farther on, the laundry, a saw-mill and grist-mill and other machinery, and a granary.'

Apart from the production of their own furniture and other

necessities, such as brooms, measures, pails, tubs, mops, mats, sieves, washing machines, and chimney cowls, the Shaker workshops turned out a great number of these articles for sale in the world, where they were marketed by the trustees, who, with the resulting funds, bought wholesale those commodities that the Shakers were unable to produce for themselves, such as tools and machinery of certain kinds. Even in this field, however, the Shakers are credited with various inventions. They claim to have perfected the first circular saw in America; they designed their own mower-and-reaper, printing-press, planing machine, tongue-and-groove machine, revolving harrow, pea-sheller, and metallic pen. An elderess of the Harvard Society invented cut nails and a double-spinning-head, and at the time of her death was experimenting with false teeth, of which she had already produced a set in wax.

The economy of Shaker societies was, however, mainly agricultural, and each society, if not each family, had its own home farm. Here again, they produced not only their own necessities, but also a surplus for sale. The quality of their garden seeds, medicinal herbs and roots, and of their preserved fruit and vegetables earned them a reputation that reached right across the continent. Following the precepts of Mother Ann that they should all earnestly labour with their hands—including the elders and elderesses—and that they should do all their work as though they had 1,000 years to live, and as though they were going to die to-morrow, the Shakers produced craftsmen of the highest skill, with a disinterested application to their work, and a communal spirit in the execution of it, that are reminiscent of the mediæval artisans.

The simplicity enjoined by religious belief and the utility adopted as a labour-saving principle by a group of people who employed no servants (apart from seasonal hired labour ᵢin the fields) resulted in furniture and other products that were of revolutionary design, for, while avoiding the 'vanities' of the world and the 'luxury' of nineteenth-century ornamentation, they produced work of a spare and graceful beauty that has only been re-discovered in our own age of 'functionalism'.

Nordhoff remarks that an eternal Sabbath stillness reigns in a Shaker family, 'there being no noise or confusion, or hum of busy industry at any time, although they are a most industrious people'; and all writers testify to the scrupulous neatness and cleanliness, the evidence of order, simplicity, and regularity, that were everywhere to be seen. Industrious they certainly were, rising at 4.30 in summer and at five in winter; and ordered they were also, regulating their lives to a great extent by a prescribed and detailed ritual, as may be seen in the following extract from the 'Orders and Gifts' posted in the sisters' retiring-room: 'Every person must rise from their beds at the sound of the "first trumpet", kneel in silence on the place where you first placed your foot when getting out of bed. No speaking in the room unless you wish to ask a question of the sister having the care of the room, in that case whisper. Dress your right arm first. Step your right foot first. At the sound of the "second trumpet", march in order, giving your right side to your superior. Walk on your toes. Fold your left hand across your stomach. Let your right hand fall at your side. March to your workshop in order. No asking unnecessary questions.'

After the first spell in the workshops, or in the fields, came breakfast. Meals were eaten in silence in the dining-hall, sisters at one table, brothers at another. 'You must not cast your eyes at the brothers' table. Sit with your eyes cast on the floor. Kneel in silence before eating. Clasp your hands, pinching down the forefinger of each hand with the thumb. Leave the table in the same order in which you go to it. Go directly to your workshop. Never look at the world's folks.'

Their diet was simple. None ate pork, and a great many ate no meat of any sort, some even refusing all food produced by animals—including milk, butter, and eggs. For this reason, two tables were sometimes laid, one with meat, the other without. A great quantity of fruit and vegetables was eaten. Tea, coffee, and ardent spirits were forbidden, unless recommended for medicinal purposes by the physician attached to each society. (Also, each family had its own infirmary and nurses.)

The greater part of the day was spent in labour, but the evenings were given up to study and meditation, to religious meetings and other spiritual occupations. On most days, everyone was in bed, with lights out, by nine or 9.30, having previously spent an hour in silent meditation, seated upright upon a chair in the retiring-room.

At first sight, this seems a spartan and even a stultifying life; but it is worth remembering that the rules and regulations of any society seem more fierce on paper than they do in practice, when they are not always observed absolutely to the letter. It is also worth remembering that membership, even of the Church Order, was voluntary, and could be renounced, as Elkins renounced it, at any time. We should not assume, therefore, that the Shakers were unhappy because they were subject to restrictions and repressions that might seem to us to be unbearable. The facts of Shaker craftsmanship alone, deny unhappiness. No one who was frustrated, repressed, discontented, or ill-adjusted to life could have produced such simple and eloquent work, which breathes the air of tranquillity and fulfilment. It is only when we begin to cast an eye on the tortured furniture, the gaudy and tawdry trappings, and the grotesque upholstery of the 'world' at the same period that we can see the products of frustration and neurosis. Whatever psychologists might make of the peculiar religious attitude of the Shakers, the Shakers themselves found fulfilment in it.

What we would call 'amusement' was unknown to the Shakers in their heyday. Books of the world were frowned upon, instrumental music was forbidden, tobacco was looked at askance. There were no paintings, no performances of plays, no games, indoor or outdoor. News from the outside world was received by extracts from the newspapers, read out and censored by the elders once a week. For the rest, the Shakers depended for their relaxation upon the learning of new hymns and hymn tunes, many of which were gifts from the spirit world; upon singing and conversation; upon visits arranged once a week between brothers and sisters—usually four or more aside—for some elevating purpose.

Many nights were spent in religious service, in 'labouring to be good'; and ritual songs and dances, with spiritual manifestations, were the most important features of these services or meetings. Brown has thus described the type of meeting that took place in the earlier days of Shaker history: 'Trembling, shaking, twitching, jerking, whirling, leaping, jumping, stamping, rolling on the floor or ground, running with one or both hands stretched out and seemingly impelled forward the way one or both pointed; some barked and crowed, and imitated the sound of several other creatures—these were the gifts of mortification. Also hissing, brushing, and driving the devil or evil spirits out of their houses; often groaning and crying out on account, as they said, of the remains of the evil nature in them, or for the wicked world; at other times rejoicing by loud laughter, shouting and clapping their hands.'

Such were some of the manifestations of zeal with which they laboured towards God, incidentally finding release and dissipation of the libido that was at other times so rigorously pent. If the frequency of these extreme demonstrations of earlier days was later diminished, their character remained very similar throughout the nineteenth century. In the years between 1837 and 1847 there was such an intensification of spiritual manifestations that great excitement was provoked in the 'world' itself; and curious members of the public, and enemies of Shakerdom, made it advisable for the Shakers to close their doors to all applicants and visitors. Most of the songs in 'strange tongues', of which there are dozens, date from this period, as does the *Holy, Sacred, and Divine Roll and Book, from the Lord God of Heaven to the Inhabitants of Earth*, in which revelations abound, and the holy angels bear such names as Ma'ne Me'rah Vak'na Si'na Jah, Assan 'de La'jah, and Michael Van'ce Va'ne; while some of the songs are mixtures of strange tongues and plain English:

> Lo all vo, hark ye, dear children, and listen to me,
> For I am that holy Se lone' se ka' ra an ve'. . . .

Anyone who wishes to examine these remarkable songs, together with the tunes to which they were sung, and the dances to which they sometimes formed the accompaniment, should consult *The Gift to be Simple*, by Edward Deming Andrews. Almost every song had its appropriate accompaniment of gesture cr dance, some of the movements being highly complex. The meetings of which they formed so essential a part usually opened with a hymn, followed by brief addresses from an elder and an elderess. These preliminaries over, the ranks were broken and a dozen of the brethren and sisters, forming a square on the floor, began a lively hymn tune, in which all the rest joined, marching round the room to a quick step, women following men, and all often clapping their hands rhythmically.

The dances were varied by reforming the ranks, and were interspersed with speeches from men and women, with songs, and with a curious shuffling dance while marching. 'Occasion-ally', wrote Nordhoff (in 1875), 'one of the members, more deeply moved than the rest, or perhaps in some tribulation of soul, asks the prayers of the others; or one comes to the front, and bowing before the elder and elderess, begins to whirl, a singular exercise which is sometimes continued for a considerable time.' At any moment an instrument might become entranced, calling out, 'Shake! Shake! Shake!! There's a great spirit on you—shake him off! off! off!! Christ says shake him off! Christ says you must come down low! low! low!!' or the Devil might enter their assemblies in person, which was a visitation they much enjoyed, for the Devil was always defeated, being despatched with a ritual kicking motion accompanied by 'a bursting yelp, in imitation of a gun'. Sometimes Christ or Mother Ann came to them with presents of golden potatoes, oranges, cakes, plum puddings, syllabubs, or jellies, and with various kinds of fruit unknown on earth. Mother Ann owned a wine-press in Heaven with which she could extract the juice of the 10,000 different kinds of grape that grow in the celestial fields. It was therefore a simple matter for her to bring wine to her children, which the instrument decanted into imaginary cups that were taken with such eagerness by the believers that they soon began to reel, stamp, shout, and laugh with sheer intoxication; though there were some, Elkins tells us, particularly among the younger generation, many of whom left the Shakers when they came of age, who secretly, if not openly, mocked these extreme examples of hallucination.

Spiritual manifestations might cause a great physical orgy that would keep the Shakers up far beyond their usual hour of retirement—sometimes, indeed, all through the night; but spirits also came to them quietly, with a message of comfort or warning, or asking the prayers of the assembly, and on such occasions the elder would ask all to kneel in silent prayer for a short period. All the Patriarchs, Prophets, and Martyrs came to the Shakers, announcing that they had joined the Shaker Church. Alexander, Napoleon, Washington, and Franklin—to mention only four men of a different calibre—were frequent visitors, Alexander being particularly interested, on a visit to the Harvard society, to discover that a descendant, bearing his name, was among the believers; and when he was told that Mother Ann had selected this very sister as a medium or instrument, 'his joy knew no bounds'.

Among large gatherings of spirits, what Shaker society could hope to rival the experience of Harvard, on whose Holy Hill no less than 40,000 once assembled? And among innumerable individual visions, many of which have been recorded in Shaker journals and diaries, it would be hard to find one more picturesque than that which tells of a vast Figure driving a hoop with a flaming torch down the side of a mountain twenty-five miles high. As the hoop bounded against rocks and stumps, a loud groaning was heard, and a voice cried out: 'O holy Virgin! O holy St. Peter! O all the Saints in the Calendar have mercy on me!' It was then observed that the Figure was no other than the Devil bowling Pope Leo down to Hell—the unfortunate Pope having had his feet joined to the crown of his head with 'cement made of all the souls he had damned'.

The visions, portents, miracles, healings, and messages received were endless. They included every field of experience that wishful-thinking, compensation, hallucination, and hysteria could encompass. They brought joy and triumph, ecstasy and exhaustion, release and fulfilment; above all, together with those songs and dances which now form part of the folk-lore of America, they formed a ceremonial that was the most effective means of binding together the Shaker societies; and because such ritual had a deeper meaning than a constitution, a manifesto, a conference, or a banquet, the Shaker Church outlived many secular communities.

The Shaker experiment made both negative and positive contributions to the history of utopian societies. We may regard the restrictions upon personal liberty, the authoritarian government, and the unnatural suppression of sexual impulses as heavy sacrifices to make in the interests of a communal society that lasted for 150 years. Yet their positive contributions to the communal ideal were important. Almost alone among such communities, they produced skilled craftsmanship and a folk art of their own. Their insistence on absolute equality between men and women was revolutionary. So also was their tolerance of race and colour—for they were the only people of their time to include both Jews and Negroes in their settlements. They fought slavery, war, and the worst aspects of society at that time, not by pleading with a world in which their voices would have been lost, but by offering what they considered to be a model of the good life. 'To the mind of the simple, unsophisticated Shaker', wrote Elder Frederick Evans, who had been a radical journalist before joining the Shakers, 'it seems marvellously inconsistent for any human government to be administered for the sole benefit of its own officers and their friends and favourites; or that more than one half the citizens should be disfranchised because they happen to be females, and compelled by the sword to obey laws they never sanctioned, and ofttimes in which they have no faith, and to submit to taxation where there has been no previous representation; while still millions of other fellow-citizens are treated as property, because they chance to possess a darker-coloured skin than their cruel brethren. And again, that the members of the same religious body or church should be divided into rich and poor in the things of this temporary world, but who are vainly expecting that, in the world to come, they shall be willing to have eternal things in common! And when this same unjust and unequal administration is confirmed and carried out in the most popular religious organisations of Christendom, the Shakers think the climax of absurdity, tyranny, and oppression well-nigh attained.'

These wrongs the Shakers put right within the boundaries of their own societies; and if their demands upon life were few, if they employed hired labour on a small scale, if they owned property in land, if their communism did not extend beyond the confines of a single society, they nevertheless held together through the cohesive force of these very limitations. By thus maintaining a stabilised society, the ordering of which was so successfully conducted, the Shakers made their greatest contribution to the community movement; for however peculiar their religious beliefs and practices may have been, there is no denying the common-sense and practical efficiency which they brought to bear upon the organisation of their industries and daily lives. Dickens, in his *American Notes*, might scoff at their 'grimness', and many observers might criticise their binding ritual, but these restrictions were essential to their success.

They were the first to demonstrate that community life could be something more vital than the doleful, monastic seclusion of the *Woman in the Wilderness* or the *Ephrata Cloister*. Theirs were the first societies endowed with that practical energy that was a characteristic of the revivalist period. They were the first to show that communities could be prosperous, neat, orderly, and of long duration. Their fame spread far. Robert Owen studied first-hand reports of them in Scotland, and was thus encouraged to make his own experiments; they were visited, for advice and observation, by founders of communities throughout the nineteenth century. They provided a solid and enduring foundation for others to build upon.

CHAPTER FOUR

REVOLUTIONS, REVIVALS, AND A DREAM

I other climes
Where dawns, with hope serene, a brighter day
Than e'er saw Albion in her happiest times,
With mental eye exulting now explore,
And soon with kindred minds shall haste to enjoy
(Free from ills which here our peace destroy)
Content and bliss on Transatlantic shore.

Coleridge.

THE American Revolution tested the pacifist faith of the Ephratans and the Shakers, and hastened the disestablishment of the churches, thereby increasing the number of dissenting sects from which many members of communities were drawn; but apart from these minor effects, it made no immediate impact upon community experiments. As a later chapter will show, it was the after-effects of the French Revolution that were to bring about a radical change in this field. But it is worth mentioning that Tom Paine, who was perhaps the greatest moral force behind the revolt of the colonists, was responsible, soon after arriving in Philadelphia, for the founding of the first American Anti-Slavery Society—incidentally, nearly ninety years after the protest signed by Pastorius. It is also worth mentioning that Paine, who crossed the Atlantic in the same year as Mother Ann, came armed with a letter of introduction from Benjamin Franklin. Franklin, who in his early days had published some of the books of the Ephrata Cloister, had made great progress in his distinguished and versatile career by the time the American Revolution began. He was an F.R.S., and one of the most notable men of science of his day; when in America, he was a member of the

SHAKER FURNITURE. Note the row of pegs on which chairs were hung when the floor was swept.

SHAKER DANCE—THE FINAL PROCESSION. *From an engraving by A. Boyd Houghton.*
The figure on the extreme right is Elder Evans (see pp. 68, 78, 115-116). The
manual gesture was a typical movement (see p. 75).

Assembly; and in London, was the first great overseas representative of the colonists.

Paine, on the contrary, was unknown and penniless when he went to America in 1774; but twenty years later, when the second part of his *Age of Reason* had been published, he was a world figure who had given unstinted service to three nations, and had played a prominent part in two of the major revolutions of mankind. Yet when he returned to America in 1802, he was ignored by the masses who would have cheered him to the echo ten years earlier, and was venomously attacked by the outraged partisans of slavery and orthodoxy. This abuse of their former hero was occasioned by Paine's deistical views, as set forth in the *Age of Reason*; and Deism, in earlier days, had been indirectly linked with revivalism, which played an important part in the development of nineteenth-century communities.

The open acknowledgement, in three volumes of bold and sometimes scathing criticism of the Bible, of a belief which was by this time widely held in cultured circles, was typical of Paine's bravado. (Washington, Jefferson, and Franklin in America, and the youthful Coleridge and Southey in England, were only a few of the distinguished men who subscribed to the same belief, without, however, publishing their views abroad.) The reliance put upon reason, which the Deists asserted was capable of attaining certainty with regard to fundamental truths, was naturally obnoxious to the Churches; and although Deism was almost entirely confined to intellectual circles, it was part of a general drift towards secularism that affected all classes—a drift to which Jonathan Edwards, the greatest of all American theologians, had determined to put an end early in the eighteenth century. His policy, however, produced entirely unexpected results.

Edwards erected a system of thought half metaphysical and half rationalised that was one of the most intolerant applications of Calvinism ever to be made on the continent. His scorching sermons—often reminiscent of Jeremy Taylor's—threatened hell fire so effectively that it was common for members of his congregations to faint, shake, shudder, and give other physical manifestations of terror. This, of course, was exciting even to those who were not involved, and Edwards rapidly built up a large following, thus instigating, in the late thirties of the eighteenth century, that phenomenal religious revival that came to be known as the Great Awakening.

Edwards, however, who had a powerful intellect and a profound and passionate sincerity, was imitated by a host of preachers who had neither of these admirable qualities. They were merely concerned with playing upon the emotions of the people with a dexterous psychological routine. This consisted—and it is typical of almost all revivalist technique—of making each individual sinner (who was often picked out by name) feel his utter worthlessness, while at the same time planting in him a quickly developing terror of eternal torture, illustrated by graphic descriptions of satanic methods. When this terror, accompanied perhaps by violent physical manifestations, had been skilfully worked up to an unbearable pitch, the pent-up emotion was released by the sinner 'realising' his sin at the sudden behest of the preacher, or in the face of the group pressure of the congregation. As with the lunatic who hit himself on the head with a wooden mallet because it was so pleasant when he desisted, the calm that followed these painful emotions was, if it is not a contradiction in terms, ecstatic. To doubt that this calm was due to the descent of God's grace upon repentant sinners would have been a churlish reflection upon the authority of the preacher; it would also have demonstrated a degree of intellect not usually associated with simple, superstitious, and hysterical people.

Most of these frenetic demonstrations were intended to draw the people back into the Puritan Church; but they had a very different effect. The Puritan congregations had been taught that they could save themselves by a direct personal relationship with God; whereupon their most intelligent members drew the obvious conclusion that they could dispense with the ministrations of the Calvinist clergy. They therefore began to join those sects in which the theocratic element was either negligible or nonexistent; and it was due to this search for a liberal theology that the Baptists increased so rapidly during the eighteenth century. In 1740, they had twenty-one churches in New England; fifty years later they had 286; and by that time they had developed fractional sects of their own, such as the New Light Baptists, whose influence on Jemima Wilkinson and the Shakers has already been noted.

Revivalism in general, carried all along the expanding frontiers of America by such missionaries as the Wesleyans and the Campbellites, was admirably suited to the rough life of the pioneer backwoodsmen. Muscular Christianity was the perfect prescription where subtle theology and fine points of dogma would have utterly failed. Enormous camp meetings, at which hundreds, and even thousands, of people came together from the surrounding districts, were a regular feature of frontier life just before the turn of the century. Dancing, shaking, and jerking with all but Saturnalian abandonment, the virile pioneers were enabled, for at least one week in the year, to sublimate desires that were at all other times strictly proscribed by the conventional puritanism of their lives. The famous Kentucky Revival of 1800, which had so excited the Shakers, was probably attended by no less than 15,000 people: it was part of a tradition that was to persist for several decades, embracing the great Nettleton and Finney revivals, providing one reason for the peculiar inception and rapid growth of the Mormons, and exerting a strong influence, as late as 1840, on the founder of the Oneida Community.

Revivalism exerted an influence on American communities that was only exceeded in importance by that of the ideas which arose out of the French Revolution. Meanwhile, somewhat earlier in date, the fall of the Bastille was partly responsible for the utopian dreams of two young Englishmen.

The repercussions in England of that tremendous event are well known. In 1789 even the most level-headed and cautious of republicans felt much the same as the brethren of *The Woman in the Wilderness* had felt when they saw what seemed to them to be a portent of the Millennium. It appeared that deliverance from all earthly tyranny was at hand, and that an era of unexampled freedom and equality must follow:

> Not favoured spots alone, but the whole Earth,
> The beauty wore of promise. . . .
> The inert were roused, and lively natures rapt away!

Such was the mood. And Wordsworth was not the only con-temporary poet to welcome the French Revolution--Southey and Coleridge were also deeply affected. Such sympathies were dangerous, however. The Government that forced Tom Paine to flee the country, and the mob violence that destroyed Joseph Priestley's house at Birmingham, did not intend to tolerate radical opinions or activities. The forces of reaction stood firm. Liberty, it seemed, must be sought elsewhere—and why not in America, where the Revolution had been successful? Priestley had already settled there; Southey and Coleridge planned to follow him.

These two young men, who first met at Oxford in 1794, when Southey was nineteen and Coleridge twenty-one, envisaged an ideal community which would combine the innocence of the. patriarchal age with the knowledge and experience of European culture. 'We preached Pantisocracy and Aspheterism every-where', wrote Southey to his brother. 'These, Tom, are two new words, the first signifying the equal government of all, and the other the generalisation of individual property.'

Pantisocracy and Aspheterism—delightful words! But what action did they evoke in the minds of their makers? Thomas Poole, the most practical and perhaps the most devoted friend of the group, has left us some details of the proposed colony. It was to consist of twelve men and twelve ladies, all of whom would be known to each other before the scheme started. While the men worked the soil, the ladies would care for the children and keep house. Life would not be strenuous—the men, it was thought, would have to work only two or three hours a day to maintain the colony; for the rest of the time, they would pay the greatest attention to the cultivation of their minds, indulging in much study and discussion on the basis of a small but compre-hensive library. As to other matters, all would be free to follow their inclinations. They might hold whatever religious beliefs they pleased; they might leave the colony at will; and there was a tentative proposal that the marriage contract should be dissolved if either party should desire it. A contribution of £125 by each member would be sufficient to cover all their initial expenses; and they proposed to embark in April 1795.

How Coleridge and Southey were joined by a third poet, Robert Lovell, and how all three soon found themselves engaged to the daughters of a family Southey had known since childhood, is common knowledge. Lovell and Mary Fricker, Southey and Edith, were betrothed without misgivings; but Coleridge entered upon his engagement to Sarah with the reluctance of a man still yearning for an earlier love. His lack of enthusiasm in this respect, however, was amply made up in pantisocratic zeal. While on a walking tour, he had already talked Pantisocracy in half the inns of Wales; and on another tour with Southey in the West Country had won the sympathetic interest of Thomas Poole. Also, before parting from Southey at Bristol, Coleridge had attempted to raise funds for the expedition by persuading Cottle, the publisher, to promise an advance on some poems. Coleridge's enthusiasm, however, was raised to its highest pitch by an encounter in London with an American land-agent, who painted a delectable picture of colonial life. Coleridge and his friends should settle in Pennsylvania, he advised, for there they would meet with no hostility from the Indians. He knew the very place for them— on the banks of the Susquehanna. . . .

Susquehanna! There was a softness, a certain exotic, languorous, musical beauty in the name. Coleridge found it enchanting—and even inspiring. His *Monody on the Death of Chatterton* must be revised, he decided, to include a reference to this magic-sounding river—in fact, to Pantisocracy itself:

O Chatterton! that thou were yet alive!
Sure thou would'st spread the canvas to the gale,
And love with us the tinkling team to drive
O'er peaceful Freedom's undivided dale;

And we, at sober eve, would round thee throng,
Would hang, enraptured, on thy stately song,
And greet with smiles the young-eyed Poesy
All deftly masked as hoar Antiquity.

Alas, vain Phantasies! the fleeting brood
Of Woe self-solaced in her dreamy mood!
Yet will I love to follow the sweet dream,
Where Susquehanna pours his untamed stream;
And on some hill, whose forest-frowning side
Waves o'er the murmurs of his calmer tide,
Will raise a solemn Cenotaph to thee,
Sweet Harper of time-shrouded Minstrelsy!
And there, soothed sadly by the dirgeful wind
Muse on the sore ills I had left behind.

Also, he decided, he would write a book on Pantisocracy—a book that would include 'all that is good in Godwin'. Susquehanna was indeed an inspiration, for Coleridge made another decision—with what eventual effect is not recorded—to take lessons in carpentry, as a preparation for his future life.

Southey, meanwhile, had drawn up a list of eighteen probable Pantisocrats—including all the Frickers. Coleridge, however, began to have qualms when Southey wrote to him. He had heard that Southey intended to introduce domestic service into the colony; and he doubted whether the Frickers were Pantisocrats at heart; but his deepest misgivings were due to the fact that he was now certain that he did not love Sarah. . . .

Money, as always, was also a problem. Even Coleridge realised that one could not live on the mere name 'Susquehanna', however enchanting it might be. How were the Pantisocrats ever to raise their fares to America? It was true that by lecturing and writing, and by soliciting the aid of such a kindly man as Cottle, they had already made a little money; but it seemed to vanish as soon as they'd made it.

As the months dragged on, the dream evidently began to wear a little thin. People to whom they outlined their plans thought them mad, and Southey's aunt, with whom he lived, turned him out of her house when she heard of the scheme. Such reactions were to be expected—but the suggestion of a sympathiser that they should prepare for their American adventure by establishing themselves on a co-operative basis in Wales was thoroughly vexing. It took Coleridge some time to adjust himself to this abominably cautious proposal—and the dream was becoming threadbare. Moreover, he still distrusted Southey's intentions; and when he learnt that Southey's private resources were to remain his individual property, and that everything was to be privately owned except a farm of 5 or 6 acres, his patience came to an end. 'In short', he wrote, 'we were to commence partners in a petty farming trade. This was the mouse of which the mountain Pantisocracy was at last safely delivered.' Thus, but much more voluminously, did he write an indictment of Southey, and thus did the two men become estranged.

Coleridge's indictment was the penultimate blow to Pantisocracy. It was Southey, and not the Fricker sisters, as is so often alleged, who killed the scheme. Having secretly married his Edith, he seized the opportunity to sail to Lisbon with his uncle in November 1795. Coleridge, however, was haunted by the dream for some years—a dream that was symptomatic of the times, and characteristic of the poets who indulged in it.

Perhaps it is fortunate that the scheme failed, for it is difficult to picture Coleridge swinging an axe or Southey driving a plough with any success—even for 'two or three hours a day'. Perhaps, on the other hand, it is regrettable that some such energetic and capable sympathiser as Thomas Poole was unable to start a small community in America. It might have stood a better chance of success than the grandiose scheme that was actually the first nonsectarian experiment. This also was conceived by an Englishman —but thirty years were to pass before it would be established.

The communities that were to be founded in the intervening years—the first one in Pennsylvania, at no great distance from the Susquehanna—were very different in character from the Coleridgean dream. Composed of stolid German peasants and artisans who worked a full day, they afforded little opportunity for the cultivation of the mind, and enjoined adherence to a particular set of religious beliefs.

CHAPTER FIVE

RAPPITES AND ZOARITES

> When Rapp the Harmonist embargoed Marriage
> In his harmonious settlement—(which flourishes
> Strangely enough as yet without miscarriage,
> Because it breeds no more mouths than it nourishes,
> Without those sad expenses which disparage
> What Nature naturally most encourages)—
> Why called he 'Harmony' a state sans wedlock?
> Now here I've got the preacher at a deadlock.
>
> *Byron: Don Juan, Canto XV.*

THE Shakers who had crossed the Atlantic with Ann Lee were very few in number. In contrast to this emigration of a mere handful of settlers, several of the communities that were founded in the first half of the nineteenth century were to draw their membership almost entirely from Europe, by the boatload. Such was the case with the Germans, who had been crossing the Atlantic in ever-increasing numbers since the establishment of their first colonies in Pennsylvania. Among those who were to form communities early in the new century were the 600 followers of George Rapp, who arrived in 1804, and 200 Separatists under Joseph Baumeler, who arrived in 1817. They were followed, in 1843—a year before the founding of Dr. Keil's first community of Germans already resident in America—by 600 Inspirationists under the leadership of Christian Metz.

The first two groups, with whom we shall deal briefly in this chapter, were very similar. Both came from Württemburg; both had broken away from the Lutheran Church and were Quietists; both were organised by energetic and practical leaders; both, at one time or another, adopted celibacy; and neither of them had intended to form communities when they left Germany. Unlike the German Pietists of the previous century, they do not appear to have possessed any outstanding intellectual talent, or to have indulged in any extravagant mystical or metaphysical speculations. Their membership was composed mainly of artisans and peasants; they therefore came to America well equipped to win a living from the land.

George Rapp was the son of a small farmer and vinedresser. He received a moderate education and helped his father on the farm. Being a devoted Bible student, he was particularly impressed by the contrast of the life around him with that of the social order prescribed in the New Testament; and it was not long before he began to deliver sermons on such matters to a small congregation that assembled in his house on Sundays. The clergy of the Lutheran Church regarded this small sect as the nucleus of a dangerous heresy—which was, of course, duplicated in dozens of similar Separatist groups—and the Rappites were accordingly fined, imprisoned, and subjected to other forms of persecution which helped them to grow from a mere house-party to a substantial body of 300 families.

By the time he was forty-six, Rapp had saved enough money from his farm work to enable him to sail to Baltimore (in 1803) with the object of finding land on which he and his followers might settle and pursue their religious life without fear of persecution. He bought 5,000 acres of virgin land north of Pittsburg, in the Conoquenessing valley, and on the 4th July 1804 the first contingent of his followers, 300 in number, arrived at Baltimore. A few weeks later the second boatload, containing an equal number of emigrants, landed at Philadelphia. During the first winter, while Rapp and his best workmen were building houses for them, the main body of the colonists was scattered throughout Maryland and Pennsylvania, working on farms. In 1805 they were all called together, and formally organised themselves into the Harmony Society,[1] numbering about 750 men, women, and children.

---

[1] 'The principles of which, being faithfully derived from the sacred Scriptures, include the government of the patriarchal age, united to the community of property adopted in the days of the Apostles' (Articles of Association).

Discovering that they included among their members many who were too old, too infirm, or too poor to be able to maintain themselves, the Society resolved to adopt communism. The members agreed to place all their possessions in a common fund, to adopt a uniform and simple style of dress and of house, and to labour for the good of the whole body. The usual provisions were made for the care of the sick and of orphans; and a generous clause was inserted by which anyone leaving the society was to be repaid his original contribution, or if he was poor, and had been unable to make a contribution, he was to be given a donation on leaving. (This latter provision was abolished in later years.) In the first year they built about fifty log-houses, a church, a school, a grist-mill, a barn, and some workshops; they also cleared 150 acres of land. In the following year they cleared a further 400 acres, built a saw-mill, a tannery, and a storehouse. They grew wheat, rye, hemp, flax, and poppies from which they made sweet oil; they owned the first merino sheep in the colony and set up a woollen mill. They also planted a vineyard and built a distillery in which they made whisky that became famous in the district. These two latter items make a heartening break with the traditions of the earlier communities. Although the Rappites were not great whisky-drinkers, they liked to drink wine, and this may well be one reason why they appear to have been more mellow and human than some of their abstemious predecessors. They also enjoyed their food, and did not stint themselves. Rising between five and six, they ate a light breakfast; at nine they lunched; at twelve they dined; at three they were ready for *vesper brodt*; between six and seven they rounded off the day with supper—and were in bed by nine.

Mellow and human though they may have been, a religious fervour gripped them in 1807, and they resolved to adopt celibacy and to give up the use of tobbaco. No community ever changed from the married to the celibate state with such ease; husbands and wives continued to live together, with their children, in the houses they had always occupied, but ceased as if by magic from conjugal intercourse. Some members withdrew from the community when celibacy was adopted; but for those who remained no precautions were taken, no rules were made; strength of religious conviction was considered to be—and apparently was—sufficient.

Harmony was now relatively prosperous; but the site had two defects: it had no water communication with the outside world and the soil was unsuitable for vine-growing. In 1814, therefore, the community bought 30,000 acres of land in the Wabash Valley of Indiana and sold their original settlement with all it contained for $100,000. An advance party of 100 began the building of their new home, also called Harmony, and by 1815 the entire community had been moved. Harmony, Indiana, prospered to such a degree that it became an important business centre for a considerable region, selling its products in the branch stores of the neighbourhood as well as at Harmony itself. With added wealth, it also acquired large accessions of members from Germany. One hundred and thirty friends and relatives from Württemburg joined the community in 1817, bringing the total population up to about 700. The best possible proof of their satisfaction with the communistic life, and perhaps also of their communal wealth, is the fact that in 1818 they burnt, by unanimous consent, the book in which were written the amounts each family had originally contributed to the common fund.

Harmony, Indiana, was now extremely prosperous, but the site had several defects: the people suffered from ague and malarial fevers, and found their neighbours unpleasant. In 1824, therefore, they sold the town and 20,000 acres of land to Robert Owen for $150,000, and bought land at Economy, north of Pittsburg, and not far from their original home. An advance party of ninety cleared the land and laid out the new town. By 1825 the entire community had been moved for the third and last time. At Economy the Harmonists enjoyed greater prosperity than they had ever known before. The nearness of Pittsburg and the cheap transport on the Ohio River favoured the sale of their manufactures; they had a beautifully situated as well as a healthy home, enough young blood among their members to give them enthusiasm for new enterprises, agreeable neighbours, and a wealth of experience which was useful to them in designing the town of Economy.

Nordhoff, who visited the town in the early 'seventies describes it as standing 'in the midst of a rich plain, with smiling hills behind, protecting it from cold winds in winter; a magnificent reach of the river in view below; and tall hills on the opposite shore to give a picturesque outlook. The town begins on the edge of the bluff; and under the shade-trees planted there benches are arranged, where doubtless the Harmonists take their comfort on summer evenings, in view of the river below and of the village on the opposite shore. Streets proceed at right angles with the river's course; and each street is lined with neat frame or brick houses, surrounding a square in such a manner that within each household has a sufficient garden. The broad streets have neat foot-pavements of brick; the houses, substantially built but unpretentious, are beautified by a singular arrangement of grape-vines, which are trained to espaliers fixed to cover the space between the top of the lower and the bottom of the upper windows. This manner of training vines gives the town quite a peculiar look, as though the houses had been crowned with green.'

The writer adds that even at that date, when one might 'meet only occasionally some stout, little old man, in a short light-blue jacket and a tall and very broad-brimmed hat . . . or some comfortable-looking dame, in Norman cap and stuff gown', Economy was still regarded as 'a model of a well-built, well-arranged country village'. He describes how a specially large house was built for Father Rapp (since he was obliged to entertain many visitors and strangers of distinction) and how this house 'stands opposite the church; and has behind it a spacious garden, arranged in a somewhat formal style, with box-edgings to the walks, and summer-houses and other ornaments in the old geometrical style of gardening. This was open to the people, of course; and here the band played on summer evenings, or more frequently on Sunday afternoons; and here, too, flowers were cultivated, I am told, with great success.'

The Duke of Saxe-Weimar, who visited Economy in 1826, only one year after it was founded, wrote an enthusiastic account of his visit:

The warehouse was shown to us, where the articles made here for sale or use are preserved, and I admired the excellence of all. The articles for the use of the society are kept by themselves; as the members have no private possessions, and every thing is in common, so must they, in relation to all their wants, be supplied from the common stock. The clothing and food they make use of is of the best quality. Of the latter, flour, salt meat, and all long-keeping articles, are served out monthly; fresh meat, on the contrary, is distributed as soon as it is killed, according to the size of the family, etc. As every house has a garden, each family raises its own vegetables and some poultry, and each family has its own bake-oven. For such things as are not raised in Economy, there is a store provided, from which the members, with the knowledge of the directors, may purchase what is necessary, and the people of the vicinity may do the same. . . .

Mr. Rapp conducted us into the factory again, and said that the girls had especially requested this visit that I might hear them sing. When their work is done, they collect in one of the factory rooms, to the number of sixty or seventy, to sing spiritual and other songs. They have a peculiar hymn-book, containing hymns from the old Württemburg collection, and others written by the elder Rapp. A chair was placed for the old patriarch, who sat amid the girls, and they commenced a hymn in a very delightful manner. It was naturally symphonious, and exceedingly well arranged. The girls sang four pieces, at first sacred, but afterward, by Mr. Rapp's desire, of a gay character.

Their factories and workshops are warmed during the winter by means of pipes connected with the steam-engine. All the workmen, and especially the females, had very healthy complexions, and moved me deeply by the warm-hearted friendliness with which they saluted the elder Rapp. I was also much gratified to see vessels containing fresh sweet-scented flowers standing on all the machines. The neatness which universally reigns is in every respect worthy of praise.

There is something especially endearing in these glimpses of life at Economy as compared with life in some of the earlier religious communities. These people were obviously not fanatics. They did not find it necessary to torture themselves or to deny themselves beauty and simple joys—and whether or not the picture of bliss is overdrawn, there can be no doubt that they were happy and contented people who lived quietly and pleasantly.

Into the midst of this paradise, however, a serpent was introduced—a gentleman named Bernhard Müller, who had created himself 'Count Maximilian de Leon'. Arriving at Economy in 1831 at the head of a little band of German followers, he wormed his way into the confidence of the community and then began to advocate all kinds of worldly pleasures, including marriage. So adept a schemer with such smooth, insinuating manners and such plausible expressions of piety was this ordinary adventurer that he succeeded in effecting a serious division among the Harmonists. Eventually two factions faced one another in bitter enmity, and when they were separated, it was found that 500 members remained true to Rapp, while 250 had been persuaded to follow the 'Count'. 'We knew not even who was for and who against us', declared the man who drew up the lists of the two parties of adherents; and when the result was declared, the same man added that Father Rapp, with 'his usual ready wit', quoted from the Apocalypse: 'And the tail of the serpent drew the third part of the stars of heaven, and did cast them to the earth.' . . .

By a mutual agreement, the third part of the stars of heaven were then cast out of Economy within three months, taking with them only their clothing and household furniture and relinquishing all claims upon the property of the society; but they were generously given $105,000 by the Rappites. They left Economy in the summer of 1832, and set up a communistic society (called the New Philadelphia Society) ten miles away. Here they wasted the money they had received, and after fruitless endeavours to extort more money from the Rappites, the 'Count' and his followers moved on to Grand Ecore, near Natchitoches, in Louisiana, where he died of cholera the following year. The community property was then divided, and there was a third move to Germantown, La., though some De Leonites afterwards joined Dr. Keil's community of Bethel. The prosperity of Economy was almost unaffected by this upheaval, which its financial resources were apparently well able to withstand. They afterwards suffered—in common with almost all communities—

several lawsuits at the hands of discontented ex-members, but all judgements were given in favour of the society.

The success of the community was due largely to the combination of Father Rapp's spiritual leadership with the remarkable administrative ability of his adopted son, Friederich. Friederich not only brought the 600 colonists across the Atlantic without a single mishap, but also organised the two transfers of the entire community, with all its possessions, from its original settlement to the succeeding ones. The management of such complete and smooth-working removals in those days was no mean feat, and the latter withdrawal, from Indiana, was admired by several observers.

Father Rapp himself, described as tall, well-built, blue-eyed, and of a kindly disposition, was a benevolent autocrat. His ready wit, his genuine affection for the colonists, and his innate gift of leadership inspired so much confidence in his followers that he was able to rule them with the minimum of discipline and with fewer rules and regulations than were to be known in any other community. Extremely vigorous, and never wasting a moment of his time, he lived to be ninety, preaching two sermons on the Sunday before his death. Shortly before he died, expecting the Second Coming, he confessed: 'If I did not know that the dear Lord meant I should present you all to Him, I should think my last moments come.' This millennial outlook, shared by his followers, together with their prosperity, their celibacy, and the loss of a leader upon whom they were more dependent than were the members of most communities, contributed to the decline of the society—which, however, lasted until the beginning of the present century.

Joseph Baumeler—or Bimeler, as he came to be known in America—was a very different man from Father Rapp. He had been first a weaver and then a teacher, and was a man of considerable knowledge and ability; but he lacked Rapp's qualities of leadership, wit, gaiety, and imagination. He was apparently a somewhat heavy, sombre, and solemn man. On Sundays, for instance, he invariably delivered a long discourse on some edifying subject such as religion, morals, manners, housekeeping, thrift, or homæopathy—discourses which were gathered, at his death, into three ponderous octavo volumes. He was also in a less commanding position than the leader of the Harmonists, and perhaps this combination of character and circumstance may account for Zoar's lack of beauty and comfort, of neatness and finish, such as existed at Economy. Nordhoff, who visited Zoar in 1874, was shocked by the fact that after fifty-six years of existence the town had neither pavements nor 'regularity of design', and he noted that the houses needed painting, and that the whole place had a shabby and neglected air.

Although the Zoarites, like the Rappites, were Quietists, who believed in obedience to the law, but also in freedom to worship as they pleased, they were a more aggressive body of people than their countrymen. Consequently, they were more severely persecuted in Germany, where they had refused to send their children to the Lutheran schools and to allow their young men to serve as soldiers. After some years of the usual flogging, imprisonment, and paying of fines, they were enabled to emigrate by the financial aid of some English Quakers. On arrival in America, they bought 5,600 acres in the wilderness of Ohio.

Baumeler and a few able-bodied men went out to take possession of the land, and built their first log-house in December 1817. In the spring the rest of the group followed, and, being entirely without resources, had to obtain employment with neighbouring farmers in order to pay for the separate properties on their tract of land—for at this time they had no thought of setting up a communistic society. They soon decided to do so, however, for the same reasons as those which had weighed with the Rappites. After some weeks of discussion, the articles of agreement were signed in April 1819.

As soon as they adopted the community life, their problems became less acute. All those who had been working in the countryside were called in, and it was found that there were about 225 men, women, and children. At first they crowded into a few

ROBERT OWEN. *From a contemporary print.*

small log houses, pinching and scraping, living within their very small means, and as much as possible off their own produce. They were mostly careful and laborious peasants, and some of them still had to work for neighbouring farmers; indeed, they would have found life exceedingly difficult but for a fortunate chance which set them on their feet in 1827, when a canal was dug in their neighbourhood. By obtaining a contract to do part of the work for $21,000, and by selling their produce to the contractors, they made enough money to pay off the debt on their land, and thereafter were never again troubled by poverty.

At first they were celibates, but in order to ensure the continuation of the community they began to permit marriage (about 1830). They permitted marriage—but Bimeler taught that God only tolerated it, and did not approve of it; therefore they did not approve of it. Nevertheless, Bimeler himself married and had a family of children; it is even said that the abandonment of celibacy by the community was due to the fact that Bimeler could not resist the attractions of a young girl who had been assigned by the community to wait on him. The Bimelerites were endogamous; if anyone wished to marry outside the community, he had no alternative but to leave it. Young people wishing to marry were obliged to consult and obtain the permission of the trustees, who were responsible for providing the couple with accommodation and furniture. Until 1845, when more orthodox customs were adopted, children lived with their parents only until they were three years old, when they were placed in special houses—one for girls and one for boys—never again coming under parental control.

In 1832, when the community, by the accession of new immigrants, attained its greatest strength in numbers, it was incorporated under the laws of Ohio, taking the name of 'The Society of the Separatists of Zoar'. Under its constitution, which was revised in the following year, the affairs of the community were vested in three trustees, who served for three years, but might be indefinitely re-elected. The trustees appointed the supervisors of the industries, and directed each member to do the work that was most readily compatible with his desires and abilities. While holding office the trustees had almost unlimited power; but they, together with the standing arbitration committee of five, which settled all disputes within the community, and all other officers, such as the agent, who acted as commercial intermediary with the outside world, and the cashier, who was the treasurer, were elected, in accordance with the laws of the state, by the entire adult membership. These elections took place annually by ballot and the majority vote. Thus, as regards the machinery of government, Zoar was more democratic than most communities. There was no president in name, and the constitution itself was subject to amendment by a two-thirds vote. Bimeler, unlike Father Rapp, was accountable to the standing committee, and was elected only so long as he had the confidence of the society.

The society was divided into two classes, one of probationers and children, the other of full members who, after a year's probation, had signed the covenant, thus being entitled to vote and hold office. The probationers surrendered all their money—which was returnable upon production of a receipt—and were obliged to place their children under the exclusive guardianship of the trustees; but they did not have to give up their property. Unlike the Shakers or the Perfectionists, they had no daily meetings or rituals to keep alive their earnestness or piety, but on Sundays they had three meetings, at one of which extracts were read from Bimeler's discourses, which, says Nordhoff, they were careful not to call sermons. They did not practice audible or public prayer, they did not celebrate baptism or the Eucharist, they avoided all set forms and ceremonies, had no religious hierarchy, and addressed everyone as 'thou', only uncovering their heads or bending their knees before God.

They played music, which was almost their only form of entertainment, but did not permit dancing. They possessed no library, and their books were restricted to religious treatises, some sacred songs by Bimeler, Terstegen's hymns, and the 2,574 pages of Bimeler's discourses. They were a sober, quiet, orderly, industrious, and thrifty people, entirely unintellectual, and satisfied with the barest necessities of life. They rose at six, or at dawn in summer, breakfasted at seven, dined at twelve, and supped at six in the evening. They drank cider and beer, but were forbidden to smoke, although some of the younger members apparently did so. They were usually in bed by about nine o'clock. They lived in separate houses, each house containing several families, and each family managing its own affairs, cooking for itself, but obtaining bread from a general bakery.

After the cholera epidemic in which Count de Leon perished, the Zoarites were obliged to employ hired labour to replace the numbers of people they lost; and they never relinquished the practice. Growing steadily wealthier, acquiring more land, building woollen factories, flourmills, tanneries, and machine shops, they owned about 7,000 acres of land in 1874, and were reputed to be worth more than $3,000,000. During this increase of wealth, they suffered the usual litigations concerning the proper disposal of the property of seceders, and were rewarded with the usual judgements in favour of the community by the Ohio courts.

Comfortable within a very narrow and unimaginative definition of the word, prosperous with the prosperity of thrift, stolid, plain in religion and plain in dress, unemotional and obstinately set in a perennial routine, the Zoarites slowly plodded on through time, accumulating their just meed of octogenarians and gradually acquiring those 'dull and lethargic' appearances of which Nordhoff writes, until, without a de Leon to test their faith, or a vision to excite some spark of life in them, they began, probably out of sheer boredom and pique, to squabble among themselves in a desultory manner, which ended, after an increasingly acrimonious conflict, in the dissolution of the community in 1898.

The failure of the Zoarites may be partly ascribed to lack of religious enthusiasm. They showed none of that intense or fanatical zeal that kept alive the faith of the Pietists and the Shakers;

nor, even in their early days, were they stimulated by the great waves of religious excitement that swept along the western frontiers of the States. Revivalism did not touch these stolid German peasants—nor, of course, were they affected by the aftermath of the French Revolution. For the first two decades of the century the repercussions of that cataclysm were felt only in Europe—but they gave birth to ideas that were to prove of far greater consequence, when brought to America, than any native influence on community life.

CHAPTER SIX

NEW HARMONY

Ah, soon will come the glorious day,
Inscribed on Mercy's brow,
When truth shall rend the veil away
That blinds the nations now.

The face of man shall wisdom learn,
And error cease to reign:
The charms of innocence return,
And all be new again.

From an Owenite poem.

THE main force of the French Revolution had been directed against the aristocracy. Hatred of those who had abused their privileges for so many years blinded the fanatical leaders of the Terror to almost all other issues. Heads must roll even while industrial exploitation went unchecked; and the rabble armies of the Directorate must loot and pillage foreign countries in the name of a Republic that was no less aggressive and imperialistic in its tendencies than the old régime. The effect of this new tyranny upon the intellectuals of the period, who had hailed the storming of the Bastille with joy, was profound. Most of them turned away in disgust. In England, Wordsworth, Coleridge, and Southey plunged deeper into the romanticism which they had already begun to explore before the Revolution took place. The main trend in social philosophy, also, was away from violence. Just as the Anabaptists had turned away from the violence of Münster, so did French socialists—such as Saint-Simon and Fourier—forswear the methods of the Terror. In Wordsworth's phrase, 'they toil'd, intent to anatomise the frame of social life', and in drawing up schemes for the reorganisation of society some of them embraced doctrines that were almost as fantastic in certain respects as were the Rosicrucian and Theosophical beliefs of the early Pietists.

Saint-Simon and Fourier were born before either the American or the French Revolutions, and were as much opposed to the use of mob violence as to the tyranny of monarchs. They considered that their recommendations were practical, but in fact both men were predominantly dreamers endowed with the romantic attitude of the age, and for this reason were referred to by Marx as 'utopian socialists'.

With Count Henri de Saint-Simon, who was born in 1760, and who fought in the American Revolution, we are not greatly concerned, except to note that his ideas form a connecting-link between the eighteenth and nineteenth centuries. He sought to reorganise society upon the basis of a new spiritual power and a new religion that would meet the demands of an industrial age. He looked upon industrialisation as a benefit to mankind, and, being blind to the differences between labour and capital, proposed that the old feudal and military systems should be superseded by an industrial order controlled by industrial chiefs, while the spiritual direction of society was to pass from the Church to men of science. The essence of the new religion, and the means by which the new society was to be achieved, were to be embodied in the words, 'Love one another'. The principles of equality of opportunity and abolition of privilege that had been proclaimed in 1793 were to be retained; but the significance of Saint-Simon's teaching lies in the fact that he added to this principle the proposition that men should organise society in the manner most advantageous to the greatest number. Thus, he directed attention upon the amelioration of poverty and distress, without, however, expressing himself clearly upon the vexed question of private property. This matter was dealt with by his followers, who desired 'that all instruments of labour, land, and capital, which now form, subdivided, the inheritance of private means, should be united in one social fund, and that this fund should be operated on principles of association by a hierarchy, so that each one will have his task according to his capacity, and wealth according to his work'. Hierarchy is a dangerous word; and it is evident that the Saint-Simonian panacea might have resolved itself into a rigid form of State socialism.

The Saint-Simonian church and religion that came into being within a year or two of the Count's death in 1825 was faced with the sort of problems that occur throughout the history of communities. Having no tyrannical God to appease for the fall of man, which they repudiated, the Saint-Simonians dared to seek a new happiness by abolishing that dualism of the spirit and the flesh that had vexed countless generations of Christians. In this they were revolutionary; but in proclaiming the emancipation of women (which they justified by the Shaker-like assumption that God was bisexual) they were led to attempt a system of free-love that brought their church to an end in the law-courts. In these respects, their beliefs led them to daring secular solutions of problems that we have already met in religious communities in America. Thus their moral tenets represent a transitional phase, just as their proposed hierarchical system of State socialism represents a compromise between the authoritarianism of the past and the autonomous associative ideas that were already being proposed by others—by Fourier, for instance.

The ideas of Charles Fourier, who was born in 1772, are so wildly extravagant, so chaotic, so entertaining, and nevertheless so important to the future of community experiments in America that they will be dealt with separately in a later chapter. It will be sufficient, at this point, to state that his theories were based upon an apocalyptic conception of the world which postulates a period of harmony that is to endure for 35,000 years. During this blissful period the world will be organised upon the basis of self-contained co-operative units known as 'phalanxes'. Each phalanx will contain about 1,750 people, who will live upon their own produce and exchange surplus goods with neighbouring phalanxes. In these settlements industry will be made attractive, and nothing will be omitted that might conduce to the happiness and fulfilment of their inhabitants. The problem of the family will be solved by a peculiar form of polyandry; and private property is to remain inviolable.

Fourier never lived to see the practical application of his theories; but in England there existed a man with social ideals that were similar to Fourier's, although they were not worked out in such detail or accompanied by such bizarre fantasies. This was Robert Owen, whose life is sufficiently well known to make any general reference to it here unnecessary.

Although the fundamental ideas of Owen and Fourier were similar—the establishment of small ideal communities, in which man, who is essentially good, might escape the foul environment which alone makes him bad—they differed in several respects. One way in which they differed was that Fourier did not believe in the equality of human beings or in community of goods, whereas Owen, at least during one period of his life, seems to have believed in both. A difference of fortune also existed: Owen had gained wealth and a European reputation from his reforms at New Lanark and could afford to finance his own schemes and reckon on respectful attention to them from influential persons. Fourier, who was penniless, could only wait hopefully for the advent of a sympathetic millionaire.

Robert Owen arrived in America with a flourish. The fame of his industrial reforms at New Lanark had preceded him, and it was known that many great men of the age—as well as sovereigns and princes—had paid him homage. Had he not appealed, vainly, but with typical optimism, to the benevolence of Czar Nicholas of Russia, and had he not submitted plans for industrial communities to the Congress of Sovereigns at Aachen, in 1818?

'I am come to this country', he announced in April 1825—in the old Rappite church, by then converted into the Hall of New Harmony—'I am come to this country to introduce an entire new system of society; to change it from an ignorant, selfish system to an enlightened social system which shall gradually unite all interests into one, and remove all causes for contest between individuals.' It would not be possible, of course, to work this miracle overnight. Even the optimistic Owen realised that; but he sincerely believed that the miracle could be wrought in the space of three years. Only a few weeks previously, he had explained to the President of the United States and a vast audience of the most eminent men in the country how he would rid the human race of evil. Man, as he had reiterated time and time again over the length and breadth of England, was the creature of his environment. One had only to change the environment—and hey presto!—man himself would change.

The change of environment would begin with new buildings, models of which Owen had exhibited at his lectures in Washington. An ideal community consisted of a hollow square 1,000 feet long, in which were to be found a complete school, academy, and university. Lecture-rooms, laboratories, a chapel, a library, ballrooms, committee-rooms, and rooms for reading and recreation were to be housed in the large buildings in the centres of the sides, and in the corners of the square. Kitchens, dining-halls, laundries, and other domestic departments would occupy the space between these larger buildings; above them, the first and second stories would contain the living quarters of married couples, while the third floor was set aside for unmarried people and children over two years of age. Each department was to be supplied with gas, water, and all modern conveniences; while from the windows there would be a beautiful and extensive view, embracing a river and an island. . . .

Meanwhile, until this model could be transformed into reality, Owen and his followers would have to be content with the village of New Harmony as it stood. Here, with buildings enough to house about 1,000 people, and with twenty thousand acres of land that had been cultivated by the Rappites, Owen proposed to set up his 'new empire of peace and goodwill', which would lead 'in due season, to that state of virtue, intelligence, enjoyment, and happiness which it has been foretold by the sages of the past would at some time become the lot of the human race'. He was convinced that the truth of his principles and the advantages of community life would spread 'from Community to Community, from State to State, from Continent to Continent, finally over-shadowing [sic] the whole earth, shedding light [sic], fragrance and abundance, intelligence and happiness upon the sons of man'.

Having delivered himself of this superb prospectus, Owen had only to invite 'the industrious and well-disposed of all nations' to come to New Harmony and help found the new civilisation. This he did—and they came. They came in their hundreds. In six weeks 800 had assembled, men and women of all classes and vocations, embracing dozens of different nationalities, creeds, professions and trades. Some were inspired by Owen's grandiose vision and were prepared to devote themselves earnestly and sincerely to the realisation of his rather vague plans; but many were attracted by his wealth and his reputation as a philanthropist. The latter expected to step into a paradise rather than to help make it. Moreover, there was nothing in the constitution of the Society to prevent anyone—even if undesirable—from joining it; consequently anyone did. And when they arrived at New Harmony there was nothing—not even an immediate practical or economic plan—to unite them. To make matters worse, Owen, the sole owner and only person effectively empowered to shape and guide the community, left New Harmony almost immediately to go to England, and did not return for more than six months.

Lacking any binding force, and differing widely in their interpretations of communitarianism, the people of New Harmony ran through five different constitutions in a year, split into four separate communities within the parent community, and, according to an observer, 'continued strangers to each other in spite of all their meetings, their balls, their frequent occasions of congregating in the hall, and all their pretence of co-operation'.

The Preliminary Society of New Harmony was formed on 1st May 1825. Its constitution, which began with the generous statement that the society was 'instituted generally to promote the happiness of the world', placed Owen in charge of the community for three probationary years. (Owen had enough common sense to realise that men brought up 'in an irrational system of society' could not be expected to adopt a rational one without preparation.) For the first six or seven months, working under a committee of control during Owen's absence, the society slowly began to stir itself. An increase of accommodation was the most urgent necessity: carpenters and masons were at once employed on converting the existing buildings so that they would house a population that was nearly twice as large as that of the Rappites. There seems to have been a lack of skilled artisans, but various trades and industries were set in motion, a newspaper was produced, schools were organised, and enough entertainment was provided to keep down the rowdiness and disorder to which there was a tendency even in the early days. Agriculture, however, seems to have been much neglected; and when undertaken, to have been inefficient.

Superficially, the community appeared to be prospering; encouraged by the panegyrics of the *New Harmony Gazette*, which never failed throughout its existence to echo the sublime optimism of Owen, it was kept busy and hopeful: in July had not the first new Owenite Community been established at Yellow Springs, Ohio? And by Christmas had not the population of New Harmony reached 1,000?

When Owen returned in January 1826, followed by his famous 'Boatload of Knowledge', the Preliminary Society was in good heart. If its doors had then been temporarily closed to further members, and if those who had been found undesirable had been expelled, careful planning and prudent guidance might have led to the consolidation of a society which, within the three years allotted to it, might have reached a common decision as to its permanent form. Unfortunately, Owen returned with the fixed idea of establishing the Community of Equality at once. On January 25th, therefore, the second constitution was proposed, by which the community, which had hardly become used to the first one, was to be reorganised on the basis of community of property, with a general assembly as the chief authority, and a council of six as its executive. This was adopted, with slight modifications, in February.

It was adopted; but it was so vague as to practical economic working methods of accountancy and distribution, that it was open to almost any interpretation. The constitution of the Preliminary Society had also been vague, but it had been possible to make it work. It was because it did not work as well as it might have, that everyone had looked to Owen's return for something more definite; but when the hypnotic influence of his oratory had subsided, the New Harmonites found that they had been deprived of what little practical guidance they had. 'This was "liberty, equality, and fraternity" in downright earnest', wrote Robert Dale Owen, the son of the founder. 'It found favour with that heterogeneous collection of radicals, enthusiastic devotees to principle, honest latitudinarians, and lazy theorists, with a sprinkling of unprincipled sharpers thrown in.' Services to the community were no longer to be rewarded in proportion to their worth, as under the Preliminary Society, but equal privileges and advantages were assured to every member of the community. It was resolved that all members of the Preliminary Society who signed the constitution within three days could, with their families, become members. Most of them signed, but some refused; and a group of the latter, who objected to Owen's deistic beliefs, made plans to start a separate community. Owen granted them land about two miles from the Rappite settlement, and 150 installed themselves there in log cabins. This society was known as Community No. 2 or Macluria, after William Maclure, the most impressive member of the Boatload of Knowledge, President of the Philadelphia Academy of Natural Sciences from 1817 until his death in 1840, 'Father of American Geology', and an innovator in America of the Pestalozzian system of education. Macluria lasted nine months.

Within a fortnight of adopting the second constitution, New Harmony became so disharmonious that the majority of members begged Owen to resume personal control. Accommodatingly, he did so, and succeeded in restoring a certain amount of order. The number of idlers was greatly reduced; workshops and farms became more productive. The *Gazette*, which had been jubilant at the introduction of the Community of Equality, was now even more jubilant at the introduction of its successor.

Owen, however, had only papered over the cracks; for in

March a second schism took place, and one more community was set up on the New Harmony estate. It was settled mostly by English farmers, who were skilled workers but strong drinkers, and were therefore opposed to Owen's teetotal beliefs. It was named Feiba Peveli, the strange title being the invention of Mr. Stedman Whitwell.[1]

Internal division had now become one of the main preoccupations of the New Harmonists. Maclure, who was alarmed by this tendency, proposed that New Harmony should be divided into several communities 'as being the best and perhaps the only way to apportion the labour either justly or accurately, and to reduce the responsibility of payments within the sphere of the previous habits of calculation; education and amusements to remain upon the same footing as before'; and one correspondent in the ever-helpful and serene *Gazette* even suggested names for these prospective societies—names such as Lovedale, Everblest, Glee, Lovely, Voltaire, Socrates, and Peace Glen.

Owen, with some modifications, met these demands in a third constitution, which divided Community No. 1 (as it was called) into three sections. These in their turn were found to be unworkable, largely owing to the fact that the most responsible members had gone to Communities 2 and 3, leaving behind a large number of incompetents and parasites. This division took place in March; and before the end of the year there were more constitutions.

[1] Whitwell was a London architect and a social reformer who liked to spend his time writing verses and making drawings of elaborate community palaces. Brought to America by Owen, he noticed with disgust the tendency to name one town after another 'Washington' or 'Springfield', and decided that this poverty of invention must be stopped. Each locality was to be given a distinctive name which would express in words the latitude and longitude of the place, thus enabling it to be located geographically once the key was known. Letters were substituted for numerals in a complex system of ciphers, to which were added rules for pronunciation of the names arrived at and advice for overcoming various technical difficulties. New York, had Whitwell had his way, would have become Otke Notive and London, Lafa Vovutu. Lockwood tells us that the 'principal argument in favour of the new system presented by the author was that the name of a neighbouring Indian chief, "Occoneocoglecoco-cachecachecodungo", was even worse than some of the effects produced by this "rational system" of nomenclature'.

With each controversy, each schism, and each new constitution, New Harmony lost more members. By June, however, Owen had not even begun to waver in his optimism. On 4th July 1826, he produced what seemed to him to be the most memorable manifesto since the Declaration of Independence, of which this date was the fiftieth anniversary. This was his famous 'Declaration of Mental Independence', in which he averred 'that man up to this hour has been in all parts of the earth a slave to a trinity of the most monstrous evils that could be combined to inflict mental and physical evil upon the whole race. I refer to private or individual property, absurd and irrational systems of religion, and marriage founded upon individual property, combined with some of these irrational systems of religion.' This uncompromising statement, which undoubtedly tickled Owen's fancy and flattered his sense of showmanship, was scarcely likely to heal the breach between the religious and non-religious members—a breach that could hardly have been wider in any community. However, the *Gazette* was thereafter dated in the first and second years of Mental Independence. ...

Towards the end of the year, when his ingenuity had been taxed to the full to invent new constitutions, and when some irreverent members had made arrangements for an imposing funeral procession to put New Harmony symbolically in its grave, Owen at last began to have doubts. They came too late, however; the tide was ebbing fast. Early in the new year Owen offered parts of the estate for sale; a waxworks and puppet-show appeared in the settlement; gin-houses were opened. In March, eighty people departed by boat with the intention of ascending the Ohio in order to found a community near Cincinnati. The granary, public eating-house, cook-house, meeting-house, and sitting-rooms were deserted; the few remaining members were obliged to take their meals in the boarding school.

In April, Owen and Maclure sued each other over financial arrangements, having become disillusioned with one another's educational policies. By June, when Owen left for New York on his way to England, the community, as a community, was finished. Owen, however, delivered lectures painting attractive pictures of ten new colonies settling on portions of the New Harmony estate. These, which he had advertised for, did not actually exist; Owen remained what he had always been—an incurable addict of hallucinatory optimism.

The original optimism, had it been applied to facts rather than fancies, would have been by no means unjustified; for no communitarian experiment had ever been, or ever was to be, started under such favourable circumstances. Entering ready-made homes, and taking over thousands of acres of farmsteads, orchards, vineyards, and cultivated fields, the Owenites escaped the usual pioneering toil, started free from debt, and were able to rely upon the financial resources of a wealthy philanthropist. Yet the project failed before it ever became a true community.

Some of the reasons which contributed to its disintegration have already been mentioned: failure to select members, absence of any binding force, and the vulnerable impetuosity of Owen himself. The sectarian communities had assimilated their members gradually, over a number of years, after many tests of good faith; they were bound by a common belief, and united, in the critical early years, by a life-and-death struggle for existence. Moreover, their personnel consisted almost entirely of men and women who were used to hard work, and whose intellectual and æsthetic needs were extremely few; and they had no grandiose notions of transforming the world.

With the Owenites, however, it was very different. The large number of intellectual and middle-class members did not mix well with those of humbler origin. Maclure and the distinguished scientists and educators that he brought with him were always travelling about the country or absorbed in their own private interests; and when they attempted manual labour, as did Thomas Say, the greatest American geologist of his time, they were thoroughly unfitted for it. The Duke of Saxe-Weimar, who visited New Harmony in 1826, has left a description of this distinguished man 'with his hands covered with hard lumps and blisters, occasioned by the unusual labour he was obliged to undertake in the garden'.[1] He has also described how 'the better-educated members kept themselves together, and took no notice of the others'; how, at a ball, the lower classes did not participate in the dance, but read newspapers which were scattered over the side-tables; how the 'higher classes of society had put on the new costume,[2] and made a party by themselves'; and how a 'delicately brought up' young lady almost wept with vexation when she was called to 'the servile employment' of milking.

Paul Brown, a carping but not entirely unreliable critic, mentions the 'individual sufferings from the privations and embarrassments arising out of the continual shifting of arrangements'. At the end of 1826 'Money was in higher repute than in any other town, and became almost an object of worship. . . . Every one was for himself, as the saying is.'

Here, then, were sufficient reasons for failure. By 1830, every Owenite community—of which there had been about a dozen, including those on the New Harmony estate—had ceased to exist. Owen, who had announced that he would 'introduce an entire new system of society', had proved incapable, on this occasion, of uniting 1,000 men and women in a common enterprise. Yet, in his farewell address, he said that he felt that results had been achieved which justified the experiment; and it is possible to agree with him, for his philanthropic idealism provided an opportunity for a number of educational reformers to start work of considerable importance.

Owen himself, even in his early days, had been a pioneer in educational reform. When he visited de Fellenburg's Pestaloz-

---

[1] Robert Dale Owen (in *Threading My Way*) describes the same type of experience: 'I had previously tried one day sowing wheat by hand, and held out until evening, but my right arm was comparatively useless for forty-eight hours thereafter.'

[2] 'That for the man consists of white pantaloons, buttoned over a boy's jacket, made of light material, without a collar; that of the woman of a coat reaching to the knee, and pantaloons such as little girls wear among us. These dresses are not universally adopted, but they have a good appearance.'

DESIGN FOR AN OWENITE COMMUNITY. *One of Stedman Whitwell's many drawings* (*see footnote on p.* 109).

zian School at Hofwyl, he found that very few modifications
were necessary in order to bring his own schools up to the same
standard; indeed, these New Lanark schools were Owen's
proudest exhibit at that establishment, and they drew a considerable number of visitors whose main interests were education first
and general social reform second. Among such visitors, in 1824,
was William Maclure. He introduced himself to Owen, and the
two men discovered that they had much in common. Both were
rich, and therefore able to put their theories to the test; both had
eliminated religion from their teaching; and both severely indicted the existing social order. Maclure, however, believed in
reform by education alone, Owen in the reform of the whole
environment. This difference must have appeared to be surmount-
able, for in the following year Owen invited Maclure to New
Harmony, and when he arrived—with his boatload of distinguished collaborators—placed him in sole charge of education.
Later, however, the two men quarrelled when Owen charged the
failure of the community to Maclure's exclusive educational
policy and lack of interest in the community as a whole. There
may have been some truth in this accusation; if so, part of the
blame lies with Owen himself for permitting such a state of
affairs to exist; and whether or not Maclure's policy was disastrous
to the community as such, New Harmony would have been
deprived of its one notable achievement if Maclure had not acted
as he did.

Besides bringing Thomas Say with him in his 'Boatload of
Knowledge', Maclure brought a third geologist, Dr. Gerard
Troost, who subsequently became a professor at Nashville University, and Charles Leseur, the French naturalist who had
explored Australia. (Another naturalist, who also became a professor, the eccentric Constantine Raffinesque, frequently visited
and taught at New Harmony.) And among Maclure's education-
alists there were Professor Neef, who had been associated with
Pestalozzi's school in Switzerland, and two other Pestalozzian
teachers, Mme. Frotageot and Phiquepal d'Arusmont. This was
an impressive list of names; and the individuals included in it were

to exert a considerable influence upon the educational system of the nation. Their opportunity occurred with the disintegration of New Harmony as a community, for Maclure had by this time obtained complete freedom to conduct his educational experiment as he pleased.

This experiment was the most ambitious and inclusive that had yet been attempted in America, and perhaps anywhere else. It established the first kindergarten, the first infants' school, the first distinctive trade school, the first school system offering the same educational advantages to both sexes, and the first self-governing or 'free' school. It also determined upon co-education in all its schools. It not only introduced the Pestalozzian system of teaching to the American nation (which was later to adopt it everywhere), but also contributed directly to its eventual success by acting as a training centre for teachers who were to popularise the system when they left the community. In the same way, Robert Dale Owen became the most notable advocate in America of 'free, equal, and universal schools', the legislative father of the Indiana free-school system—which was adopted throughout the Middle West—and a begetter of the Smithsonian Institution.

This was a record of which any unsuccessful communitarian society could be proud. The influence of New Harmony, however, was not confined to educational matters. Robert Dale Owen was also a great champion, in the Indiana legislature, of women's rights. He procured for women the right to own and control their separate property and their individual earnings during marriage; he modified the state divorce laws so as to enable a married woman to secure relief from an habitually drunk or cruel husband; and he secured for widows the absolute ownership of one-third of their deceased husband's property. In this latter campaign he was undoubtedly influenced by the remarkable work of Frances Wright, who was one of the first arrivals at New Harmony and had accompanied the Rappites to Pennsylvania in order to study their society.

Fanny Wright, the ward of Jeremy Bentham, the intimate friend of Lafayette and of many European reformers, the advocate of complete universal suffrage, the political, moral, and religious radical, and the courageous champion of emancipation for Negroes and women, deserves to be placed beside Lloyd Garrison, on the one hand, and Mary Wollstonecraft, on the other. Her community of Nashoba, which was intended to educate and liberate Negro slaves, is of exceptional interest. While Frances Wright was resident at Nashoba, there was a possibility of modest success. Unfortunately, she became ill, and was obliged to leave. During her absence details of free-love associations between Negroes and whites were published by the uncompromising reformer who took her place as head of the community. This was more than the public could stand, and a great outcry was raised against Frances Wright and all that she represented. She returned with Robert Dale Owen in 1827, when an attempt was made to place Nashoba on an associative rather than a communal footing, but this was unsuccessful, and the scheme soon came to an end.

After the failure of New Harmony, when the *Gazette* was removed to New York—changing its title to the *Free Enquirer* —it was edited for several years by Robert Dale Owen and Frances Wright, both of whom also delivered lectures on many aspects of social reform. In close sympathy with them were two young Englishmen who had arrived in New York in 1820— George Henry Evans and his brother, Frederick William. They published successively *The Working Man's Advocate*, *The Daily Sentinel*, and *Young America*. Although these newspapers demanded equal rights for women and the abolition of 'chattel slavery and wages slavery', they placed emphasis upon educational and land reform. The former demands, however, were endorsed by 600 journals in different parts of the United States and eventually resulted in the formation of a political Working Men's Party in New York State. In the city of New York, where this party amalgamated with the Whigs, it succeeded in electing four of its candidates to the Legislature. Thus, in its last direct manifestation in the Labour Movement of America, Owenism scored a small triumph.

It is interesting to note that Frederick William Evans, the

radical journalist, abandoned freethinking circles for Shakerdom in 1831. He became that Elder Evans—the most notable Shaker born in the nineteenth century—whose name is already familiar.

With this completion of the circle that began when Robert Owen was encouraged to found a community of his own by hearing of the success of the Shakers, it would be pleasing to end; but a word remains to be said of New Harmony itself. It was not abandoned; many of the scientists and other intellectuals remained in residence; and in 1839, when Owen's son, David Dale Owen, was appointed U.S. geologist, he established there the head-quarters of the U.S. Geological Survey, where it remained until 1846, when the Smithsonian Institution was completed. The little town was also responsible, through the example and industry of its Working Men's Institute and Library, for the growth of 144 public libraries in Indiana. Maclure, who financed the scheme when it started, can thus add to his other claims for recognition that of being the first founder of free libraries. In 1874, fifty years after the Rappites had left their former home, they purchased the dilapidated old church, demolished it, and converted it into a school building which they presented to the town as a memorial to Father Rapp. These admirable people completed their good work by spending a further $2,000 on repairing the building in which the Working Men's Institute and Library were housed.

CHAPTER SEVEN

EXCITEMENTS AND INSTITUTIONS

One man renounces the use of animal food; and another of coin;
and another of domestic hired service; and another of the State. . . .

Emerson.

NOYES, in his *History of American Socialisms,* points out with his
usual acumen, that 'a vast spiritual and intellectual excitement is
one thing; and the *institutions* that rise out of it are another. We
must not judge the excitement by the institutions.' Thus, although
New Harmony and the smaller communities associated with it
had died out by 1830, the work of Robert Dale Owen and Fanny
Wright agitated the country and actually found its way into the
programme of the Democratic Party. 'The excitement about
Owen's ideas, which was really the Owen movement, reached its
height about 1830; and the embers of it are in the heart of the
nation to this day.' Moreover, Owenism prepared the way for
Fourierism: 'The same men, or at least the same sort of men that
took part in the Owen movement were afterward carried away
by the Fourier enthusiasm. The two movements may therefore
be regarded as one; and in that view the period of the great
American socialistic revival extends from 1824, through the
final overwhelming excitement of 1843, to the collapse of
Fourierism after 1846.'

Noyes has also shown how revivalist and socialistic excitement
alternated with one another, Nettleton (in 1817) preparing the
way for Finney (in 1830), just as Owen had prepared the way
for Fourier. Certainly, in the ten years between 1830 and 1840,
when no new communities were started, the main activity was
in the religious field. The disestablishment of the Churches, begun

at Rhode Island and given an impetus by the American Revolution, was completed in 1833 with the conquest of Massachusetts, the last stronghold of authoritarianism. The revivalism of the frontier permeated everywhere among the former minority churches and their fractional sects, among the 'come-outers', and among the small groups that were constantly being formed and re-formed about local preachers. In such an environment, the Church of Jesus Christ of the Latter-Day Saints, founded by Joseph Smith with only six followers, in 1830, grew so rapidly that its membership was at least 15,000 when Nauvoo was established ten years later.

The general history of the Mormons, which has so often been told, lies outside the scope of this book. Two aspects of their sensational story must, however, be mentioned. These are the co-operative and communistic schemes with which they experimented in the 'seventies, and the significance of their polygamy. The former phenomenon will be dealt with in a later chapter; the latter may be alluded to at once. Mormon polygamy was part of the general attack that was everywhere being made upon the institution of monogamy. Celibacy among the Shakers and Rappites, and the system of complex marriages which we shall encounter at Oneida, are other examples of this attack; and there can be little doubt that, whatever immediate sanctions for these unorthodox practices were advanced by those who introduced them, they served a useful purpose in binding such societies together. They necessarily involved a direction of interest towards the group rather than towards the individual.

Owen, without the binding force of either a common religious impulse or a radical attack upon the accepted relationship of the sexes, had also attempted to direct attention towards social, or communistic, interests at New Harmony—and had failed to do so. In four of the five communities that were started immediately before the Fourierist campaign, the reaction from Owenistic communism was clearly evident. While advocating combination and association, they directed as much attention towards the individual as towards the society itself. Hopedale was an attempt to combine individual and common interests, members being permitted to hold property and carry on business independently of the community; the Northampton Association was co-operative rather than communistic; Brook Farm was a joint-stock undertaking; and the ephemeral Fruitlands represented the very soul of an eccentric individualist. Before describing these communities, which initiated the most crowded and excited phase of nineteenth-century experiments, and which brought to a close the period of ten years in which revivalism was dominant, one man, who anticipated the change in outlook from communism to individualism, deserves consideration.

Josiah Warren was an orchestral leader and an inventor, established at Cincinnati, where at the age of twenty-five, having patented a new type of oil lamp, he was running a factory for the production of it. When Owen visited the city in 1824, Warren followed him to New Harmony, where he became conductor of the orchestra. He stayed two years and left, unlike many, without bitterness or cynicism, attributing the failure of the community to suppression of individuality, lack of initiative, and absence of personal responsibility. The basis of all future reform, he decided, must be absolute individual liberty. Everyone must be free to dispose of his person, his property, his time and his reputation as he pleased—but always at his own cost. And since New Harmony had convinced him that any theory of social reform must be put to the test, he began his first practical experiment of this kind by opening the Equity Store at Cincinnati, in 1827.

The Equity Store became popularly known as the Time Store since Warren used a clock to determine the amount of compensation due to him. Customers paid Warren, in cash, the actual cost price of the articles they wished to buy, and in addition handed him a labour note representing the amount of time Warren had spent in attending to them; and Warren gave labour notes, representing the time spent upon the manufacture of an article, to those who brought him goods to sell. In spite of the difficulties involved in valuing various kinds of labour on the basis of time, the Store was a great success. It cut out the middleman's immense profits, perfectly equated demand with supply, and encouraged individual tradesmen to ignore the petty restrictions of quite unnecessary apprenticeship.

Thus encouraged, Warren set himself to learn several trades—such as wood- and metal-working, type-founding and printing—in order that he might be better qualified to start a co-operative industrial village. This idea he actually put into practice in the village of Equity, Ohio, which led to some interesting experiments in industrial and practical education. Unfortunately, it soon had to be abandoned owing to the malarial condition of the neighbourhood. Immediately following the abandonment of Equity, Warren entered upon a new phase of his life, which was to coincide with the interim period between the Owenite and Hopedale communities. At this time, apart from explaining the principles of equity in one of the most remarkable weekly newspapers ever printed,[1] Warren devoted his energies to invention, and did not return to social experiments until 1842, from which time he was to be constantly occupied with such schemes until 1860—but we shall hear more of him before that date.

Individualism combined with social responsibility and religious liberalism was the principle upon which the Hopedale Community was founded. Adin Ballou, the Christian Socialist who founded it, had been expelled from the Rhode Island 'Christian Connection' for subscribing to Universalism. Joining his relative, Hosea Ballou, he then became a leading figure in the Universalist Society, but believing that all hope of universal salvation had been conveniently forgotten by the complacently orthodox ministers of this formerly liberal church, he withdrew from it, taking with him a number of ministers who shared his conception of a struggle for social justice as being

[1] *The Peaceful Revolutionist,* which had an existence of several months. Bailie tells how Warren invented and built the press upon which it was printed, made the type-moulds, cast the type and the stereo-plates, wrote the articles, set them up, and printed off the four sheets of the paper—the typography of which was 'conspicuously neat'.

the true means of salvation. Thus was organised the Massachusetts Association of Universal Redemptionists, from which the Hopedale Community was born in January 1841.

Starting with a joint stock of $4,000, Ballou's company bought 600 acres of land near Milford, Massachusetts. Here they built about thirty houses, a chapel, and several large workshops; and within ten years their membership had risen from thirty to 175. The nature of the community has been better described by its founder than by anyone else. 'It is', he wrote in 1851, 'a Church of Christ (so far as any human organisation of professed Christians, within a particular locality, have the right to claim that title), based on a simple declaration of faith in the religion of Jesus Christ, as He taught and exemplified it, according to the Scriptures of the New Testament, and of acknowledged subjection to all the moral obligations of that religion. No precise theological dogmas, ordinances or ceremonies are prescribed or prohibited. In such matters all members are free, with mutual love and toleration, to follow their own highest convictions of truth and religious duty—answerable only to the great Head of the true Church Universal. But in practical Christianity this Church is precise and strict. There its essentials are specific. It insists on supreme love to God and man—that love which "worketh no ill" to friend or foe. It enjoins total abstinence from all God-contemning words and deeds; all unchastity; all intoxicating beverages; all oath-taking; all slave-holding and pro-slavery compromises; all war and preparations for war; all capital and other vindictive punishments; all insurrectionary, seditious, mobocratic and personal violence against any government, society, family or individual.'

This statement of belief and practice would have been largely subscribed to by most dissident sects in the heretical tradition from the Middle Ages to the nineteenth century. Clear and uncompromising, it echoes the faith of the Primitive Church. In addition to these religious preoccupations, however, Hopedale was also concerned with social duties. 'It is', Ballou continued, 'a moral power anti-slavery society, radical and without compromise. It

is a peace society on the only impregnable foundation of Christian
non-resistance. It is a sound theoretical and practical woman's
rights association. It is a charitable society for the relief of suffering humanity, to the extent of its humble ability. It is an
educational society, preparing to act an important part in the
training of the young. It is a socialistic Community, successfully
actualising, as well as promulgating practical Christian socialism
—the only kind of socialism likely to establish a true social state
on earth. . . . It affords a most desirable opportunity for those who
mean to be practical Christians in the use of property, talent, skill
or productive industry, to invest them. Here those goods and gifts
may all be so employed as to benefit their possessors to the full
extent of justice, while at the same time they afford aid to the less
favoured, help build up a social state free from the evils of
irreligion, ignorance, poverty and vice, to promote the regeneration of the race, and thus resolve themselves into treasure laid up
where neither moth, nor rust, nor thieves can reach them. Here
property is pre-eminently safe, useful and beneficent. It is Chris-
tianised. So, in a good degree, are talent, skill, and productive
industry. . . . Such is the Hopedale Community as a civil state. . . .
There is no Red Republicanism in it, because it eschews blood;
yet it is the seedling of the true democratic and social republic,
wherein neither caste, colour, sex nor age, stands proscribed, but
every human being shares justly in "liberty, equality and fraternity." . . . It guarantees to all its members and dependents employment, at least adequate to a comfortable subsistence; relief in want,
sickness or distress; decent opportunities for religious, moral, and
intellectual culture; an orderly, well-regulated neighbourhood;
fraternal counsel, fellowship, and protection under all circumstances; and a suitable sphere of individual enterprise and responsibility, in which each one may by due self-exertion elevate himself
to the highest point of his capabilities.'

This extract from an extraordinarily extensive catalogue of
claims made on behalf of the community, although undoubtedly
sincere, leaves more than a suspicion of wishful thinking on the
part of its author; for he envisaged 'an indefinite number of

Communities, scattered far and wide throughout the land and world, which were to be coordinated and organically united in a great ecumenical federation styled "The Practical Christian Communion".' This programme proved too ambitious, and the first constitution, of which it formed a part, was replaced by a second, in 1847. This provided that the affairs of the community should be placed in the hands of a board of trustees—and for a time there was general improvement in the financial and industrial state of the community; but there was apparently some source of discontent, since monthly meetings were instituted in the following year, which were 'designed to consider and take action upon such instances of more or less reprehensible conduct on the part of members as might have been made public, to correct existing abuses, to allay strife and bitterness, to reconcile alienated feeling, to restore harmony when broken or disturbed, and to apply the proper remedy to all known offences and misdemeanours; and also to talk over in an informal, friendly and confidential way whatever was calculated to help repress and hold in check the lower tendencies of human nature, to overcome bad habits, resist temptation, stimulate the better nature, and develop in all our souls the graces and power of the Christian character and life. They were to be fraternal character and life. They were to be fraternal tribunals for obtaining judgement upon overt acts of folly and wrong, and at the same time schools for mutual discipline and culture in the things that pertain to the Kingdom of God.'

With this adoption of a system of mutual criticism that was a common feature of many communities—designed to promote greater solidarity—Hopedale acquired the one ingredient of success that it had lacked. In 1852 it reached the peak of its prosperity, and even managed to weather the storm of a 'free-love episode' which caused much scandal, and resulted in the expulsion of the offenders. By 1854, there were 235 members, and an attempt was made to found a new colony at Union Grove, Minnesota. This, however, soon failed owing to trouble with Indians and lack of support from Hopedale—which, by 1856, had got into serious difficulties, from which it never recovered.

This crisis in its affairs was caused by Ebenezer Draper and his brother, who together owned three-quarters of the community's stock. The Drapers were sharp businessmen who became alarmed at the ambitious plans of the community. Withdrawing their stock, they invested it in their own manufacturing company, and became virtual owners of what was now no more than a model industrial village. Thus, through the powerlessness of the community to control individual holdings, it brought about its own downfall. 'Its glory had departed; its sun had set forever', wrote Ballou; but he refused to join those members of the community who had accused the Draper brothers of treachery and bad faith, humbly maintaining that the experiment had failed 'because as a whole we lacked the Christlike wisdom and virtue necessary to the successful prosecution and final triumph of such an undertaking'. It would have been more correct to ascribe the failure to a different cause—that over-confidence in the goodness of human nature which alone could have allowed two unscrupulous persons a loophole through which they could control the fate of 200. Thus, in spite of its otherwise adequate social machinery and its practical idealism, this attempt to combine communal and individual interests was brought to a sudden end by an oversight in its constitution—namely, the failure to restrict individual holdings in the company.

The community of Skaneateles, founded in 1843, very nearly suffered the same fate as Hopedale, though with less excuse; since, contrary to the practice of other communities founded in these years, it was organised upon a communistic basis. This characteristic, together with its repudiation of religion, placed it in the Owenistic tradition. It was founded by John A. Collins, famous in the eastern states as General Agent of the Massachusetts Anti-Slavery Society, and organiser of 100 Anti-Slavery Conventions. It was his practice, immediately after organising one of these meetings, to call a socialist convention in the same place, thus building up a considerable following.

In October 1843, having resigned from his other duties, he bought a farm of 350 acres and, imitating Owen, issued a general invitation to the public to join him. By the following January the new community had been formed, with 150 members; and in the same month was issued the first number of its newspaper, the *Communitist*.

A few weeks previously Collins had read to his prospective associates a statement of the principles which he considered essential to the formation of a community; and it is interesting to note that Collins, like Owen and Ballou, not to mention many men who were to follow, persisted in the belief that the advantages of his community might be 'ultimately secured to all the inhabitants of this globe'. In order 'to work out this great problem of human redemption', religion must go by the board. All forms of worship should cease, and belief in any special revelation of God to man was to be discountenanced. 'While we admire the precepts attributed to Jesus of Nazareth, we do not regard them as binding because uttered by Him but because they are true in themselves, and best adapted to promote the happiness of the race; therefore we regard the Sabbath as other days; the organised church as adapted to produce strife and contention rather than love and peace; the clergy as an imposition; the Bible as no authority; miracles as unphilosophical; and salvation from sin, or from punishment in a future world, through a crucified God, as a remnant of heathenism.'

If they had no use for religion, they were equally contemptuous of governments, disbelieving 'in the rightful existence of all governments based upon physical force; that they are organised bands of *banditti*, whose authority is to be disregarded: therefore we will not vote under such governments, or petition to them, but demand them to disband; do no military duty; pay no personal or property taxes; sit upon no juries; refuse to testify in courts of so-called justice; and never appeal to the law for a redress of grievances, but use all peaceful and moral means to secure their complete destruction'.

As to positive beliefs, they determined upon absolute

community of property, 'forever after yielding up their individual claims upon it'; championed monogamy in opposition to 'licentiousness, concubinage, adultery, bigamy and polygamy'; and were resolved upon the adoption of a vegetarian diet, and the abandonment of narcotics and stimulants. When it was found that there was not unanimous approval of these principles, the *Communitist* made amends by stating simply: 'Our principles are as broad as the universe, and as liberal as the elements that surround us. . . . We estimate the man by his acts rather than by his peculiar belief. We say to all, Believe what you may, but act as well as you can.'

Acting as well as he could, however, at first induced Collins to repeat a mistake made by Owen; for although he claimed the right to reject undesirable characters, he refused to appeal to any outside authority to help him do so; and being a believer in non-resistance, he found himself at the mercy of plausible impostors and rogues, one of whom, described by Hinds as a 'long-headed, tonguey Syracuse lawyer', succeeded in obtaining temporary control of half the estate. Collins, fortunately, was rich enough to buy him out and persuade him to leave; and wise enough to abandon the views—and the nebulous constitution—which had almost brought disaster to the group.

The actual end of Skaneateles was due to a decision that must be almost unique. After two or three years of prosperity which doubled the value of the property, Collins apparently tired of the scheme. Or perhaps the conflict between his principles of non-resistance and the necessity of using some sort of force in order to eject undesirables put too great a strain upon his idealistic nature. At all events, he decided that 'the community idea could not be carried out in practice', and, calling a meeting of members, he explained his feelings, deeded the estate to them, and departed 'like one who had lost his nearest and dearest friend'.[1] Most of the members withdrew soon afterwards, and the community quietly dissolved.

[1] Noyes, *History of American Socialisms*.

The Northampton Association, like Skaneateles, did not adopt any religious creed; nor was any particular form of worship enjoined. There was a weekly meeting, at which all had the right to express their opinions freely and at which it soon became evident that there was a serious division between those who approved of card-playing, dancing, and other amusements and those who thought them improper. At first this difference of views led to acrimonious debate, which resulted in the withdrawal of a number of members; but later, religious and ethical differences were accepted without causing a disturbance.

The Northampton Association of Education and Industry was formed by David Mack, Samuel Hill, George Benson, William Adam, and a handful of others who held their first meeting in April 1842, when they adopted a preamble, constitution, and laws. They were soon joined by others who, like them, were in search of a purer, freer, and more earnest life than could easily be found within any particular sect or within the framework of ordinary capitalist society. Worthy motives and a desire to lead the good life were the only criteria of membership.

The Association was co-operative rather than communistic. Wages were paid—equally to both sexes, and at a similar rate for all work—and a small charge was made for food and lighting. In this respect the Association was similar to Fourierism; as it was also to some extent in housing sixty or seventy of its members in a single building. It is said that the members—of whom there were never more than 130 at any given time—were satisfied with extreme simplicity of diet and of dress. This was just as well, as the community speedily became impoverished. Beginning with 500 acres of land, six dwelling-houses, a silk factory four stories high, a saw-mill and other property—of which the total value was $31,000—they incurred a debt of $11,000 at purchase. This they had hoped to pay off, but, owing to further expenses and to the withdrawal of certain members who owned stock, the debt was increased fourfold and became altogether crippling. A subscription which was opened in the hope that more stock would be taken up proved unsuccessful, and in 1846 the affairs of the Association were wound up.

At Brook Farm we shall find ourselves standing upon the threshold of these Fourierist schemes; but for the moment we shall describe only its early period, before its conversion to Fourierism.

George Ripley, who founded the Farm, had been a minister of the Unitarian Church until he had encountered in it the same lack of liberalism that Adin Ballou had met with in Universalism. Ripley therefore resigned his ministry in 1841, and at the same time, by leaving Boston to start the Farm, left the society of the Transcendentalists. Transcendentalism—at any rate in its New England form—came into being when Emerson, who had also been a minister of the Unitarian Church in Boston, extended the the beliefs of that church until they could find a place for the nascent evolutionist science of the day and the newly explored mysticism of the East. Transcendentalism was thus a humanist religion 'with an unswerving witness in the soul', open to evolutionists, monists, and pragmatists, as well as to anyone who believed 'in an order of truth that transcends the sphere of the external senses'. It was the faith of the American Romantic Revival in literature—of Emerson, Thoreau, and Hawthorne—and it inspired the humanitarianism of Bronson Alcott, Theodore Parker, Margaret Fuller, Elizabeth Palmer Peabody, and many others.

Ripley would have welcomed the participation of these people in his experiment, but, with the exception of Hawthorne, who joined the Farm, their support was lukewarm. Emerson, indeed, was to refer to Brook Farm as 'a perpetual picnic, a French Revolution in small, an age of reason in a patty-pan'—a statement that bears little relation to the truth. That the Brook Farmers were determined 'to secure as many hours as possible from necessary toil' is true; but they wished to do so in order that they might use this leisure 'for the production of intellectual goods'. They hoped to be able to provide, 'not only all the necessaries, but all the elegances desirable for bodily and for spiritual health: books,

Considérant Del

DESIGN FOR A FOURIERIST PHALANSTERY, *by Victor Considérant* (*see p.* 139). *Like Whitwell's design, it was an unrealised ideal.*

apparatus, collections for science, works of art, means of beautiful amusement'[1]—all of which were to be held in common. Here, at last, was an aim worth any amount of preliminary toil—an aim the fulfilment of which would supply the one great deficiency of even the most successful communities that already existed. Even if Brook Farm had started with no other end in view than this, it would have justified itself; but it would not have been a perpetual picnic, for no group intent upon self-support and the acquisition of leisure could afford to neglect the toil that was necessary in order to achieve them.

The Farm, however, had no such limited aims: consisting largely of intellectuals, it suffered a little, perhaps, from the characteristic awe with which such people are inclined to look upon manual labour and the good earth. 'We meant to lessen the labouring man's great burthen of toil by performing our due share of it at the cost of our own thews and sinews', wrote Ripley; and the Farmers paid all labour, whether manual or intellectual, at the same rate, on the principle that as the labour becomes merely bodily, 'it is a greater sacrifice to the individual labourer to give his time to it; because time is desirable for the cultivation of the intellect, in exact proportion to ignorance. Besides, intellectual labour involves in itself higher pleasures, and is more its own reward, than bodily labour.' (Hawthorne, whose experience of manual labour recalls that of Thomas Say, Robert Dale Owen, Adin Ballou,[2] and many other intellectuals, would certainly have agreed with the latter part of the above quotation. His bodily toil was performed not only at the cost of his thews and sinews, but also at the cost of the work for which he was fitted. After the day's work, he found that he had no energy left for writing.)

One of Ripley's most earnest aims was the abolition of domestic servitude. Accordingly, it was abolished, and in 1844 he was able to report to the New York Convention of Associationists

[1] Elizabeth Palmer Peabody in *The Dial,* January 1842.

[2] He was frequently, he said, so tired by his labour in the fields that he would lie down under a haystack earnestly praying that he might never rise again.

that 'we have now for three years lived at Brook Farm and have
carried on all the business of life without it. . . . We do freely,
from the love of it, those duties which are usually discharged by
domestics.' In a community which fulfilled the two conditions of
success named by Noyes as of primary importance—namely,
religious principle and previous acquaintance—a social equality
was realised that put New Harmony to shame. This success was
undoubtedly due, also, to the limited number of members, which
made a compact and easily manageable group.

Beginning with only twenty members, the Farm never had
more than seventy or eighty. They all helped assiduously to cultivate the 160 acres, and succeeded in setting up several small industries as well. Most of the members paid for their board out of
their wages for labouring, but in the case of inability to work due
to sickness or old age, support was guaranteed—as it was, of
course, to women and children. Stockholders, however, when they
did not work, were subject to a charge which never exceeded the
interest on their shares. Although co-operative in principle, the
Farm had a genuine communal spirit, which included free
education and the purchase of all the necessities of life at wholesale
prices.

Some efficiency may have been lost owing to lack of practical
experience; and also owing to the adoption of a system by which
all took turns at the various types of work; but what was lost
in efficiency was thus made up in the personal interest of each
member in the experiment. They lived in an atmosphere that was
enlivened by intellectual tolerance and free discussion; their
nightly dances, their frequent picnics and boating parties, their
performances of plays, their pageants, tableaux, and charades all
testified to a free contentment that is rare among community
members. Their success lay partly in the modesty of their aims,
which never included the conversion of the world, and partly in
the good faith of their members, among whom there was never
a Count de Leon, an Ebenezer Draper, or a 'long-headed, tonguey
Syracuse lawyer'.

Even so, it is doubtful if Brook Farm could have succeeded

without its school, from which the greater part of its income was derived. This school, in which the development of creative ability and the selection of subjects for study were given prominence over meaningless discipline, is justly famous. The excellence of its methods is reflected in the success of its students—among whom were George William and James Burrill Curtis, Father Isaac Hecker (the future organiser of the Paulist Fathers), and General Francis Barlow, who became Attorney-General of New York. Orestes Brownson and George Bancroft both sent two sons to the school, and Margaret Fuller's younger brother was also a pupil.

The Farm, in its idyllic setting near the Charles River, with pine woods, lush meadows, and gently rolling hills surrounding it, was near enough to Boston for frequent visits to be made by various eminent sympathisers and well-wishers; yet it was a complete, self-contained, and spontaneous colony, with a vivid and refreshing personality of its own, requiring neither assistance nor interference from without. Interference, in the form of Fourierism, was brought to it, however; and although this was due to the wishes of the majority of the members, the results—described in the next chapter—were deplorable.

Transcendentalism, with which Brook Farm was connected (although it did not actually espouse it), was certainly the mainspring of Fruitlands, to which Emerson's description of Brook Farm as a perpetual picnic might with more truth have been applied. In this case, however, the picnic would have provided limited nourishment, for the Fruitlanders would neither use nor consume anything which caused suffering or harm to any living creature. Their diet was strictly of the pure and bloodless kind, completely devoid of all animal substances.

'The pure soul', wrote Bronson Alcott, the founder of the community, 'by the law of its own nature, adopts a pure diet and cleanly customs; nor needs detailed instruction for daily conduct. The greater part of man's duty consists in leaving alone much that he is in the habit of doing. Shall I sip tea or coffee? the inquiry may be. No. Abstain from all ardent, as from alcoholic drinks. Shall I consume pork, beef or mutton? No, if you value health or life. Shall I stimulate with milk? No. Shall I warm my bathing water? Not if cheerfulness is valuable. Shall I clothe in many garments? Not if purity is aimed at. Shall I prolong my dark hours, consuming animal oil, and losing bright daylight in the morning? Not if a clear mind is an object. Shall I teach my children the dogma inflicted on myself, under the pretence that I am transmitting truth? Nay, if you love them intrude not these between them and the Spirit of all Truth. Shall I become a hireling, or hire others? Shall I subjugate cattle? Shall I trade? Shall I claim property in any created things? Shall I adopt a form of religion? Shall I become a parent? Shall I interest myself in politics? To how many of these questions, could we ask deeply enough, could they be heard as having relation to our eternal welfare, would the response be—"Abstain. Be not so active to do as sincere to Be".'

'Be not so active to do . . .'

What did they do? They rose at early dawn, took first a cold plunge, second a music lesson, and third a breakfast of the grains, fruits, nuts, and herbs that were native to the locality. The morning was then spent in following 'some occupation' until the vegetarian lunch, when usually some 'interesting and deep-searching conversation gave rest to the body and development to the mind'. Further 'occupation', either in- or out-of-doors, according to the state of the weather, carried them on to the evening meal, when they again engaged in deep discussion until sunset, when they went to bed.

Since Alcott, the most spontaneous of men, believed that work should rely not so much on reasoning or skill as on 'the spirit's dictates', it is hardly surprising that his tiny community lasted only from the spring to the autumn of 1843. That Alcott was 'sincere to Be' is indubitable, but he was at once an extreme individualist and a man with a deep sense of social responsibility. Spurning Hopedale and Brook Farm—both of which communities he had been invited to join—as too gross and commonplace to satisfy his ethereal desires, and owing the financial backing of Fruitlands to his English disciple, Charles Lane, who was a most erratic and temperamental fanatic, Alcott was unable to distinguish between spiritual ideals and practical possibilities. Refusing to 'exploit' animals even for draught, refusing to wear wool because sheep would feel the loss of it and cotton because slaves produced it, using pine knots and bayberry wax for illumination, or sitting in darkness when these were unobtainable, planting vegetables at the wrong season, and deserting the community at harvest-time, neither Lane nor Alcott were ever able to adorn the lovely heights upon which their 100-acre farm was situated with the orchards and vineyards they had planned.

When the community failed, Alcott, braver than all other Transcendentalists in that he attempted to put its principles to the test, retained his faith. Lane, after spending the winter in the Shaker Society at Harvard because he thought he had embraced celibacy for life, returned to England, where he was shortly afterwards married.

At the time when Fruitlands failed, Brook Farm was on the verge of conversion to Fourierism. Its financial arrangements and its system of interchangeable occupations had already given it two Fourierist characteristics, and although Miss Peabody's article in *The Dial* of October 1841 included a disclaimer of Fourierism, it is probable that many of the Farmers had by that time read Brisbane's *Social Destiny of Man* (which had been published in 1840) and were eager to give Fourier's system a fair trial.

By 1843, the volume of Fourierist propaganda had reached proportions that were not only unprecedented but also never to be repeated in the history of communities. Fourier, however, had died six years before this remarkable activity, and perhaps it was well that he had; for the foolhardiness with which most of his followers attempted to realise his dreams would have greatly distressed this meticulous Frenchman.

CHAPTER EIGHT

FOURIER AND FOURIERISM

The Series distribute the Harmonies.
The Attractions are proportionate to the Destinies.

S O M E indication of the fantastic imaginings of Charles Fourier has already been given in an earlier chapter. The temptation to describe his extraordinary cosmological and social systems at length is almost irresistible, but since an entire book could hardly do justice to the sublime madness and the occasional gleam of sanity that are contained in the six or more volumes of Fourier's works, a mere résumé of his most important arguments and propositions cannot hope to convey more than an outline of the fantasies that await the reader of those fascinating books.

Fourier's work was largely conditioned by an unfortunate event that took place early in his otherwise uneventful life. His father, a wealthy merchant, left a fortune of nearly a quarter of a million francs; but the whole of this inheritance was lost in the French Revolution. When Fourier later received a tiny legacy from his mother, he set himself to invent a system of society that would prevent the recurrence of revolution, preserve his own petit-bourgeois class, and also abolish the appalling conditions of labour that were everywhere prevalent. His criticism of society developed into a criticism of the world. It was not merely that social wealth was unevenly distributed, or that the sufferings of the poor cried aloud for relief—the whole scheme of things was wrong from top to bottom of the universe. God, Fourier insisted, had created a universe on an ordered and harmonious plan, but so far he alone had realised what that plan was. '*Moi seul*', he writes time and time again, 'I alone comprehend the true plan and the means of fulfilling it.'

Since God created an harmonious universe, there must be an

harmonious relationship between everything that exists—a relationship depending upon the law of Attraction. Just as this law governs the movement of the heavenly bodies, so is it used by God to govern men; for God has thoughtfully distributed attraction and repulsion in such measure as will enable us to fulfil His plan. Every repellent task, for instance, has an attraction for somebody at some time; and if we choose to impose monotony and drudgery upon ourselves or others, that is our fault, and not God's. God, indeed, has given us passions that constantly impel us towards change and the experience of pleasure—in fact, it is through the passions that the law of attraction operates. All of them—carefully analysed, subdivided, and catalogued by the meticulous Fourier—all of them are good passions, and lead towards pleasure. It is only the environment with which we have surrounded ourselves that makes them bad. Like Owen, Fourier advises us to change our environment in order to abolish evil.

When our passions are fully gratified, as they will be in the ideal society, they will not only conduce to pleasure, but they will also serve useful ends by leading to the spontaneous association of human beings for the purposes of work. The smallest of such associations will be known as a Group, and it should consist of at least seven persons in order that it may be divided into Subgroups—two persons in each wing representing the 'ascending' and 'descending' extremes of tastes and tendencies, and three in the centre to maintain an equilibrium. Thus the two wings will engage with each other, and will also combine to engage with the centre, in friendly rivalry and competition. There will be Groups for every conceivable occupation, from that of growing roses—with one Group assigned to each colour or variety of rose —to that of raising poultry or driving elephants in the Burmese jungle. The division of labour is, in fact, unending in its ramifications and possibilities, since the Groups not only compete within themselves, wing against wing or wings against centre, but also against one another, and as many as thirty or forty groups may be engaged in rose-culture alone. Moreover a number of Groups— at least five—will constitute a Series, which again has its centre and two wings. Thus there will be an horticultural Series, a live-stock Series, an office-management Series, and so on. Finally—if anything can be called final in Fourier's intricate system of interdependent parts—the Series will unite to form a Phalanx, which ought to contain between 1,620 and 1,800 individuals.

It is important to stress the fact that all the members of a Phalanx are to be individuals and not mere cogs in a complex social machine. Free choice of occupation and movement from one Group to another and from Series to Series was provided for in order to make industry attractive by constantly varying the work—and the fellow workers—of any given person. In fact, Fourier suggests that the average individual will belong to no less than thirty or forty Groups, in each one of which he will probably work no longer than an hour and a half or two hours on end. Within the limits of a Phalanx, therefore, everyone ought to be able to fulfil himself completely.

The Phalanx should cover an area of about three square miles, of which the greater part will be given over to fields, orchards, and gardens. Somewhere on this estate will be the Phalanstery—the vast, three-story communal building that will house all the inhabitants of the Phalanx and provide them with every amenity they could possibly desire. The Phalanstery, like the groups and Series, will consist of a centre and two wings in which will be found apartments, a hotel, ballrooms, council-chambers, a library, workshops, dining-hall, kitchens, nurseries, schools, recreation-rooms, sanatoria, and so on. Granaries and stables will be housed in a building that will close the fourth side of the square—and in the quadrangle thus formed parades and festivities will be held, while from here also the Groups will set out each morning in orderly formation, with banners flying.

The property of the Phalanx will be represented by shares of stock, but every member need not be a stockholder, nor need a stockholder be a member. The Phalanx will keep accounts with every member, giving him credit for work, at certain fixed rates, and charging him for board, lodging, and other expenses. At the end of the year the profits of the Phalanx will be divided in the ratio of five-twelfths to labour, four-twelfths to capital, and three-twelfths to skill or talent. Among the members—of whom seven-eighths will be farmers and mechanics, and the rest capitalists, artists, and scientists—there will be no jealousy with regard to this division of profits, since all occupations are interchangeable, and each member may become a capitalist. In the same way the Phalanstery will provide humble and sumptuous apartments, banquets and simple fare, elegant and plain clothing—so that everyone may live according to his means and desires.

Work will be rewarded according to its usefulness, and the most disagreeable work will receive the highest pay. The beneficent passions so operate in children as to grant them pleasure in playing with dirt and refuse; they will therefore combine, in scavenging groups known as 'The Little Hordes', to do that work which is most repellent to adults—for which reason they will be honoured more highly than any other group, taking their place at the head of all parades and receiving the Salute of Esteem.

These are the saner ideas among those that are scattered with such abandon and are developed with such serious, absurd, minute, and obsessional detail in the pages of Fourier. Unable to linger over the many descriptions of enormous feasts, or to describe the great battle of the contending armies of cooks; having no time in which to investigate the pages of furious denunciation devoted to the Sixty Malevolent Characteristics that have transformed civilisation into 'a sink of corruption', nor space in which to reproduce a specimen of that blissful concurrence of pleasures, heaped one upon another, that constitutes a *parcours*; leaving regretfully the Chancellory of the Court of Love, the Corporations of Love, and the whole peculiar system of polyandry-cum-concubinage, and turning our backs upon a theory of immortality that entails a complete and detailed system of transmigration, we can only offer as compensation the briefest summary of Fourier's cosmology.

The stars and planets, it appears, are sentient beings like ourselves. Animated by the same passions that move us, they fall in love and reproduce their kind; moreover, they pass through the periods of infancy, youth, maturity, and decay; they die, like the moon, which contracted a fever from the earth shortly before the Flood; and they are responsible for the presence or absence of certain flora and fauna on earth. The average life of a planet is 80,000 years, half of which period is spent in 'ascending vibrations', and the other half in 'descending vibrations'. Within these periods there are—as we might expect—many subdivisions; as far as the earth is concerned, there are thirty-two in all, and we are now in the fifth of these periods. When we reach the eighth, in some thousands of years, we shall enter the period of Harmony. Remarkaole events will then take place. Men will grow tails equipped with eyes; dead bodies will be transformed into aromatic airs drifting gracefully through interplanetary and interstellar space; an atmospheric phenomenon known as the 'Polar Crown' will begin to distil perfumed dew; six new and scintillating moons will replace the miserable creature with which we are now burdened; the sea, losing all saltiness, will turn into lemonade; the climate will everywhere be the same—ideal, as in the Garden of Eden; and wild beasts will be replaced by lovable and docile creatures—'anti-lions', 'anti-sharks', etc.; in these islands, we shall even benefit from this latter process to the extent of 'anti-rats', 'anti-bugs', and 'anti-fleas', which is consoling in view of the unfair advantage that might otherwise be gained by Africa or Bengal.

It is during this miraculous period that Fourier's ideal society will really come into its own. The Phalanxes will spread over the entire land-surface of the globe until there are exactly 2,985,984 of them; they will unite the whole human race into a brotherhood; there will be but one language and a single, uniform mode of life. Constantinople will be the capital of the world, and in it will live the Omniarch, or world-ruler, assisted by 3 Augusts, 12 Cæsarinas, 48 Empresses, 144 Kalifs, and 576 Sultans, whose functions, by some strange omission on Fourier's part, are never fully described. It is possible, however, that these impressively-named potentates were invented by Fourier for the sole purpose of tempting ambitious millionaires to finance an experimental

Phalanx; for Fourier never gave up hope that some wealthy man would enable him to realise his dreams. He even kept a list of 4,000 candidates for this honour; and towards the end of his life inserted an advertisement in the newspapers saying that he would be at home at a certain hour every day if any philanthropist should wish to visit him.

Poor Fourier! This childish faith was but one aspect of the magnificently childlike constructions of his mind—a splendid compensation for his own drab life. The groaning tables and the sexual indulgences of Harmony were invented by a timid bachelor living in one furnished lodging or cheap hotel after another—a man whose imagination, being able to change the nature of the sea, chose to change it into lemonade; a man who was no doubt best loved by the cats on whom he lavished so much affection. It is difficult not to feel for this professed sociologist a sympathy and an admiration that such men usually fail to inspire; he can, indeed, arouse in the breast of the traveller returning exhausted from the conventional Utopia or from the Proudhonian or Marxist realms a combination of love, delight, and wonder that is usually reserved for the tellers of fables and fairy stories, and the great weavers of myth and legend.

Fourier was found dead, kneeling at his bedside, on 10th October 1837. The inscription on his tombstone is an epitome of his life's work:

> Here lie the remains of Charles Fourier.
> The Series distribute the Harmonies.
> The Attractions are proportionate to the Destinies.

Although Fourier did not live long enough to see the widespread adoption of his social theories or to witness the many attempts that were made to put them into practice, he did live long enough to acquire two enthusiastic young disciples. Victor Considérant gathered a nucleus of followers about him, and began a small Fourierist movement in France about 1832. In this year a newspaper, Le Phalanstère, was launched, and a M. Baudet-Dulary, député for the Seine-et-Oise, set up the first community on an estate near the forest of Rambouillet. Both failed: the newspaper in 1834, and the community—from lack of capital—earlier. In 1836, however, *Le Phalanstère* was revived as *Le Phalange*, and steadily increased its circulation until, in 1843, it had acquired sufficient readers to become a daily, *La Démocratie Pacifique*. The practical application of Fourierism, however, was never to make much headway in France, partly because Fourier's works were available in their entirety and offered obvious advantages to critics, and partly owing to the nature of the political situation—which, indeed, was responsible for the suppression of *La Démocratie Pacifique* in 1850.

It was Fourier's second disciple, Albert Brisbane, who, by bringing his master's doctrines to America, initiated a widespread Fourierist campaign. Brisbane was a young American of liberal education who at the age of eighteen went to Europe to study social philosophy. Having spent some time working under Cousin and Hegel, and having flirted with the theories of Saint-Simon, he eventually found what he was looking for in Fourier's treatise, *L'Association Domestique-Agricole*, which he picked up by chance. The words 'attractive industry' acted upon him with the effect of a revelation. He threw down the book, he tells us, 'and commenced pacing the floor in a tumult of emotion . . . carried away into a world of new conceptions'. Fortunately, Brisbane, having discovered the most practical idea in Fourier's entire works, was level-headed enough to cling to it, and to discard the more fanciful speculations of his master. After making an exhaustive study of Fourierism—under Fourier and his associates—Brisbane returned to America. Some years later, in 1840, his *Social Destiny of Man* appeared, containing a clear and simple statement of all that was essential in Fourierism for the initiation of practical experiments, and excluding anything that might give offence or reflect upon the dubious mental condition of his master.

Horace Greeley, editor of the *New Yorker*, was converted overnight by Brisbane's book, and became the most useful recruit; for two years later, when he was editing the influential *New York Tribune*, he offered Brisbane a regular column in it for the exposition of Fourierism. In the spring of 1842 a frontpage headline in the *Tribune* announced:

ASSOCIATION; OR, PRINCIPLES OF A TRUE
ORGANIZATION OF SOCIETY.

This column has been purchased by the Advocates of Association, in order to lay their principles before the public. Its editorship is entirely distinct from that of the *Tribune*.

This ingenious arrangement not only permitted the Associationists to air their views, but also increased the sale of the *Tribune* by obtaining for it all those readers who were interested in social problems. Brisbane's explanatory articles, practical advice, and announcements of meetings gradually began to have an effect upon the public; and Greeley, in spite of his disclaimer on behalf of the *Tribune*, not only helped the cause by making frequent editorial allusions to the Associationists, but also by speaking in public, helping to organise meetings and Phalanxes, and finally, by pledging his property to Association.

Propaganda on behalf of the movement now came from all sides. In 1843 Brisbane started *The Phalanx*, which ran for two years until superseded by *The Harbinger,* which became a Fourierist journal with the conversion of Brook Farm in 1844. During the four years of its existence this little paper contained innumerable articles by Ripley, Charles A. Dana, John S. Dwight and William Henry Channing; T. W. Higginson, James Russell Lowell, J. G. Whittier, and Margaret Fuller were also important contributors. Parke Godwin, the son-in-law of William Cullen Bryant, and Associate Editor of the *Evening Post*, was won over to Fourierism, and wrote four books and many articles on the subject. Brisbane obtained control of the *Chronicle,* a small daily, and the *Democrat*, a monthly magazine. But these were merely the New York channels of propaganda; there were also three or four journals issued by Phalanxes in other states, and many lecture tours and meetings.

The enemies of Fourierism might call the movement 'infidel'

or 'mad' for all they were worth; its doctrines nevertheless achieved a wonderful popularity, calling forth abundant sympathy and encouragement, and provoking constant debate and discussion. Associations and Conventions of Associationists began to spring up everywhere, but especially in the north-eastern states, where a particularly sharp economic crisis had recently caused much unemployment. The anti-slavery movements also helped the growth of Fourierism; for as the former movement gathered momentum it began to include as one of its aims the abolition of wage-slavery as well as chattel-slavery, and such men as John A. Collins (of Skaneateles) were as active in advocating the one cause as the other. The Fourierist programme of attractive industry on a co-operative basis could not have been brought forward at a more opportune moment; it not only made an instant appeal to those who were suffering from the economic crisis, but also to those idealists and humanitarians who wished to relieve such suffering without embracing any doctrine so dangerously radical as socialism or communism.

Fourierist propaganda was so ably conducted and so well received that it brought results which were embarrassing to the leading Fourierists. Once indoctrinated with the general idea of Association, the impetuous public took the initiative into its own hands. In their impatience and enthusiasm, hundreds of misguided labourers and artisans were headed for disaster. Instead of carefully planning their schemes in advance and concentrating upon a few substantial experiments, they frittered away capital and effort on dozens of ill-organised adventures. Out of more than forty such experiments, only three were to survive longer than two years, and only another three longer than fifteen months.

Fourier had always warned his followers against hasty and ill-conceived attempts to establish a Phalanx. He was particularly emphatic on this point, since the Phalanx, unlike most communal schemes, did not pretend to be a civilisation in microcosm, but was intended to be a fully established and integral part of a world system. Whereas the Shakers, the Rappites, and the Owenites concentrated upon the spirit of community life, and were prepared to develop organically and empirically, the Phalanx was to observe Fourier's cosmological and social laws to the letter. It was to spring into being complete in every detail of a predetermined pattern. Fourier had insisted upon an initial membership of at least 1,600 and a capital of about a million francs, and although these demands had been reduced by Brisbane to a membership of 400 and a capital of $400,000, the leading Fourierists in America were not prepared to make further concessions. All through the disastrous period of small-scale and poverty-stricken experiments they held to this ideal of large and wealthy Phalanxes; and when the ruins of Fourierist enterprise lay scattered about them, they maintained that no fair trial of the system had been made. In a letter to the *Oneida Circular*, which had given an account of Fourierist Associations, Brisbane pointed out that none of them had realised a single one of the conditions laid down by Fourier: 'Not one of them had the tenth, nor the twentieth part of the means and resources—pecuniary and scientific—necessary to carry out the organisation he proposed. In a word, no trial, and no approach to a trial of Fourier's theory has been made. I do not say that his theory is true, or would succeed, if fairly tried. I simply affirm that *no trial* of it has been made; so that it is unjust to speak of it, as if it had been tested.'

There is much truth in this complaint, which in some respects is unanswerable; but in many cases the Phalanxes courted disaster by actually fulfilling one of Fourier's conditions. Since they did not possess either the requisite capital or membership, many Associations apparently decided to make up for these deficiencies by purchasing either the required amount of land, or as much land as they could afford to buy—regardless of its quality and situation. Thus they came into possession of barren wildernesses or malarial-infested swamps miles from any centre of communication, often devoid of water supply and building material, and usually heavily mortgaged. Instead of living in palatial Phalansteries, they huddled together in miserable log huts;

and far from raising abundant crops and orchards of luscious fruit, they often starved—either because the soil was sterile or because they lacked experience in agriculture.

'Think of the great hope at the beginning; the bitterness of the end', writes Noyes. 'Plodding on their weary march of life, Association rises before them like the *mirage* of the desert. They see in the vague distance magnificent palaces, green fields, golden harvests, sparkling fountains, abundance of rest and romance; in one word HOME—which is also HEAVEN. They rush like the thirsty caravan to realise their vision. And now the scene changes. . . .'

'The great hope at the beginning' was certainly illustrated in many cases. 'We have implements, some stock, and some machinery', wrote one ephemeral Phalanx, 'but what is better than all we have honest hearts, clear heads, and hardy limbs.' Heart, head, and limb may have been admirable, but they couldn't make barren soil productive. Such optimism was repeated time and time again, only to be succeeded by disappointment and bewilderment. Even the Clermont Phalanx, which was ideally situated and started with a magnificent fanfare of trumpets, ended within two years with a debt of $19,000. Macdonald, who travelled with the two successive boatloads of Associationists who sailed up the Ohio to take over this new Phalanx, has described these journeys: 'There were about one hundred and thirty of us. The weather was beautiful, but cool, and the scenery on the river was splendid in its spring dress. The various parties brought their provisions with them, and toward noon the whole of it was collected and spread upon the table by the waiters, for all to have an equal chance. But alas for equality! On the meal being ready, a rush was made into the cabin, and in a few minutes all the seats were filled. In a few minutes more the provisions had all disappeared, and many persons who were not in the first rush, had to go hungry. I lost my dinner that day; but improved the opportunity to observe and criticise the ferocity of the Fourieristic appetite. We reached the domain about two o'clock p.m., and marched on shore in procession, with a band of music in front, leading the way up a road cut in the high clay bank; and then formed a mass meeting, at which we had praying, music, and speech-making. I strolled out with a friend and examined the purchase, and we came to the conclusion that it was a splendid domain. A strip of rich bottom-land, about a quarter of a mile wide, was backed by gently rolling hills, well timbered all over. Nine or ten acres were cleared, sufficient for present use. Here then was all that could be desired, hill and plain, rich soil, fine scenery, plenty of first-rate timber, a maple-sugar camp, a good commercial situation, convenient to the best market in the West, with a river running past that would float any kind of boat or raft; and with steamboats passing and repassing at all hours of the day and night, to convey passengers or goods to any point between New Orleans and Pittsburg. Here was wood for fuel, clay and stone to make habitations, and a rich soil to grow food. What more could be asked from nature? Yet, how soon all this was found insufficient!'

The second boatload set out, and arrived, with similar festivity: 'We left Cincinnati triumphantly to the sound of martial music, and took our journey up the river in fine spirits, the young people dancing in the cabin as we proceeded. . . . On landing, we formed a procession and marched to a new frame building, which was being erected for a mill. Here an oration was delivered by a Mr. Whitly, who, I noticed, had the Bible open before him. After this we formed a procession again and marched to a lot of rough tables enclosed within a line of ropes, where we stood and took a cold collation. After this the folks enjoyed themselves with music and dancing. . . .' But the music and the dancing did not last long. This Association did not die of barren soil, lack of members, or financial incompetence, but, as Macdonald wrote, of social incompatibility: 'The persons brought together were strangers to each other, of many different trades and habits, and discord was the result, as might have been anticipated.'

The Moorhouse Union, in New York State, came to an end in a few months, partly for the same reason. According to an ex-member, its population 'was composed of all nations, characters, and conditions; a motley group of ill-assorted materials, as inexperienced as it was heterogeneous. We had some specimens of the raw material of human nature, and some of New York manufacture spoiled in the making. There were philosophers and philantropists, bankrupt merchants and broken-down grocery-keepers; officers who had retired from the Texan army on half-pay; and some who had retired from situations in the New York ten-pin alleys. There were all kinds of ideas, notions, theories, and whims; all kinds of religions; and some persons without any. There was no unanimity of purpose, nor congeniality of disposition; but there was plenty of discussion, and an abundance of variety, which is called the spice of life. This spice however constituted the greater part of the fare, as we sometimes had scarcely anything else to eat.

'At first we were pretty well off for provisions; but soon the supplies began to be reduced; and in November the list of luxuries and necessaries commenced with rye and ended with potatoes, with nothing between! As the supplies were cut off, the number of members decreased. They were starved out. But of course the starving process was slower in those cases where the individuals had not the means of transportation back to the white settlements. When I left the "promised land" in March 1844, there were only six families remaining. I had determined to see it out; but the state of things was so bad, and the prospects ditto, that I could stand it no longer. I thought the whole would soon fall into the hands of Mr. Moorhouse, and I could not afford to spend any more time in a cause so hopeless. I had given nine months' time, was half starved, got no pay, had worn out my clothes, and had my best coat borrowed without leave, by a man who went to New York some time before. This I thought might suffice for one experiment. I left the place less sanguine than when I went there that Associations could succeed without capital and without a good selection of members. Yet my belief was as firm as ever in the coming abolition of conflicting interests, and the final harmonious reconstruction of society.'

The lack of honesty experienced by this unfortunate member

CHARLES FOURIER. *From an engraving after the portrait by Gigoux.*

JOHN HUMPHREY NOYES.

was evidently no exception. The Social Reform Unity of Pennsylvania, which lasted ten months, made provision in its Articles of Association for a treasury consisting of 'a suitable metallic safe, secured by seven different locks', the keys of which were to be deposited with seven different officers. Money was only to be drawn out by authority of an order signed by all the members of the Executive Council and countersigned by the President of the Unity. And Macdonald reports of another Association that it beat 'a hasty and disorderly retreat. It is said that each individual helped himself to the movable property, and that some decamped in the night, leaving the remains of the Phalanx to be disposed of in any way which the last members might choose.'

The unconquerable optimism expressed by the ex-member of the Moorhouse Union was shared by hundreds of Associationists though few perhaps were so bold as one man to whom Noyes attributes the following comment upon a failure: 'Do I censure their want of foresight? Do I regret this trial? Oh, no! It but the more forcibly confirms me in my persuasion of the practicability of our system.'

Encouraged by the optimistic propaganda—which, like that of Owen's New Harmony *Gazette*, continued ebullient to the end—and ignoring the warnings issued by Brisbane and other temperate leaders,[1] the Associationists, ever on the brink of bankruptcy or disruption, cheered one another on. In Noyes' somewhat melodramatic words, they comforted themselves with the thought that ' "They *must* succeed; they *will* succeed; they *are* succeeding!" These words they say over and over to themselves, and shout them to the public. Still debt hangs over them. They get a subsidy from outside friends. But the deficit increases. Meanwhile disease persecutes them . . . they lie idle in their loose sheds . . . sweating and shivering in misery and despair. Human parasites gather about them like vultures scenting prey from afar.

---

[1] E.g. an editorial in *The Harbinger*: 'We sincerely hope that our friends in that vicinity will concentrate their efforts on the Ohio Phalanx, and not attempt to multiply Associations, which, without abundant capital and devoted and experienced men, will, almost to a certainty, prove unsuccessful.'

Their own passions torment them. They are cursed with suspicion and the evil eye. They quarrel about religion. They quarrel about their food. They dispute about carrying out their principles. Eight or ten families desert. The rest worry on through the long years. Foes watch them with cruel exultation. Friends shout to them, "Hold on a little longer!" They hold on just as long as they can, insisting that they are successful, or are just going to be, till the last. Then comes the "break up"; and who can tell the agonies of that great corporate death!

'See how pathetically these soldiers of despair with defeat in full view, offer themselves to other Associations, and take comfort in the assurance that God will not drive them from the earth! See how the heroes of the "forlorn hope", after defeat has come, turn again and re-organise, refusing to surrender! . . .'

There were, however, some partial successes among these many failures.

Of the three most successful Phalanxes, the North American, located near Red Bank in Monmouth County, New Jersey, lasted twelve years; the Wisconsin Phalanx, in Fond du Lac County, lasted six years; and Brook Farm, with a total existence of five years, spent only two of them as a Phalanx.

The North American Phalanx was established in September 1843, and although it began with a membership of less than eighty and a capital of only $8,000, it was generally regarded as the testing-ground of Fourierism in America. Brisbane, Greeley, Parke Godwin, Channing, and Ripley all helped to prepare for the experiment and were afterwards frequent visitors. Within a short time of its foundation, the temporary dwelling-house was replaced by a three-story Phalanstery with a frontage of 150 feet. A large grist-mill and other mills and workshops were erected, and an impressive agricultural domain was laid out. The famous Fourierist orchards at last made their appearance, and even if Fourier's instructions assigning a Series of Twelve Groups to the raising of twelve varieties of the Bergamot pear were not carried out to the letter, the orchards nevertheless covered 70 acres. They raised fine crops of wheat, potatoes, tomatoes, melons, and other vegetables; and they kept their fields and farms in better trim than those of their neighbours. Since a high proportion of the members were apparently 'cultured and refined', this was no mean achievement. These members, however, do not seem to have paid much attention either to cultural pursuits or to education. It is true that they owned a library, took in all the leading journals of the movement, and ran a school, but the absence of 'facilities for education and mental improvements' were remarked by several observers. Probably the members concentrated upon the primary work of making the Phalanx a sound business proposition. In this they were highly successful, raising the value of the property to $80,000 in nine years. They were probably wise to concentrate their attention upon financial matters, for in doing so they avoided all the stresses and strains which poverty and insufficiency bring. To judge by the accounts frequently published in Fourierist journals, they were·a happy and contented people. N. C. Neidhart reported that they 'appeared to be a genial band, with happy, smiling countenances, full of health and spirits', and the following account, in *The Harbinger*, of July 4th celebrations at the Phalanx is idyllic, even if allowance is made for partisan exaggeration:

As soon as the moisture was off the grass, a group went down to the beautiful meadows to spread the hay; and the right good will, quickness and thoroughness with which they completed their task, certainly illustated the attractiveness of combined industry. Others meanwhile were gathering for dinner the vegetables, of which, by the consent of the whole neighbourhood, they have a supply unsurpassed in early maturity and excellence; and still others were busy in the various branches of domestic labour.

And now the guests from New York and the country around having come in, and the hour for the meeting being at hand, the bell sounded, and men, women and children assembled in a walnut grove near the house, where a semicircle of seats had been arranged in the cool shade. Here addresses were given by William H. Channing and Horace Greeley, illustrating the position that Association is the truly consistent embodiment in practice of the professed principles of our nation.

After some hour and a half thus spent, the company adjourned to the house, where a table had been spread the whole length of the hall, and partook of a most abundant and excellent dinner, in which the hospitable sisters of the Phalanx had most satisfactorily proved their faith by their works. Good cold water was the only beverage, thanks to the temperance of the members. A few toasts and short speeches seasoned the feast.

And now once again, the afternoon being somewhat advanced, the demand for variety was gratified by a summons to the hay-field. Every rake and fork were in requisition; a merrier group never raked and pitched; never was a meadow more dexterously cleared; and it was not long before there was a demand that the right to labour should be honoured by fresh work, which the chief of the group lamented he could not at the moment gratify. To close the festivities the young people formed in a dance, which was prolonged till midnight. And so ended this truly cheerful and friendly holiday.

This Association was wise enough to adopt a careful system of admission. Intending members were invited to become visitors for a month or two, after which time they could be admitted as probationary members for one year, full membership then being conferred or withheld by the Association.

Profits were divided among the Groups and Series according to Fourier's scale. Fourier's system of wages was also followed; the highest wages were paid for repulsive or exhausting labour; less wages for less repulsive labour; and still less for agreeable labour. No one could earn more than 10 cents an hour, no one less than 6; but special rewards were paid for skill and talent in any branch of industry. Free choice of occupation was given to everyone, and payments were made monthly, while profits were divided yearly. Macdonald's account of his second visit in July 1852 will give an indication of the low cost of living, and explain the system of bookkeeping. By this date the North American had adopted 'the eating-house system. At the table there is a bill of fare, and each individual calls for what he wants; on obtaining it, the waiter gives him a check, with the price of the article marked thereon. After the meal is over, the waiters go round and enter the sum marked upon the check which each person has received in a book belonging to that person; the total is added up at the end of each month and the payments are made. Each person finds his own sugar, which is kept upon the table. Coffee is half-a-cent per cup, including milk; bread one cent per plate; butter, I think, half-a-cent; meat two cents; pie two cents; and other things in like proportion. On Mr. Holes' book, the cost of living ran thus: breakfast from one and a half cents to three and a half cents; dinner four and a half cents to nine cents; supper four and a half cents to eight cents. In addition to this, as all persons use the room alike, each pays the same rent, which is thirty-six and a half cents per week; each person also pays a certain portion for the waiting labour, and for lighting the room. The young ladies and gentlemen who waited on table, as well as the Phalanx Doctor (a gentleman of talent and politeness), who from attraction performed the same duty, got six and a half cents per hour for their labour.'

This visit of Macdonald's was made only two months before the Phalanx entered its tenth year. It alone had survived all the forty or fifty Fourierist experiments, but was not to last much longer. The subsidence of the great effervescence of the early 'forties had left it in a peculiarly isolated position. Apart from religious communities, it had no rivals and no apparent successors, unless the Icarians, who had only just arrived in America and were already in difficulties, could be so regarded. At this moment, also, the North American was weakened by the disaffection, on religious grounds, of a considerable number of members and stockholders who withdrew to form the short-lived Raritan Bay Union. When Macdonald returned in the autumn of 1853, the psychological state of the North American was summed up in his report when he wrote that he 'felt assured they were "sticking it" '. Their spirit had certainly fallen sadly, and when a fire destroyed their mills and workshops in 1854, they had no will to continue, in spite of offers of assistance.

Like the North American, the Wisconsin Phalanx made a very careful selection of new members. Beginning with only twenty, and increasing to 180 in a year, they built a large dwelling-house and saw-mill in the midst of an uninhabited prairie. Their land was therefore cheap without, in this case, being poor in quality. They built a small township, Ceresco, and became incorporated by the state laws, one of their members even running for Governor on the Free-Soil ticket. With a very small initial capital and over 700 acres of land, they succeeded in outstripping all other Fourierist organisations in financial prosperity, providing the only example of a Phalanx that dissolved without loss to its founders and stockholders. This success is attributed to the organisational ability of Warren Chase, the founder, who retained almost unlimited control of the Phalanx from beginning to end. Having paid cash down for their land, these Associationists started free from debt; and since the founders were obliged to trek many miles into the prairie with cattle and horses, pitching tents until they could build a dwelling-house, they were endowed with a hardy pioneering spirit which, added to the fact that they were experienced farmers, enabled them to overcome all initial difficulties. This tough and realistic attitude was also responsible for the fact that they paid little attention to cultural or educational facilities; and, apart from their outstanding financial success, they are one of the least interesting of the Fourierist Associations. According to Macdonald, who quotes an unnamed observer who saw the whole progress of the Phalanx, 'the love of money and the want of love for Association' were the causes of its breaking up. 'Their property becoming valuable, they sold it for the purpose of making money out of it.' The dissolution took place in 1850, the sale of the property yielding 108 per cent. of the investments.

Financial success, as such, had never been known at Brook Farm. In that gracious little colony it had never been sought, for, provided the Farmers were able to pay their way, they asked only for leisure in which to enjoy the arts, cultivate the mind, and shape a humanitarian social philosophy. Avoiding all social formalism and religious dogma, and applying to their society 'the principles of justice and love . . . in accordance with the laws of Divine Providence',[1] the Farmers, who owed their organisation to an ex-minister, came near to being a religious community; and although their organisation into four departments—of General Direction, Education, Finance, and Agriculture—and their method of paying for labour were simplified adaptations of Fourierist principles, there had always been a vociferous anti-Fourierist minority at the Farm. This minority was responsible for entering a caveat in the recommendations of the National Convention of Associationists, held in New York in April 1844. But by this time Ripley, Dana, and other prominent members had been converted to Fourierism, and the Farm had consented to the metamorphosis implied by the new title, 'The Brook Farm Phalanx'.

With the conversion of the Farm, the Fourierist movement reached the height of its power and prestige. Brisbane and Greeley, flattered no doubt by this crowning achievement of their propaganda, swamped the little colony with pompous and impressively dull lectures on the details of Fourierist organisation; they also arranged long discourses on morality that could easily have been better delivered by the pupils of the Brook Farm School. But now the school itself was neglected for interminable discussions concerning Groups and Series; and although the injection of so much Fourieristic claptrap at first acted as a stimulant, raising the membership and causing a whirlwind of unnatural activity, the reaction from it rapidly followed. *The Harbinger*, which became the most important Fourierist journal, brought the germs of officialdom to the Phalanx, and they infected not only lectures and meetings, but also amusement, which no longer grew organically from the peaceful activities of a group of people united by a gentle culture, but was organised into whist drives and other deadening pastimes. Theatrical entertainments, readings from the classics, costume parties, and picnics gradually ceased; Emerson, Thoreau, and other literary figures no longer paid visits to the Farm. The unique atmosphere which had infused every activity of the Farmers with spontaneity and enjoyment had gone.

[1] Articles of Association.

The accession of new members brought dissensions and disturbed the delicate balance of social unity. Beneath all the patient labour and fervid enthusiasm that went into the building of the great Phalanstery, there was a jaded and discontented spirit. After costing the Farmers two years of constant labour, and the greater part of their available funds, the Phalanstery caught fire and was burnt to the ground within a day of its completion, in the spring of 1846. After this disaster—which foreshadowed the fire that brought the North American Phalanx to an end—the Farmers had neither the spirit nor the financial resources for further endeavour. Within a year the community dissolved and the property was sold.

Fourierism was already in decline. Had the fire not occurred, the community might have lasted as long as the North American Phalanx, or longer; but if it had done so, it is difficult to suppose that the original spirit of Brook Farm could have been recaptured. In some respects the Farm was lucky. For three years it achieved an ideal that had never been equalled in community life, and if we find it convenient to blame Fourierism for the destruction of this ideal, and a fire for the destruction of Brook Farm as a Phalanx, it is worth remembering that a worse tragedy than either event might have occurred at any moment after the first happy years. The Farm might have shared the ignominious fate of so many communities, petering out amid an unseemly wrangle of dissension.

Thus ended the hectic fever brought from France. When it had subsided, the association of individuals in community had been almost discredited, just as the development of communistic societies had been temporarily checked by the failure of New Harmony. Communism, however, which was still being pursued by all the established religious societies, and by three new ones, was to be given a further trial in 1848 by the followers of another French utopian writer, Emile Cabet.

Meanwhile, the individualist approach had not completely died out. It was being quietly developed by Josiah Warren.

Warren, to whom J. S. Mill was indebted for the phrase 'The Sovereignty of the Individual', can be regarded as the first American anarchist. He shared the aptitude of many men of that persuasion for self-reliance combined with mutual co-operation. His individual gifts were as remarkable as his social theories, and sound common sense ensured the practical application of both; but his social experiments have been eclipsed by larger schemes of the same kind, and his inventions have never received the recognition they deserve.[1]

Warren's preoccupation with printing, which has been mentioned, was the logical development, in a practical man, of a desire to propagate his own views of society. Like the founders of many communities who published their own newspapers, Warren realised that the popular Press would not be likely to welcome his theories. It was for this reason that he had produced the *Peaceful Revolutionist*. Becoming more and more absorbed in the technical problems of printing, he eventually produced in 1840 an entirely new press of revolutionary design. The first number of the *South-western Sentinel*, published on 28th February 1840, proudly announced that it was 'the first newspaper probably in the world which was ever printed on a continuous sheet. Our press or printing machinery is the invention of Mr. Josiah Warren, of New Harmony. He has brought a series of experiments extending through nine years to a successful close, and this machine, which he calls his speed press, is one of the results.'

The 'result' was twenty-five years ahead of its time; for it was not until 1865 that a similar machine was successfully placed on the market by William A. Bullock of Philadelphia. Warren's machine, in fact, was too revolutionary for the printers. Fearing that it would throw them out of work, they continually sabotaged the press until Warren, tried beyond endurance, removed it and broke it up. In spite of this experience, however, Warren remained undaunted and persevering. By 1846

[1] Except from William Bailie, whose short biography, published in 1906, is the main source of information on Warren.

he had brought his stereotyping inventions to a degree of perfection at which such good results could be obtained by the process that its possibilities seemed unlimited; and at the time of his death he had made further improvements which, although they have never been accorded the praise they deserve, have been incorporated in the process of stereotyping that is still in use.

Warren's stereotyping patents brought him $7,000, which he used to found a new Equity village; but he had meanwhile opened another Time Store—on this occasion at New Harmony. At first it was vigorously opposed by other shopkeepers, who feared for their own trade, but when it began to bring down retail prices throughout the district, it received such overwhelming popular support that its success was ensured. 'I will venture to assert', wrote Warren, 'that no institution, political, moral, nor religious, ever assumed a more sudden and extensive popularity than the Time store of New Harmony. But it was principally among the poor, the humble, and the down-trodden. None of those who had been accustomed to lead, none who had anything to lead with, offered the least assistance or aid, nor scarcely any sympathy, though they did not attempt to deny the soundness of the principles. . . . When all the stores in the surrounding country had come down in their prices to an equilibrium with the Equity store, the custom naturally flowed back again to them, and the next step was to wind up the Time store and commence a village.'

In 1844 Warren had delivered a lecture at the Clermont Phalanx in Ohio. He was not deceived by its excellent site and prospects—so vividly described by Macdonald—and prophesied the failure of the scheme. When it did fail, after little more than two years, Warren acquired land within a mile of it and established his second village, which he courageously named Utopia. Each family owned its own house and its own plot of land, exchanging labour on equitable terms by means of labour notes, which were used in every transaction and provided for all necessities. One man built himself a brick cottage one and a half stories high with a cash outlay of only $9.81—every other expense being covered by labour notes.

Warren's purpose in founding Utopia was to show that people with little or no financial resources could, by co-operation on a basis of equity, lead lives as satisfactory as those of ordinary citizens in the outside world. In this he was successful; but the abolition of capital, other than that represented by the labour force of the villagers, restricted their dealings with neighbours. The surrounding land was valuable, and, not having the capital to purchase it, most of the Utopians, after about four years, moved to Minnesota, where land was cheap and easily obtainable.

In 1850, when the Fourierist gale of propaganda had blown itself out, Warren went to New York and Boston on a lecture tour. His quiet, authoritative manner and the reasonableness of his proposals for individualistic co-operation gained him a number of followers who had become disillusioned by the windy rhetoric of the Fourierists and by the failure of so many Phalanxes. Among these converts was Stephen Pearl Andrews, formerly a leading Fourierist, and an influential writer. In the following year Andrews published his *Science of Society*, which contains the best exposition of Warren's views; and he was an enthusiastic supporter of Warren's next enterprise, begun in the same year—his third village, named Modern Times.

This was situated on Long Island, about forty miles from New York, and, partly owing to its proximity to the city, was more successful than Warren's previous communities. It received much publicity—mainly from the *Tribune*—which was not always welcome, bringing many visitors who came merely to satisfy their curiosity. Most of them had no idea of what was being attempted at Modern Times, and had no desire to learn. They found about 100 settlers who had worked hard to clear the rough land for their market-gardens and who had built themselves rather primitive houses while awaiting the prosperity which they were sure would follow their system of equity. Some of these visitors remained and, owing to their fundamental lack of sympathy and their eccentric behaviour, became a general nuisance. They became a nuisance because Modern Times, like many anarchist or near-anarchist communities, held to its principles of complete toleration. While it had no proper constitutional machinery for excluding undesirables, it was also not prepared to resort to law or force in order to do so. Most of these eccentrics were harmless enough in themselves—there were, for instance, a polygamist and a nudist—but journalists in search of sensational news focused their attention upon them until it seemed to the public that there could not be a normal human being in the village. When one woman began to dress in masculine style, a newspaper reported that 'the women of Modern Times dress in men's clothes and look hideous'. When another woman died as the result of attempting to live on nothing but a diet of beans, it was announced that 'the people of Modern Times are killing themselves with fanatical ideas about food'. Such publicity brought nothing but a troublesome notoriety to the colony, which eventually sought to avoid further experiences of the same kind by changing its name to Brentwood.

The colony continued to prosper in a quiet way, in spite of the undesirable notoriety that was forced upon it. It is a remarkable testimony to the individualist form of association that Modern Times held together without any central government. While its inhabitants were completely independent of one another, they were always ready to co-operate for any purpose that required combined action; and in their attractive little village, with its broad avenues, tree-shaded streets, and well-cultivated gardens, they might have continued to live happily for many years. Unfortunately, the panic of 1857, which threw 20,000 people out of work, ruined a manufacturing business that was the mainstay of the community. The Civil War followed, and spoilt all chances of further development.

Modern Times endured long enough to prove that Warren's theories were capable of practical application. It had demonstrated, in a quiet but effective manner, that there was an alternative to Fourierist association other than communism. Warren, who did not return to the village after 1860, lived quietly for the remaining years of his life. He died in 1874.

Warren's anarchism—like his inventions—was ahead of its time. Communism was still the preferred basis of organisation in communities, as was shown by three groups that were formed some years before Modern Times.

CHAPTER NINE

RACIAL AND RELIGIOUS COMMUNISM

Wives, submit yourselves unto your own husbands, as unto the Lord.

Eph. v. 22.

APART from the Shakers, the most firmly established and longest-lived communities in America were all German sectarian groups. The Rappite Society lasted ninety-eight years, the Zoarite eighty-three; and the Inspirationists of Amana, now flourishing in their one hundred and twenty-fourth year, spent eighty-seven of those years in a state of successful communism. All these groups, together with the shorter-lived German societies of Bethel and Aurora (1844–81) and the Swedish colony of Bishop Hill (1841–62), stand outside the main stream of development in community life. It is significant that three of them had not originally intended to adopt communism, and therefore did not set out with any preconceived notion of challenging the validity of the family as the basis of community life. Even the celibate Rappites lived in separate houses, continuing the family relationship in all respects, save that of sexual intercourse; and those societies that set out with the intention of abolishing private property made no attempt to alter the conventional relationship of the sexes. In none of these societies, therefore, was there any interest in the emancipation of women—a problem with which all the most important communities were preoccupied. The Inspirationsists, in fact, gave women no authority at all. Similarly, these groups were less interrested in education and general enlightenment than any society other than that of the Shakers. Nor did they participate in the anti-slavery or industrial reform movements. It is a matter almost of astonishment that the Inspirationists, whose society was founded during the height of the Fourierist and anti-slavery movements, while a great economic depression was in progress, were hardly affected by these stirring events. They were not quite unaffected, however; for the growing industrialism of Buffalo was one reason for their removal to Amana. Like the other groups already mentioned, they wished simply to live at peace, in isolation. The fact that three of these groups were so successful, in spite of the fact that two of them lacked the usual safeguards that bind such societies together, is probably due to the stolid temperament of the German peasants of whom they were composed, rather than to leadership or religious zeal—although it is true that when Dr. Keil died, both his communities dissolved within four years.

Dr. Keil arrived in America in 1838, and set up as a physician in New York. He was no ordinary doctor, but a mystic who used animal magnetism and a book of prescriptions reputed to have been written in human blood. In fact, he appears to have inherited in a slightly grotesque form some of the characteristics of the German Pietists and Rosicrucians. Unfortunately, no one could witness to the authenticity of his wonderful prescription book, since the good doctor burnt it with 'awe-inspiring formalities'[1] when he became a Methodist. But he was not a Methodist for long. His next role was that of one of the two Witnesses of the Apocalypse, in which character he announced that he was to be worshipped, and predicted that he would be slain in the presence of his followers after a fast of forty days. By this time he had formed a small sect of his own.

Keil's people were soon joined by the remnants of the 'Count de Leon's' followers—that same 'Count de Leon' who had caused so much trouble among the Rappites, and who had died of cholera in 1833. Keil, who was in need of a new occupation and a means of support, was probably encouraged by these new adherents to start a community. They began to plan one along Rappite lines, but without including celibacy as one of their

[1] Nordhoff, p. 306.

objects. In 1844 they secured 2,500 acres in Missouri and set up the community of Bethel, which ten years later had almost doubled its acreage of land and had a population of 650. It owned a distillery, grist-mills, saw-mills, woollen mills, and all the workshops and other buildings that are commonly found in communities.

Although they were at first very poor and troubled by disease —in spite of the doctor's remarkable qualifications—they succeeded by sheer economy and hard work in raising their standard of living to a level they could have attained only by communal effort. When this satisfactory degree of prosperity had been reached, Keil once again became restless. He envisaged a larger community somewhere on the Pacific coast, and in 1855 set out with an advance party of eighty. They settled temporarily in Washington Territory and then in 1856 established the community of Aurora in Oregon, not on the coast, but fifty miles inland, south of Portland. Many families from Bethel followed their leader to this new settlement, and by 1870 there were about 400 people on the 18,550 acres at Aurora and about 200 at the first community.

Keil was president of both societies, and revered by all his followers as their temporal and spiritual leader. A short, burly man, with blue eyes, he had whitish hair and a white beard when Nordhoff met him in the 'seventies. 'He seemed excitable and somewhat suspicious; gave no tokens whatever of having studied any book but the Bible, and that only as it helped him to enforce his own philosophy. He was very quick to turn every thought toward the one subject of community life; took his illustrations mostly from the New Testament; and evidently laid much stress on the parental character of God. As he discussed, his eyes lighted up with a somewhat fierce fire; and I thought I could perceive a fanatic, certainly a person of a very determined, imperious will, united to a narrow creed.' Keil was certainly patriarchal and autocratic, and there is no doubt that he held his followers together by the force of his own personality. At Aurora he had as advisers four elders whom he selected; at Bethel he was represented by a nominal leader assisted by six trustees; but in both cases his followers were so united in aim that little exercise of authority was necessary in practice. Matters of vital importance to either community were discussed by all members, and their consent was obtained before a decision was reached. Government was therefore extremely simple; and so were the daily lives of the members.

Like the Rappites and the Zoarites, most of them were stolid German peasants. Plain living, rigid economy, and a strictly utilitarian outlook deprived them of all purely decorative, comfortable, æsthetic, or intellectual accessories. No carpets, easy chairs, or pictures furnished their scrupulously clean little dwellings. Apart from Bibles, hymn-books, and an occasional medical treatise, they owned no books. In their schools they taught nothing but 'the three R's'. Their women dressed plainly in sunbonnets and calico. Their men for the most part did not smoke; and there were no cases of drunkenness. Apart from an occasional dance and a band that played on Sundays, they lacked all amusement. Sundays were devoted to quiet recreation—a little music, perhaps, and the rather monotonous pastime of 'visiting'. On alternate Sundays they attended a simple service in church. Otherwise they had no regular meetings or formalities.

Family life based upon strict monogamy within the society was the foundation of their existence; community of land and property was their social justification; and work occupied a greater part of their lives. Although every man was expected to work for the good of all, there were no set hours, and no set occupations. Work was interchangeable according to the need of the season; outside labour was hired for the harvest; and the products of their leisure hours were sold for pocket money. They owned general stores, from which householders drew what they needed, without accounts being kept; a drug-store run by the community doctor;[1] and a general store at which their neighbours could make cash

---

[1] At Bethel Nordhoff noted two drug-stores, one of which was 'large enough . . . to accommodate with purges and cathartics a town of twenty-five hundred inhabitants'.

purchases. At Bethel, Nordhoff was distressed to see liquor being sold to hired labourers, but consoled himself with the fact that it was done 'in a very quiet way'.

Some shops and businesses at Bethel were owned by ex-members of the community, who were allowed to stay on at the settlement; and this was one feature that made the community unique. Communism and individualism were oddly combined; the small houses and gardens, and the purchasing of goods with money earned from poultry-keeping and other hobbies, were balanced by common effort in field and workshop, and the free issue of all necessities. This policy, which could have been disastrous—especially when combined with the looseness of organisation, absence of ritual, and freedom to work or remain idle—was surprisingly successful, probably owing to a complete lack of imagination on the part of the members. They were unimaginative even with regard to utilitarian matters, never displaying the inventive skill that was common in other sectarian communities, nor lightening their labour by simple devices that would have cost them little thought or effort. Nor did they care a hoot for the appearance of their settlements. Nordhoff had already noted the general untidiness of the streets when Hinds, writing of Bethel, remarked that there was 'scarcely a pretence of a sidewalk in the place, though the soil is of that adhesive clay which renders sidewalks so indispensable to comfort in walking. Grunting pigs foraged everywhere at will; and a big wood-pile exposed to all the storms, encumbered the street opposite every house.' They took life easily, he adds—'perhaps too easily'; and Nordhoff, at Aurora, had detected the results of a 'too monotonous existence. The young women are mostly pale, flat-chested, and somewhat thin. The young men look good-natured, but aimless. The older women and men are slow in their movements, placid, very quiet and apparently satisfied with their lives.'

Such criticism is almost identical with that which has already been levelled at the Zoarites. Unlike the Zoarites, however, the Bethel-Aurorans had no sound democratic constitution, nor any spectacular wealth, and when their founder died in 1877, neither community survived him by many years. Bethel dissolved in 1880, and Aurora in 1881.

The organisation of the Swedish community of Bishop Hill, which was founded two years after the establishment of Bethel, was as dangerously loose as that of Keil's communities; and in this case it brought about the disruption of the society. And whereas Keil's prophesy that he would be slain in the presence of his followers was never fulfilled, Eric Janson, the founder of Bishop Hill, did meet with this unusual end.

Janson had already come near to death in 1834, and the experience, common enough in the history of conversion, filled him with an insatiable desire for spiritual knowledge and holy works.[1] In 1834, he met Jonas Olson, the leader of some Swedish Pietists or Devotionalists, and having impressed Olson by greeting him with a severe rebuke for his lack of zeal, the two men became partners in a fervent anti-Lutheran campaign. The usual persecutions followed, especially as Janson was regarded as a potential Wat Tyler. He was arrested six times, had a price put upon his head, and escaped only because he was favoured by the King. Eventually he was smuggled into Norway by his followers, and thence to America, where he determined to found a socialistic theocractic community.

The first boatload of emigrants arrived in America in October 1846, to occupy a site that had already been selected by a small advance party. Some of the men are said to have covered the whole distance from New York to Illinois on foot, but most of them travelled by canal and by lake to Chicago. All except the weaker women and children tramped the 100 miles from Chicago to Victoria, and also from there to Bishop Hill, near Red Oak Grove. (Bishop Hill was so named in honour of Janson's birthplace.) Other parties of emigrants continued to arrive until 1854.

[1] While ploughing, he was subjected to an attack of 'rheumatism' so severe as to render him unconscious. When he recovered consciousness, God spoke to him, telling him that if he should 'ask anything in My name, I will do it, saith the Lord'. This disturbing combination of direct and reported speech had such an effect upon Janson that when he arose his pains had gone—never to return.

With the exception of a small farmhouse and 80 acres of cultivated land, their new home contained no buildings and nothing
but unbroken land. By 1848 there were 800 of them, of all ages
and classes. Emigration, paid for by the wealthy members, had
left them almost without means, and they were obliged to shelter
themselves in any cave or cranny they could find. Winter and
summer alike they lived in primitive shelters covered with turf
and dug against the sides of the hills. Using whatever rough stone
was available, they improvised hand-mills for grinding corn, and
some members, turn and turn about, worked night and day at
nothing else, in order to provide the one staple food on which
they could rely. In their damp, overcrowded, and ill-ventilated
caves and shelters, half-starved and constantly plagued with
fever, they were an easy prey to disease. One hundred and fourteen of them died of cholera in a single fortnight, while Janson,
described as tall and angular, with abnormally prominent incisor
teeth, walked about among the sick cheerfully dispensing the last
blessing—'Go, die in peace'. Yet 'they counted all things as light
afflictions which endure but for a moment' and their first thought
was for a church—made of logs in a mud cave—of sufficient size
to hold 1,000 people; and their second thought was for evangelism. Janson trained twelve English-speaking disciples and sent
them out on a missionary journey in the neighbourhood.

One of the missionaries visited Hopedale, Oneida, the Rappites,
and the Shakers. The effects of his mission were mainly negative.
As a result of it, a dozen Hopedalians came to Bishop Hill, but
stayed only a short time; and the impregnable faith of the Shakers
not only resisted Jansonite evangelism, but actually converted the
missionary to celibacy. He in turn converted Jonas Olson, and
Olson forced the doctrine upon Bishop Hill. But this was in later
years.

By 1848, having borrowed money, and having received the
wages of all members who had been working for neighbouring
farmers, they bought more land, until they had 200 acres under
cultivation. Making their own bricks, they built a church and a
large four-story dwelling-house. These were followed by

numerous houses and outbuildings of wood and adobe, and by the usual mills and workshops; but the Jansonites were still in debt until 1850, when a member who had been sent to Sweden to collect several thousand dollars' worth of debts returned with them and set the community on its feet. However, they were barely established financially when their leader was killed.

Janson had permitted his cousin to marry a certain John Root —a member of the community who had served in the Mexican War—on the written condition that if Root ever wished to leave Bishop Hill he should not compel his wife to go with him. Root, who was by no means a Pietist, and should never have been admitted to the community, soon decided to leave it, and twice kidnapped his unwilling wife. She was both times rescued—with such efficiency that in bringing her back from Chicago relays of horses were provided so that the entire distance of 150 miles was covered non-stop. Root, enraged, gathered a mob which entered the village, but dispersed when it was unable to find those responsible for bringing back Mrs. Root. A second mob came, intending to burn the village, but was prevented from doing so by neighbours, who assembled, in appreciation of their industrious colonists, to protect them. Root then brought legal proceedings against Janson. The trial was held on 13th May 1850, and during the noon-recess, while Janson was standing near his counsel's table, Root entered and called him by name. As Janson turned, a bullet from Root's pistol pierced his heart.

Stunned by the news of their leader's death, the colonists waited three days for his resurrection—but even then the drama was not quite played out. During the funeral service Janson's widow stepped forward and in the presence of the congregation placed her hand upon the bowed head of Andreas Berglund, creating him guardian of the heir to the leadership until the boy should have reached his majority. For a time Berglund and Mrs. Janson led the community, but only until the return of Jonas Olson, whose qualifications were in every way superior. Mrs. Janson then joined the Shakers.

Olson, who had been prospecting for gold in California with

a party of eight men who had been sent out by Janson to obtain funds for the community, returned—without the gold—when he heard of Janson's death, and was soon installed as leader. The community now became quite prosperous. It was cleared of debt; it owned thousands of acres of fertile land, large droves of cows, sixty yoke of oxen, and 100 horses. Many new buildings had been built, and the large central dwelling-house was extended to twice its original size, so that it now had a frontage of 200 feet and was more like a phalanstery in sheer size than any building ever seen in the Fourierist Phalanxes. Its dining-hall had a seating capacity of over 1,000, in which the entire community took their meals together. Streets were laid out around a central square lined with trees; and eight outlying farms, subsidiary to the great central one, contained dormitories for the accommodation of workers during the summer months.

In 1853 the Society was incorporated under the state laws. Seven trustees, who were given full power over all the business affairs of the community, were appointed for an indefinite period, subject only to their 'good behaviour' and the veto of a majority vote of the male members. This majority vote could also be used to demand a special meeting in any emergency; otherwise there was only an annual meeting for general business and the issue of a report.

In the following year they became even more prosperous as the result of obtaining a contract to work on a railroad, and in 1856 *The Practical Christian* reported that their population was 780; their acreage of land 8,500; and their property in buildings extended far and wide over the countryside, even to the owning of town lots. They had then over 200 milking cows, and as many calves, 150 head of horses and of mules, fifty yoke of working oxen, and a stock of 600 additional cattle. They had made no less than $36,000 in one year from a crop of broom-corn, and between $150,000 and $200,000 from their railroad contract. 'The fact is', the journal adds with transparent truth, 'they are rich.' But with wealth they became unwary, even foolhardy.

It was a defect of their system of government that the trustees could engage in all kinds of dubious activities for at least a year without the members being aware of what was going on. One trustee, Olof Johnson, gathered almost all the power into his own hands, speculated wildly in real estate, and mortgaged the entire colony. His gambles failed, and he was deposed from office—but too late. In 1862 the affairs of the community were wound up, but not before Johnson, who seems to have been pitied rather than blamed, had succeeded in appointing himself and his friends as the official receivers. At the settlement, enough property was supposed to have been set aside to cancel the liabilities of the colony, but since the numerous lawsuits for bad debts that were brought against Johnson and other trustees persisted until as late as 1875, almost all this money disappeared. Thus came to a sad, but not unusual end, a community that made one of the most remarkable accelerations in prosperity ever known among similar organisations.

On the whole, the history of these Jansonists is slightly distasteful. Beginning with religious convictions which enabled them to overcome appalling hardships, they lost them more quickly than any other community holding similar views. Religious dissension rapidly distributed members among various faiths, few adhering to Janson's Pietism. They dug for gold—a filth despised by true followers of the Primitive Church; their leader was embroiled in an unseemly court action which led to his death—when no true Pietist or Devotionalist would even take oath in a court of law; and in 1861, they were so far gone in depravity that they actually raised a company of officers and men to fight in the Union army—when all true members of the heretical sects were non-resistants.

Unlike the Jansonists, the Inspirationists of Amana, who are still flourishing, have never lost faith in the main tenets of the Pietist movement from which they are descended. It is possible that their integrity has been maintained with even greater assurance than that of their compatriots and former contemporaries, the Rappites and Zoarites, on account of the more mystical nature of their early leaders. Unlike Rapp and Baumeler, the founders of the Inspirationists were 'instruments' of the will of God, in whom the current of revelation assumed a miraculous and spectacular form. Rising here in one individual and there in another, and sometimes diving underground, or 'lapsing', for a period of years, this clear stream of inspiration nourished and sustained the sect through all the usual persecutions of the sixteenth and seventeenth centuries. Its vessels or instruments had included men and women of all classes and of varying intellectual capacities; but early in the nineteenth century they were four individuals of humble origin and meagre education.

Michael Krausert, a tailor, Philip Morschel, a stocking-weaver, Christian Metz, a carpenter, and Barbara Heinemann, an illiterate serving-maid, were the instruments in question. They appear to have been blessed with common sense and organisational ability, as well as with their miraculous gift, for they did much to improve the conditions of their followers. Leading them to a manufacturing town, they found them employment and experience which they were able to put to good use in their co-operative settlements at Marienborn, Herrnhaag, Arnsburg, and Englethal, and later in America. Life in Germany, though less difficult than in earlier years, became impossible on account of their refusal to take oaths or submit to military service. In 1842, therefore, Metz, who was the accepted leader, received one of those timely and considerate revelations that we have heard of before. On August 13th he was directed to send 'several members to America to find a new and permanent home for the Society'; and on October 26th Metz landed in New York with three companions—all empowered to act for the members and purchase whatever land seemed best.

They bought 5,000 acres near Buffalo, organised themselves under the name of the Eben-Ezer[1] Society, and within three years had accommodated their 800 emigrants in four villages—Lower, Middle, Upper, and New Eben-Ezer. Some of their members were wealthy—one man contributing as much as $50,000 to the enterprise—and they prospered from the beginning, buying more

[1] 'Hitherto hath the Lord helped us'; cf. 1 Sam. vii. 12.

land and erecting more buildings as their emigrant members arrived. They found that communism, which had not been envisaged when they left Germany, was the only practical means of providing industrial, as opposed to agricultural employment for those members who were artisans; and they were once again commanded by inspiration to adopt a course of action that was essential to their survival. As a member of the community explained to Nordhoff, they 'could not have got on or kept together on any other plan'.

They were excellent business people, so that when they needed more land, instead of buying in their immediate neighbourhood, where prices had soared, they decided—or rather, were inspired —to move west. Having selected an ideal location in Iowa, they sold their entire Buffalo estate without loss—a remarkable exception to the general rule in such transactions, since the nature of most community buildings is inclined to make them unsuitable for individual use and therefore to detract from their saleable value.

The removal to Iowa was accomplished without loss, but was spread over a period of ten years. As a village was constructed in Iowa, so one was abandoned at Eben-Ezer. The first new village was laid out in 1855; the sixth and last, in 1862; and in 1859 this series of communities had been incorporated under the name of the Amana Society.[1]

The entire estate at Amana, by the time all the villages had been built, covered about 20,000 acres. Besides Amana, East Amana, Middle Amana, Amana near the Hill, West Amana, and South Amana, they also own the village of Homestead, which they bought in 1861 when the Mississippi and Missouri Railroad was extended to it. The villages lie about a mile and a half apart, each being provided with its own schoolhouse, store, tavern, shops, and factories. The villages were mostly laid out in squares, beyond which were erected the barns, mills, workshops, and other outbuildings. Each family occupied its own house of brick,

---

[1] They put the accent on the first syllable; and found the name in Song of Sol. iv. 8. But Amana, Iowa, is in a broad plain, not upon a hilltop.

stone, or wood; but assembled at common dining-halls and meeting-houses, of which there were usually several in each village. On the boundaries of the villages were a few houses occupied by hired labourers. Thus each village was an interdependent unit, managing its own affairs and keeping its own accounts, yet submitting the latter to the headquarters at Amana itself, and subject to the central government.

This government was vested in thirteen trustees elected annually by a vote of all male members. The trustees, who exercised no special authority, elected a president, and, subject to the unanimous consent of the whole thirteen, administered all the temporal affairs of the society. Since communism extended throughout the estate, a deficiency of any sort in one village could easily be made good by the surplus of another. The Society was bound together, as most successful communities usually are, by frequent meetings, both administrative and religious. The elders, who were often young men who acted as foremen and of whom there were a great many, met every evening to discuss working arrangements for the following day, and they in turn reported to a council of half a dozen older and more experienced elders in each village, which met every morning. These councils, together with the frequent religious meetings which will be described later, formed a close-knit and secure organisation that was largely responsible for the long life of the community. With the exception of Barbara Heinemann, women were debarred from all authority; but they formed a council for household management, and all unmarried women and widows over the age of thirty were allowed to vote in the annual election.

Women, and even young girls, dressed in black caps, and wore large dark-coloured shawls pinned securely across their bosoms in order to make them as unattractive as possible. They were also forbidden to wear ornaments or to let down their hair, and at all meetings sat apart from the men, and left the room before them. Every care was taken to segregate the sexes from the earliest age, boys being allowed to play only with boys, and girls only with girls—for they had been advised by one of their own early leaders to 'fly from the society of women-kind as much as possible, as a very highly dangerous magnet and magical fire'.

Such restrictions do not appear to have discouraged courtship and marriage. Perhaps they provoked them—in spite of the fact that marriage was not regarded as a praiseworthy act. In fact, newly-married couples were degraded to the lowest of the three Orders into which the society was divided, and had then to win their way back to the highest or most spiritual Order (if they had belonged to it in the first place). Weddings were solemn functions that took place at the house of the bride's father. After prayers and hymns the fifth chapter of the Epistle to the Ephesians was read slowly and with great emphasis, followed by a long and very thorough commentary by the elders—as grim an initiation to conjugal joys as could well be devised. Men were not allowed to marry until the age of twenty-four; and if they wished to contract an exogamous marriage, were excluded for one year from the society, after which time man and wife might apply for admission in the usual way.

They were systematically careful in the selection of new members, many of whom came direct from Germany. After conducting prudent enquiries, they judged upon character alone, and had a fund set aside for the purpose of paying the passage of poor families. Some applicants were admitted to full membership at once, if an 'inspiration' was received to this effect; but usually there was a two years' probation, at the end of which time the accepted novice yielded up his property and signed the constitution, which provided that he might receive his property back without interest if he should leave.

They lived simply but well, in the manner of most German communists. They ate four or five meals a day according to the season, drank home-brewed beer and wine, took coffee, and smoked. In the dining-halls men and women sat at separate tables 'to prevent silly conversation and trifling conduct'; and children also had a table to themselves. 'For those whom illness or the care of small children keeps at home, the food is placed in neat baskets, and it was a curious sight to see, when the dinner-bell rang, a number of women walking rapidly about the streets with these baskets, each nicely packed with food.

'When the bell ceases ringing and all are assembled, they stand up in their places in silence for half a minute, then one says grace, and when he ends, all say "God bless and keep us safely", and then sit down. There is but little conversation at table; the meal is eaten rapidly, but with decorum; and at its close, all stand up again, someone gives thanks, and thereupon they file out with quiet order and precision.'[1]

Every member received an annual allowance for clothing and other articles, excluding food, and could draw what he pleased from the stores, up to his limit. Purchases were entered in books owned by the purchaser, and any surplus saved out of the allowance could be carried over to the following year. Men received allowances of from $40 to $100, according to the clothing they required for the work in which they were engaged; women received from $30 to $40, and children from $5 to $10. They made all their own clothing—buying quantities of wool from neighbouring farmers—and produced a surplus sufficient to supply the countryside. They even exported some of their woollen products as far as New York.

They read mostly the Bible and religious works published by the Society; but took in certain newspapers, mainly trade journals devoted to various crafts and industries. In their schools, which were attended by children of both sexes from the age of six until the age of thirteen, the Bible, their own Catechism, and 'the three Rs' were the basis of instruction; but they were also taught music and musical notation, and much time was devoted to practical pursuits. Both sexes were taught knitting, which was regarded as a useful and industrious pursuit that encouraged repose and discouraged 'rude play'.

All frivolous amusements—cards, games, and the playing of any musical instrument other than a flute—were forbidden; so also were pictures and photographs. Their religious rules were strict and detailed, similar to those of the Shakers, advising them

[1] Nordhoff, p. 33.

to obey God and God's chosen servants without question; to study quiet and serenity; to be sober and without levity in all things; to avoid obeisance and the fear of men; and to shun the world.

They were Trinitarians. They believed in justification by faith and the resurrection of the dead; but they did not believe in eternal damnation, nor practise baptism of any kind. Their religious meetings were frequent. Every evening and three times a week in the morning they met in small groups, according to the Order to which they belonged. On Saturdays the entire village assembled in the meeting-house. Their meetings were simple, consisting of prayers, hymns, readings from the Bible, and exhortations delivered quietly in conversational tones, without any attempt at eloquence. Readings from their own sacred works were very frequent—especially from the inspired utterances of Metz; and at the large Saturday meetings the 'instruments' were sometimes moved, falling into trance, and delivering the Holy Word. Such messages were occasionally delivered at funerals and on other solemn occasions.

Metz and Barbara Heinemann were the last great 'instruments'. The former died in 1867, aged sixty-seven, the latter in 1883, when nearly ninety. In trance, they often shook severely—Metz sometimes shook for an hour—and would sit, kneel, or walk about among the congregation. 'Brother Metz used to walk about in the meeting with his eyes closed; but he always knew to whom he was speaking, or where to turn with words of reproof, admonition, or encouragement.'[1] While most of these utterances were addressed to the entire congregation, many were directed to particular individuals, who were warned in severe language against various sins, of which 'lukewarmness' was a favourite.

Both Metz and Barbara Heinemann were married, the former leaving a son. The latter had at one time been temporarily expelled from the Society for casting 'too friendly an eye upon the young men'. Two years after readmission she was again tempted by the Enemy, with a desire to marry George Landmann; and,

[1] Nordhoff, p. 47.

in spite of being made to see the error of her ways and sincerely repenting, she eventually married Landmann, was for a time under censure for doing so, and then, shortly before the emigration, regained her standing.

Christmas, Easter, and the Holy Week were their great religious festivals; but the greatest of all was the celebration of the Lord's Supper. It was also the rarest, only taking place at the direction of an 'instrument', and often not for several years. It was thought so important that it was always carefully described in writing. The account of the Lord's Supper of 1855 occupies an entire book of 284 printed pages. Brother Metz announced this particular celebration at a Saturday meeting some days before the Supper was due to take place. Many inspired utterances followed. Admonitions were delivered right and left. The wheat was sorted from the chaff by moving certain persons from one Order to another, and even the elders were subject to reproof. Everyone was commanded to 'clean out all filth, all that is rotten and stinks, all sins and every thing idle and useless'. Finally, when all the preparations were complete, the ceremony began with the elders washing the feet of the brethren of the Higher Order. Tables were then brought in, and bread and wine were blessed by the 'instrument' and served to the brethren and sisters by the Elders. A temporary adjournment followed, after which a modest supper of bread, cake, coffee, chocolate, and other light refreshment was served by specially appointed persons. A hymn was then sung and the company dispersed. When the three Orders had gone through the same ceremony—with the exception of feet-washing, which was limited to the Higher Order—a fourth supper was held for children under sixteen and such recalcitrant adults as were considered unfit to mix with others of their own age.

Such ceremonies, which would be remembered and discussed for years afterwards, were the climaxes of all the daily and weekly religious meetings that served to bind the society together with such strength; and it is likely that the 'inspiration' for such a celebration might conveniently coincide with any widespread tendency to a falling-off in proper conduct. An additional safeguard was provided by an annual examination of the spiritual condition of the community. This *Untersuchung* was conducted by Orders, beginning with the elders and working down to the children. It was extremely searching and thorough. Every member was expected to make a complete confession of his sins, his disagreements, and his disputes. If any group undergoing examination showed a tendency to be unresponsive, the examination was postponed until the attitude of the group or individuals improved. The 'instruments' played a vital part in the proceedings, bringing to light such sins as remained hidden by half-confessions, and distributing the usual admonitions and denouncements. Thus the spiritual health of the Society was ensured.

Religious publications, of which there were many, also aided this good work. Apart from their catechism, the Amanites issued numerous books relating to the inspirational history of the society, to which a supplementary volume was added every year. Their collections of hymns were equally extensive. Many of the hymns were long, containing from twelve to twenty-four verses; all were deeply devotional; and all had been given by 'the Spirit of God'. A less devotional but still pious work was that of *Innocent Amusements,* contained in about half a dozen volumes. The whole was a mass of fanciful doggerel, in which religiosity was applied to such an odd assortment of subjects as Cooking, Rain, Milk, Fog, Salve, The Ocean, A Net, Pitch, etc. And *Jesus's ABC for His Scholars,* also in rhyme, ran to 1,200 pages.

The system of religious inculcation and moral supervision was as far-reaching as that of the Shakers, and proved equally effective in maintaining social unity. Unlike the celibate Shakers, the Inspirationists needed no indulgence in frenzied dances or the gift of tongues. Even if they had been celibate, it is improbable that such lively demonstrations would have occurred. They did not occur either at Economy or at Zoar; and it would seem that the temperament of the German emigrants of the nineteenth century was not conducive either to mortification or excitement. Most of the members of Amana, according to Nordhoff, were 'quiet, a little stolid, and very well satisfied with their life'. They did not work hard: 'One of the foremen told me that three hired hands would do so much as five or six of the members'; and these characteristics were attributed by Nordhoff to 'a satisfaction in their lives, a pride in the equality which the communal system secures, and also in the conscious surrender of individual will to the general good, which is not so clearly and satisfactorily felt among other nationalities. Moreover, the German peasant is fortunate in his tastes, which are frugal and well fitted for community living. He has not a great sense of or desire for beauty of surroundings; he likes substantial living, but cares nothing for elegance. . . . I think, too, that his lower passions are more easily regulated. . . .'

They were non-resistants who admitted that they had done wrong to pay for substitutes in the army during the Civil War. Their young people did not drift away; and their old ones frequently lived to a great age. They were prosperous, contented, secure, and highly respected; and their Society endured in almost unaltered form until 1932. To-day it is nominally a corporation, but the administrative changes have made little difference to the spirit that prevails. The population of the seven villages is much the same as it ever was. This alone is a unique phenomenon among communities that have persisted to the present day. And the traditions, both of craftsmanship and social integrity, are still scrupulously observed.

CHAPTER TEN

ONEIDA

We have built us a dome
On our beautiful plantation,
And we all have one home,
And one family relation.
Oneida song.

A MERICAN communities played a significant part in American history to the extent to which they occupied themselves with problems that were vital to the nation. The Pietists of the eighteenth century had been pioneers in the anti-slavery movement; and their work was carried on in the nineteenth century by the Shakers, New Harmony, the pre-Fourierist and Fourierist Associations, and Oneida. New Harmony and Brook Farm had revolutionised education; and the emancipation of women had been achieved to some extent by all these groups, for they proved that women were capable of fulfilling as wide a variety of administrative and occupational duties as men. In the case of the Shakers this liberal attitude to the status of women was based upon their peculiar concept of a bisexual God; it was also a policy dictated to some extent, consciously or unconsciously, by celibacy, in which state the attempt of one sex to dominate the other could only have proved disastrous. In most cases, however, the liberal attitude to women was a logical consequence of the communistic attitude towards property. The Puritans—those thrifty guardians of mercantile interests and worldly goods—had proved to be the most domineering tyrants in the home, and the most unrelenting martinets with regard to the least sexual irregularity. When the power of the Calvinistic Church was challenged and in many cases overthrown by eighteenth-century secularism, and again by revivalism, the puritanical attitude to sex was also swept away.

Humanist enlightenment prepared the way for Mary Wollstonecraft, Fanny Wright, and Margaret Fuller. Reason demanded, at
the very least, that women should be allowed to exercise their
undoubted scholarly and intellectual faculties. Revivalism, on the
other hand, led to a complete revision of the attitude towards the
purely physical relationship of the sexes. The dances of the
celibate Shakers and 'The Jerks' of those who attended the
enormous camp meetings of the frontier, were similar means
of erotic sublimation, while Mormonism, with its licensed polygamy, showed a preoccupation with sex while denying the purely
intellectual concept of feminine emancipation.

The Shakers, and most revivalists, had been content to permit
the maximum amount of licence that was compatible with
absolute chastity. The complement of this licence was a rigid
system of taboo, which was observed with a ritualistic attention
to detail. Such a discipline also existed, without the correspond-
ing sublimatory licence, at Oberlin Theological Seminary, of
which the President was Charles Grandison Finney, the famous
revivalist. The students of both sexes who attended the Seminary
prided themselves upon their ability to withstand all sexual temptation. But since their spiritual muscles were in such fine trim,
the desire to exercise them was correspondingly great. How could
they be certain of their stamina and resistance—how, indeed,
could they even keep in training—without regular practice in
jumping the hurdles and leaping the ditches of sexual temptation?
Some means must be found of arousing passion in order that it
might be resisted—some means, of course, that would have the
blessing of religious sanction.

What better method could be found than that ancient custom
of taking 'spiritual wives'—a tradition handed down from the
Agapetæ of early Christian days? So, at any rate, thought Lucinia
Umphreville, who had studied these matters under Finney. She
proclaimed the doctrine in that part of New York State known
as the Burnt Over Region—in which the fires of revivalism had
flamed with an all-consuming thoroughness. Miss Umphreville
stated that perfection could be derived from passionate love,

provided the lovers lived together without indulging their carnal desires. Should they be so weak as to submit to temptation, the spiritual couples would prove that they were unworthy and ill-assorted. They would have to look for new partners, and go on experimenting and searching until the ideal partner was found. Umphrevillian Perfectionism, in fact, by making provision for lapses from grace, slyly admitted erotic possibilities by a side door. It was the very type of casuistical justification for which the Burnt Over Region had been waiting; and it was not long before a number of congregations devoted to the propagation of this form of Perfectionism, had sprung up in New England. They even possessed, in *The Battle Axe*, a newspaper devoted to their beliefs. In the middle 'thirties there appeared among these Perfectionists an earnest and eager young man who was to give the doctrine a revolutionary twist of his own by actually establishing a colony of Perfectionists who would openly practise a completely new system of sexual relations.

John Humphrey Noyes, unlike the founders of most religious communities, came of a well-established family. His father had represented Vermont in Congress, and his mother was a great-aunt of Rutherford Birchard Hayes, nineteenth President of the United States. Noyes was a born rebel, and was happily endowed with the temerity that such men require in order to achieve success. He was converted at a revival in 1831, at the age of twenty, having previously shown little interest in theology or, indeed, in the studies he had been pursuing at Dartmouth. Moving now to Andover and Yale Divinity Schools, he prepared to enter the ministry, but to enter it upon his own terms: 'If you are to be a minister,' said his father, 'you must think and preach as the rest of the ministers do; if you get out of the traces, they will whip you in.' 'Never!' replied Noyes, 'never will I be whipped by ministers or anybody else into views that do not commend themselves to my understanding as guided by the Bible and enlightened by the Spirit.' This animated reply was a prophetic utterance, for Noyes very soon got out of the traces. His trouble was that he simply couldn't believe he was a sinner. Try as he might, he couldn't summon up any feelings of deep guilt or despair. Yet this very waywardness was itself a sin in the eyes of the orthodox; and Noyes, being unable to admit it, somehow had to devise a means of abolishing sin altogether. His solution to this problem was so astoundingly simple that it amounted to a stroke of genius. In the summer of 1833, while reading the last words of the Fourth Gospel, Noyes received a sudden illumination concerning Christ's words, 'If I will that he tarry till I come, what is that to thee?' 'I knew', wrote Noyes, 'that the time appointed for the Second Advent was within one generation from the time of Christ's personal ministry'—in A.D. 70, to be precise. The Second Coming had taken place centuries ago—so long ago, in fact, that no record of the event had been preserved. The sinners had been divided from the saved, and he that sinned now, so Noyes preached, was of the devil. Noyes himself had the courage to proclaim that he did not sin, and the grace to confess that Christ had absolved him.[1] Thus, in coming to terms with an innate conviction that eternal damnation was an unnecessary and troublesome doctrine, Noyes formulated a belief that differed from those of former sectarian heresies only by its boldness and simplicity.

The implications of a Second Advent that has already taken place are bound to be far-reaching. The Shakers and the Noyesian Perfectionists, both of whom thought that they were living in a state of regeneration, believed that if they were not quite in heaven itself, they were at least close enough to it to order their lives upon heavenly conventions. One such convention for which Biblical authority existed was the absence of marriage in Heaven —where 'they neither marry nor are given in marriage'. The Shakers, who wanted to be celibate, used this text in order to justify their desires: the followers of Noyes, who did not want celibacy, used the same text to support a form of regulated promiscuity. In 1837 *The Battle Axe* published a letter from Noyes explaining his conception of the sexual relations that ought to

[1] This confession was made on 20th February 1834. The anniversaries of this date were observed at Putney and Oneida Communities.

exist between men and women. In his letter, he stated uncompromisingly that when the will of God is done on earth as it is in Heaven *'there will be no marriage.* The marriage supper of the Lamb is a feast at which *every dish is free to every guest.* Exclusiveness, jealousy, quarrelling have no place there, for the same reason as that which forbids a guest at a thanksgiving dinner to claim each his separate dish, and quarrel with the rest for his rights. In a holy community, there is no more reason why sexual intercourse should be restrained by law, than why eating and drinking should be—and there is as little occasion for shame in the one case as in the other.'

Here was boldness carried to lengths that had never before been approached. All the subconscious sexual desires of the past ten or twenty years had at last found a spokesman whom nothing could daunt, a tactician who drove straight through the enemy's lines of defence armed only with an ingenious shield of his own devising.

Since Noyes had made his unlawful system of sexual intercourse depend upon membership of a holy community, the next step was obviously to found one. In 1834 (after engaging in anti-slavery activity), Noyes had returned to his parental home at Putney, Vermont. Here he began to give Bible classes, and to convert his family to his views. Here he married Harriet Holton, granddaughter of a Lieutenant-governor of the state; and began to publish *The Witness,* which was written, composed, type-set, printed, and mailed by the family. In 1839, the group was joined by George Cragin—who had been a revivalist under Finney—and his family, and by J. L. Skinner, who married one of Noyes's sisters. Others, including William Alfred Hinds, also joined. So far there had been no formal organisation, but in 1840 the Putney Association came into being—as a purely religious body, thus described in *The Witness*:

'Our establishment, such as it is, exists in the midst of an ordinary village, and differs not in its relation to the community around from a manufacturing corporation or any other ordinary association. A few families of the same religious faith, without any formal scheme or written laws, have agreed to regard themselves as one family, and their relations to one another are regulated as far as possible by this idea. The special object of the association is not to make money, nor to exemplify the perfection of social life, but to support the publication of the gospel of salvation from sin, by papers, books, tracts, etc. Formal community of property is not regarded by us as obligatory on principle, but as expedient with reference to our present circumstances and objects. We are attempting no scientific experiments in political economy nor in social science, and beg to be excused from association in the public mind with those who are making such experiments. Our highest ambition is to be able to preach Christ without being burdensome to any, and to act out as far as possible the family spirit of the gospel. When we find a better way than our present plan to attain these objects we shall freely change our mode of living.'

They soon found 'a better way than their present plan' of living, and in 1844 adopted communism, in which change Noyes had been influenced by the example of the Shakers. With 500 acres of fertile land, seven houses, a store, and a printing office, the little community established itself upon a sound basis, combining manual labour in the afternoons with reading, writing, debating, singing and prayer in the evenings. Hebrew, Greek, and Latin were taught; and on Sundays there were chapel meetings attended by 'outsiders'. The famous weekly meetings for mutual criticism also began here; and it was at Putney, also, that Noyes first formulated his ideas of Male Continence and Complex Marriage, which were adopted by the community in 1846.

These latter practices were more than the inquisitive neighbours were prepared to tolerate. In the following year the persecution of the community culminated in the indictment of Noyes on the grounds of adultery. Noyes, who was too sagacious to play the part of a useless martyr, and who by this time was regarded by his followers as the Moses of the new dispensation, destined to lead them to a Promised Land, hastily purchased that land in another state. This Canaan consisted of twenty-three acres, with a few buildings on it, at Oneida, an excellent site in the Burnt Over Region. In 1847, therefore, it was unanimously adopted by the forty or fifty members at Putney 'that the Kingdom of God had come'. *The Witness* ceased publication and Noyes went to Oneida to take over the new estate, where in March 1848 he was joined by the greater number of his followers, the removal being completed in the following year.

During the years at Putney, they had rejected Fourierism, but 'drank copiously of the spirit of the *Harbinger* and of the Socialists; and have always acknowledged that they received a great impulse from Brook Farm. Thus the Oneida Community really issued from a conjunction between the Revivalism of Orthodoxy and the Socialism of Unitarianism. . . . In the fall of 1847, when Brook Farm was breaking up, the Putney Community was also breaking up, but in the agonies, not of death, but of birth'.[1]

The birth of Oneida Community was preceded by the conceptions of Male Continence and Complex Marriage. Both systems, although given religious justification, were invented by Noyes in order to overcome the suffering which was then the common experience of women in childbirth. Mrs. Noyes had given birth to five babies in six years, and four of them had been stillborn. Her husband could see no religious reason for permitting such pain and disappointment; but, since he disapproved of contraceptives, he advocated the practice of 'self-control', or *coitus reservatus*. At the same time Noyes the organiser, the lover of scientific method and order, was shocked by haphazard procreation, which often resulted in the birth of deformed or mentally deficient children. 'We are opposed', he wrote in *Bible Communism*, 'to random procreation, which is unavoidable in the marriage system. But we are in favour of intelligent, well-ordered procreation. The physiologists say that the race cannot be raised from ruin till propagation is made a matter of science; but they point out no way of making it so. Procreation is controlled and reduced to a science in the case of valuable domestic brutes; but marriage and fashion forbid any such system among human beings. We believe the time will come when involuntary and

[1] Noyes, p. 616.

random propagation will cease, and when scientific combination will be applied to human generation as freely and successfully as it is to that of other animals. The way will be open for this when amativeness can have its proper gratification without drawing after it procreation as a necessary sequence. And at all events, we believe that good sense and benevolence will very soon sanction and enforce the rule that women shall bear children only when they choose. They have the principal burdens of breeding to bear, and they rather than men should have their choice of time and circumstances, at least till science takes charge of the business.'

But 'amativeness' was seldom satisfied by monogamy, which 'gives to sexual appetite only a scanty and monotonous allowance, and so produces the natural vices of poverty, contraction of taste, and stinginess or jealousy. It makes no provision for the sexual appetite at the very time when that appetite is the strongest. By the custom of the world, marriage, in the average of cases, takes place at about the age of twenty-four; whereas puberty commences at the age of fourteen. For ten years, therefore, and that in the very flush of life, the sexual appetite is starved. This law of society bears hardest on females, because they have less opportunity of choosing their time of marriage than men.'

The obvious remedy for these abuses was male continence combined with complete freedom of intercourse. Such a system would also remove that discrepancy between community of goods and private possession of persons that must always be obnoxious to a logical-minded individual like Noyes; for was it not absurd that man 'should be allowed and required to love in all directions, and yet be forbidden to express love except in one direction'?

Complex marriage meant, in theory, that any man and woman might freely cohabit within the limits of the community. In practice, however, there was less freedom than might have been expected. The partners in this new form of relationship were obliged to obtain each other's consent, 'not by private conversation or courtship, but through the intervention of some third person or persons'.[1] The exclusive attachment of two persons

[1] Nordhoff, p. 276.

was regarded as selfish and 'idolatrous' and was strongly discouraged. It was usually broken up by means of 'mutual criticism' —and so were the innocent 'partialities' of one child for another. While no one was obliged, under any circumstances, to receive the attentions of someone whom he or she did not like, the propagation of children was controlled by the elder members of the community. They advised that the young of one sex should be paired off with the aged of the other sex; and at one time twenty-four men and twenty women were specially selected in order to conduct a eugenic experiment designed 'to produce the usual number of offspring to which people in the middle classes are able to afford judicious moral and spiritual care, with the advantage of a liberal education'.[1]

On the whole the system was remarkably successful. Apart from a few sorrows due to the breaking-up of an exclusive attachment, the sexual relations of the members inspired them with a lively interest in each other, and Pierrepont Noyes—one of the sons of John Humphrey—believes 'that the opportunity for romantic friendships also played a part in rendering life more colourful than elsewhere. Even elderly people, whose physical passions had burned low, preserved the fine essence of earlier associations'.[2]

It is likely that Noyes's attention was first drawn towards the religious justification of Complex Marriage at Andover Theological Seminary, where Professor Moses Stuart taught that the description of the marriage relations in Rom. vii applied to carnal man before conversion, and was not a matter of Christian experience. Noyes certainly derived the idea of Mutual Criticism from Andover, where it was practised by the students in order to further their spiritual development.

At Oneida, Mutual Criticism was the medium of all discipline. Usually a member who was confronted with a moral problem or who was conscious of some form of guilt would request a criticism; but sometimes the treatment was administered as a corrective for unacknowledged delinquency; and it was even

---

[1] Noyes, *Essay on Scientific Propagation.*   [2] *My Father's House*, p. 131.

used, as psycho-analysis is now used, as a cure for physical ailments —apparently with a number of satisfactory results. The person to be criticised would sometimes appear before the entire society, but more often before a committee selected from those who knew him best. Each member would then state quite frankly the faults and merits of the person concerned, while he sat in silence. Any tendency to spitefulness or prejudice on the part of a member of the committee would be corrected by other members, and by the knowledge that such conduct would in itself call for criticism. At the end of the session, the chairman of the committee would usually sum up and offer such advice, reproof, or encouragement as seemed necessary. No ill-feeling was provoked in the 'victim', who almost always emerged from the ordeal with a clear knowledge of how to repair his faults or avoid the causes of his distress. Like other Oneida institutions, Mutual Criticism was an adaptation of similar customs that existed in various religious communities; but it was an improvement on most of them, since it was untainted with authoritarianism.

The accommodation at Oneida was primitive, consisting of two log-houses, a log-hut, and an old saw-mill; and the community suffered several years of hardship until they were joined by Sewell Newhouse, an inventor of steel traps. The community began the manufacture of these gadgets, and was saved from financial disaster; but they made no clear profit until 1857, and were still sleeping in garrets and outhouses twelve years after the foundation of Oneida. In this time, however, they had also produced travelling bags and satchels, preserved fruit, and silk—all of which commodities were made with such care and thoroughness that the community earned a wide reputation for skilled workmanship.

Meanwhile, they had bought more land and acquired more members. At the beginning of 1849 the membership had been eighty-seven; during that year it doubled; in 1851 there were 205; in 1875, 298; in 1878, 306. Not all of these members lived at Oneida, for in 1849 a small branch community had been started at Brooklyn, and others followed at Wallingford, Newark, Putney, Cambridge, and Manlius. In 1855 some of these branches were abandoned in favour of a policy of concentration at Oneida and Wallingford.

Most of the members were New England farmers and mechanics, but there were also lawyers, clergymen, merchants, physicians, and teachers. After the completion, in the early 'sixties, of the large brick Mansion House at Oneida, they all lived under one roof, except for two or three dozen mechanics who lived near the workshops that were situated about a mile away. (These factories were fitted with the latest labour-saving machinery, and turned out 300,000 traps, and silk-twist to the value of $20,000 a year.) Nearer to the Mansion House were offices, a school (with chemical laboratory and photographic apparatus), a carpenter's shop, barns, stables, laundry, and other necessary buildings.

The Mansion House itself was centrally heated throughout, and well supplied with baths and labour-saving kitchens. It contained several large halls, a visitor's parlour, a reading and reference library of 5,000 volumes, with all the leading newspapers and journals on file, two 'family' or recreation rooms, and a large number of bedrooms. (The older members had separate bedrooms; the younger usually slept two in a room.) Also, above the dining-hall was the printing office of the *Oneida Circular*.

A firm believer in the power of the written word, Noyes had already published several journals before arriving at Oneida. He was, in fact, a prolific and energetic writer of books and pamphlets as well—most of them marked by a lucid and vigorous style. *The Berean*, published in 1847 at Putney, was an exposition of his religious views, even as *Bible Communism*, published in 1848 at Oneida, contained his social theories. The *Circular*, which superseded some earlier journals at Oneida, was a weekly paper, well produced, and well written, but distributed in a most unorthodox manner, as its own announcement will show:

The *Circular* is sent to all applicants, whether they pay or not. It costs and is worth at least two dollars per volume. Those who want it and ought to have it are divisible into three classes, viz.: 1, those who can not afford to pay two dollars; 2, those who can afford to pay *only* two dollars; and, 3, those who can afford to pay *more* than two dollars. The first ought to have it free; the second ought to pay the cost of it; and the third ought to pay enough more than the cost to make up the deficiences of the first. This is the law of Communism. We have no means of enforcing it, and no wish to do so, except by stating it and leaving it to the good sense of those concerned. We take the risk of offering the *Circular* to all without price; but free subscriptions will be received only from persons making application for themselves, either directly or by giving express authority to those who apply for them.

At the time of Nordhoff's visit, 2,000 copies were printed weekly, at an annual loss of $600—which proves the importance that Noyes set upon propaganda. Propaganda, in fact, was even introduced into the advertisement columns of the *Circular*, in a somewhat facetious manner. A few examples will suffice:

TO BROKERS

WANTED — Any amount of SHARES OF SECOND-COMING STOCK, bearing the date A.D. 70, or thereabouts, will find a ready market and command a high premium at this office.

ROOMS TO LET in the 'Many Mansions' that Christ has prepared for those that love him.

PATENT SIEVES. The series of sieves for CRITICISM having been thoroughly tested, are now offered to the public for general use. They are warranted to sift the tares from the wheat, and in all cases to discriminate between good and evil. A person, after having passed through this series, comes out free from the encumbrances of egotism, pride, etc., etc. All persons are invited to test them gratuitously.

*G*RAND FIRE ANNIHILATOR!—AN IN-VENTION for overcoming Evil with Good.
MEEK & LOWLY.

In spite of this rather tiresome evangelical playfulness, the Oneida Perfectionists were by no means narrow-minded. They encouraged freedom of enquiry and education, placed the works of Huxley, Darwin, and Herbert Spencer on their library shelves, and engaged in every form of art, amusement, and decorative embellishment that might bring them culture and happiness. They had an excellent orchestra; dances; plays; pantomimes, entertainers, and stereopticons for the children; chess, draughts, and card games; and frequent picnics. They encircled their home with a wide lawn, and surrounded the lawn with ornamental trees and shrubs. They owned summer resorts at Oneida Lake, twelve miles away, where they fished and hunted; and also at Short Beach, Connecticut, on Long Island Sound. Believing that 'every man, woman and child should be surrounded with circumstances favouring the best development of heart, mind and body, and that no one should be excluded on account of age, sex or race, from engaging in any occupation for which he or she is adapted by nature or culture', they provided, either at Oneida or Wallingford, as many complementary occupations and amenities as possible. Oneida concentrated mainly on industry, although possessing large orchards and 100 head of cattle; Wallingford paid greater attention to farming and horticulture, although it owned two small factories—one for the production of silk and one at which spoons were made. Perfect community of interest existed between these two societies, and members moved freely to and from the one or the other. They made no definite rules with regard to the time of rising in the morning or the hours of work, but encountered very little shiftlessness. (Any tendency to laziness or lukewarmness was countered by the system of mutual criticism.) Their freedom in this respect, however, was purchased by the employment of a greater number of hired labourers per head than in any other communistic society. The two communities between them employed as many as 250—all of whom were well treated—saying that, although they expected that communism would at some time displace the hireling system, 'in the meantime we propose to help our neighbours and ourselves by furnishing remunerative labour to those who are not prepared for Communism'. In practice, however, the number of hired labourers never declined, and most of the members of the community lived the privileged lives of superintendents of departments. They also frequently changed their jobs—especially the more disagreeable ones—in order to avoid monotony. (For the same reason, they sometimes changed the order of their evening meetings, their amusements, and even the times of their meals.)

Their affairs were ordered by twenty-one standing committees and forty-eight administrative departments, which together covered every conceivable activity and interest from hair-cutting and dentistry to education and silk-manufacture. The heads of all departments formed a Business Board which met every Sunday morning. At this meeting, which was open to all members, the business of the past week was discussed, and a secretary took notes of the proposals and recommendations made for the following week. The secretary's report was then read out in the Sunday evening meeting and discussed; only those proposals which received general approval were carried out. Reports of all these meetings were exchanged between the two communities.

Accounts were sent in once a month by the heads of departments, and at an annual meeting of the Business Board the work for the year was carefully laid out, estimates having been sent in to the Finance Committee, which made the appropriate allocations of money. Any member of the community could submit projects, with an estimate of the costs involved, to this meeting, and nothing was decided without general consent. In appointing members to various occupations, their inclinations and abilities were both carefully considered; but the committee responsible for these appointments could vary the employments either to suit the individual or the needs of the community. Women served on these committees, and shared in all activities, on an equal footing with men.

Their book-keeping—in the charge of a young woman—was so carefully organised that they could tell at a glance the exact financial position of any department, or of the entire community;

ONEIDA COMMUNITY DWELLING, 1850.

ONEIDA MANSION, 1867. *This shows only one wing of the building.*

they also kept a methodical inventory, which was revised annually, of all their possessions; and the same love of systematic administration was responsible for a board which revealed at a glance the whereabouts of every member on any given day.

'The men', wrote Nordhoff, 'dress as people in the world do, but plainly, each one following his own fancy. The women wear a dress consisting of a bodice, loose trousers, and a short skirt falling to just above the knee. Their hair is cut just below the ears, and I noticed that the younger women usually gave it a curl. The dress is no doubt extremely convenient: it admits of walking in mud or snow, and allows freedom of exercise; and it is entirely modest. But it was to my unaccustomed eyes totally and fatally lacking in grace and beauty.' They had no peculiar mode of addressing each other; the men were called 'mister' and the women 'miss', with the exception of those who had been married before entering the society. 'It was somewhat startling to me', Nordhoff confessed, 'to hear Miss —— speak about her baby.'

As to the babies themselves, they were cared for by the mother until weaned, when they were placed in the infants' department of the Children's House, which occupied one wing of the Mansion. Here they were cared for from 8 a.m. to 5 p.m. by nurses who worked half-day shifts. At about eighteen months the infants were promoted to another department, in which they stayed all day; and eventually at about three years of age the children left their mothers even at night, and remained in the Children's House until the age of thirteen or fourteen. During all this time parents were free to visit their children and take them for walks, whenever they wished; nor was the mother ever separated from her child for any considerable length of time, but as soon as the infant had been weaned she gradually gave up all particular responsibility for its clothing, diet, and night-care, and began to resume her place in the industries of the community.

Children were allowed to sleep as long as they wished in the mornings, and were encouraged to learn some trade or craft as well as their lessons in ordinary subjects. Before they began to take part in the industries of the community, promising talent was given an opportunity to leave the community for the purpose of special study or instruction. They sent several young men to Yale, where they took up professional studies—of medicine, law, engineering, and architecture. Others, of both sexes, were sent to factories, in order to learn new techniques and acquire thorough experience—for the community gained from their knowledge when these students returned. The inventiveness, ingenuity, and practical skill in Oneida workshops, business, and administration were largely due to this link with the world. For instance, when they began to manufacture silk, one of their students brought back a machine as a pattern; the community then made all the machines it needed in its own foundry and shops. Similarly, a young chemical student brought back the secrets of dyeing; and, apart from these derived ideas, they invented improvements of their own, such as a gadget to measure silk by the yard during winding, and another to test its strength. Many labour-saving devices appeared in the Mansion itself, of which the most interesting were the circular tables installed in the dining-hall. These, which were designed to accommodate about a dozen people each, had a stationary rim, on which were set plates, saucers, cups, and cutlery, and at the centre a revolving disc on which the food was placed. By turning the disc, each person could help himself without troubling his neighbours.

Contact with the outside world, especially with its scientific theories, did not seduce the men and women who had followed Father Noyes through all the early trials of the community. The religious basis of their existence was very real to them, and for this reason alone Darwin, Spencer, Huxley, and Tyndall were safe enough on the library shelves. By 1870, however, a new generation had grown up at Oneida—a generation that had no emotional experience of Perfectionism. These young people might be taught that the basis of their unorthodox lives was a Biblical sanction, but they were too far removed from the stirring revivalism of the 'forties to appreciate the fact. Some of them, like one of the sons of the founder, were open agnostics, and a number secretly disapproved of what seemed to them to be an immoral mode of life. A subterranean disharmony began to appear, and came to the surface in 1876, when Noyes attempted to transfer the leadership of the community to his agnostic son, Dr. Theodore Noyes. The doctor's lack of religion was bad enough, but his policy of remaining aloof from the community, and his experiments with a system of thorough regimentation, were too much. Noyes, who had retired to Wallingford, was obliged to return and resume control; but factions had already been formed that were to prove disastrous. Certain dissatisfied members were ready to support those 'outsiders' who had never ceased to attack the community on the grounds of immorality. So far, under the solidarity commanded by Noyes and by religious fervour, Oneida had survived all such attacks. Even the Presbyterian Synod of Central New York, which had appointed a committee of seven to investigate the activities of the community, had been unable to bring it to an end; and the fierce denunciations and campaigns of Professor Mears of Hamilton College would doubtless have suffered the same fate had it not been for dissension in the community itself. Noyes apparently had definite evidence that a number of his followers were prepared to support Mears, and with the same realism he had shown in leaving Putney he suddenly and secretly left Oneida on 23rd June 1876, after taking the advice of some trustworthy members. He established himself in Canadian territory, at Niagara Falls, and never returned to America. But he did not lose interest in the community, and kept constantly in touch with it, either by post or by receiving delegates who came to seek his advice. It seemed obvious that Oneida would be obliged to abandon its peculiar system of sexual relationship if it wished to survive; on 20th August 1879, therefore, Noyes sent the following list of propositions to the community:

That we give up the practice of Complex Marriage, not as renouncing belief in the principles and prospective finality of that institution, but in deference to the public sentiment which is evidently rising against it;

That we place ourselves, not on the platform of the Shakers, on the one hand, nor of the world, on the other, but on Paul's platform which allows marriage but prefers celibacy.

If you accept these modifications the Community will consist of two distinct classes—the married and the celibates—both legitimate, but the last preferred.

What will remain of our Communism after these modifications may be defined thus:

We shall hold our property and businesses in common, as now;

We shall live together in a common household and eat at a common table, as now;

We shall have a common children's department, as now;

We shall have our daily evening meetings, and all of our present means of moral and spiritual improvement.

Surely, here is Communism enough to hold us together and inspire us with heroism for a new career.

These propositions were accepted by a full assembly at Oneida, and were quickly followed by a considerable number of marriages —that state being vastly more popular than the recommended celibacy—and an attempt was now made to settle down once more to community life. Complex marriage, however, had been so much a part of the communistic pattern, and the recent disturbance had been so profound that a commission was appointed in 1880 to consider the advisability of re-organising upon a joint-stock basis. The question was discussed carefully and peaceably, and after sixteen months of study and preparation communism was abandoned. On 1st January 1881 the joint-stock company called 'Oneida Community, Limited' was set up without the loss of a single working-hour in any of the industries. The financial settlement, which was equitable, wise, and generous, included the free education of children up to the age of sixteen, when each of them received a bonus of $200 to give them a start in life. There were only half a dozen members sufficiently discontented with this arrangement to bring lawsuits—which they lost. On the other hand, there were a number of members so distressed by the abandonment of communism that they wished to set up a new community. They were, probably wisely, dissuaded from this project by Noyes.

Under the new system, members gradually began to leave the Mansion House, setting themselves up with their families in separate houses. A colony of twenty went to California; others to New York and Boston; while some fifty or more went to Niagara, where they found employment in the neighbourhood of their exiled leader.

Noyes lived on until 13th April 1886, sustained by the belief that Oneida had been planned by the heavenly powers, and still revered by the small colony of adherents who had followed him to Niagara. He was a man, wrote Goldwin Smith, 'whose ability is written on his brow, on the pages of his vigorously written books, and on the work of his organising hands'; a man with an unusual degree of moral courage and a virile faith that was tempered by wise judgement and a wide outlook.

Noyes's sound judgement and businesslike ability—which were responsible for the most interesting and one of the most successful of native American communities—were not shared by the founder of the Icarians, who came from France in 1848, when the Perfectionists had just moved to Oneida.

CHAPTER ELEVEN

ICARIA

Travailleurs de la grande cause
Soyons fiers de notre destin;
L'egoiste seul se repose,
Travaillons pour le genre humain.
Icarian song.

ÉTIENNE CABET, the founder of the Icarian communities, was some sixteen or seventeen years younger than Fourier and Robert Owen. Born a year before the fall of the Bastille, the French Revolution was only a childhood memory to him; it did not strike him, as it struck his seniors, with the full force of disillusionment midway in youth. He was able to retain a childish love of intrigue that assumed a political revolutionary form. A member of the Carbonari, and of the Insurrection Committee of 1830, he remained all his life a professional conspirator at heart. He was a man of shallower character than either Fourier or Owen, having neither the fantastic imagination of the one nor the broad visionary convictions of the other. Beside their childlike innocence, Cabet's experience appears somewhat hollow.

In recognition of his services on the Insurrection Committee, Louis Philippe appointed him Attorney-General for Corsica, hoping, no doubt, to remove a dangerous democrat from further revolutionary activity. Cabet, however, was too much of a natural conspirator to be silenced by preferment, and played such an active part in the radical movement—writing several books and publishing his own paper, *Le Populaire*—that he was soon dismissed from office. His native town of Dijon then elected him *député*, but his revolutionary attitude in Parliament resulted in his arraignment on a charge of *lèse-majesté* and he was condemned to two years' imprisonment or five years' exile. Choosing the latter, he went first to Brussels, from which he was expelled, and then to England.

In England he became a disciple of Owen, studied political history and sociology, and returned to France in 1839 with his own theories embodied in a utopian novel entitled *Un Voyage en Icarie*, which was published the following year—the same year, incidentally, as that in which Brisbane's *Social Destiny of Man* was published in America. Cabet's book is one of the dullest of its kind. Beneath a sugar-coating of fiction that is transparently thin lies the same old communist aperient, neither sickly nor bitter to the taste, but undoubtedly composed of a high percentage of common starch. It was flavoured, however, with a tincture of political gall—an ingredient that was scarce between the revolutions of 1830 and 1848. Saint-Simon and Fourier offered drugs to dream upon: Cabet appeared to offer a more fundamental medicine. His book, besides containing a history of communist theory, and recommendations for translating this theory into fact —with the usual, if rather uninspired picture of a blissful Millennium—also contained a scathing criticism of the existing social order. It was probably this latter ingredient that secured for it a popularity that was quite unexpected. It quickly became a best-seller, of which almost every working man in France had heard even if he had not read it.

Cabet was quick enough to make good use of a success that must have astonished him. Between 1840 and 1847 he devoted *Le Populaire* and a new publication, *L'Almanach Icarienne*, to the propagation of his communistic views, and by the end of the latter year was said to have built up a following of 400,000.

Cabet, who had never set out with the intention of putting his theories to the test, was now besieged with demands that he should do so. In vain did he expostulate; his warnings—like those of Fourier—that any experiment must be preceded by a long course of study and careful preparation, were lost amid popular clamour for an Icarian colony. Flattered by such success, and throwing aside what little discretion he possessed, Cabet acted the part of a communist Moses. In May 1847 he issued a flamboyantly enthusi-astic proclamation to the workingmen of France—'*Allons en Icarie!*'

It was useless, he declared, to hope for an Icaria in France. Even if governmental intolerance could be overcome, and a revolution were successful, such a revolution would not benefit the working class. A new land was needed, in which whole cities and villages could be built upon a communistic plan. Ten or twenty thousand people at least would want to take part in the founding of such a community, and a million more would join them within a short time. France was useless for such an enter-prise; America, that idyllic and unspoilt land, was the very place: '*Travailleurs, allons en Icarie!*'

Enthusiastic letters, and hundreds of offers of gifts—from seeds and jewellery to clothing and money—were showered upon the offices of *Le Populaire*. Cabet kept up the afflatus, announcing from time to time that he expected to enrol more than a million people in his scheme. But Icaria, at the moment, did not even possess a prospective site. It was high time to find one.

In September Cabet went to London to ask Owen's advice on the matter. Owen, who had already attempted to found a colony in Texas, and who was always fond of harping on the latest string he had mastered, convinced Cabet that this was the ideal location. It had been admitted to the Union as late as the preceding year and was eager for emigrants. Cabet returned to France, and might perhaps have failed to act as quickly as he did had not a Texan land-agent appeared in London in January, and had not the clamour for Icaria been as great as ever. Off went Cabet to London, and contracted pell-mell for 1,000,000 acres in Texas, binding himself to a condition that the site should be occupied by 1st July 1848.

Pleased as any man is pleased who has convinced himself that he has voluntarily taken a step that has in reality been forced upon him, Cabet announced in *Le Populaire*—under a headline that pro-claimed with graphic simplicity, '*C'est au Texas!*'—that he had secured a land flowing with milk and honey. Immediate prepara-tions were made for the embarkation of the advance party. This, of course, was bound to be of modest proportions, but soon, Cabet supposed, thousands and tens of thousands would have to be turned away, miserably disappointed at not being able to join the 1,000,000 Icarians who would by that time be living in such enviable conditions across the Atlantic.

The advance party sailed from Le Havre on February 3rd with impressive publicity. Before embarking they signed a social contract binding themselves to communism; Cabet delivered a fulsome address; and the Icarians, 'standing on the stern-deck of the ship, entoned in unison the farewell chant, *"Partons pour Icarie"*, to which the spectators responded in a thousand cries of *"Au revoir!"* '.[1] Cabet, in an effervescence of noble emotion, wrote in *Le Populaire* that he could not doubt the regeneration of the human race: 'The third of February 1848 will be an epoch-making date, for on that day one of the grandest acts in the history of the human race was accomplished—the advance-guard, departing on the ship *Rome*, has left for Icaria. . . . May the winds and waves be propitious to you, soldiers of humanity! And we Icarians who remain, let us prepare without loss of time to rejoin our friends and brothers!'

Alas for bold pronouncements and impressive opening ceremonies! Had they counted for anything, New Harmony would be an Eden to-day, and the Clermont Phalanx a land of Canaan. . . .

The Icarians, expecting a fertile soil adjoining the Red River and easily accessible by boat, were informed at New Orleans that they possessed a large tract of wilderness 250 miles from the river. Expecting 1,000,000 acres, they found that only 100,000 acres were provided for in the contract. Expecting an unbroken tract of country, they found that their land had been allocated in chess-board fashion, of which they could only lay claim to alternate squares—the intervening spaces belonging to the state; and in order to take rightful possession of even these scattered sections, they were obliged to build a log-house on each one before July.

[1] A. Sauva in *The American Socialist*.

It was an impossibility. The most they could hope to claim in this fashion was 10,000 acres. And how could they set up an efficient communist colony when each section was isolated from its neighbours?

No one could have blamed them for giving up the whole scheme. They had been tricked and trebly tricked, and tricked by proxy into the bargain. No one could have blamed them for scattering in all directions and faring for themselves as best they might. But with that mirage of Icarian bliss always before their eyes, they made no such prudent decision. Quixotically, they decided to make the best of their wretched contract. They set out on the long cross-country trek to Icaria.

They had one wagon: it broke down. They had limited supplies: they gave out. Sick, weakened by lack of nourishment, and exhausted by the long journey, the 'regenerators of the human race', the 'soldiers of humanity' practically crawled into Icaria. They built a log house and some wooden sheds and began to break up the soil. July came, and brought malaria. Four died of it. Seven more died of fatigue. Every man on the site was ill; their only doctor went raving mad; and, as if this were insufficient punishment, one man was killed by lightning. This was enough for five more members; they made off as quickly as their weak legs would carry them. The remainder hung on miserably, waiting for the second advance-party, due in September. There would be 1,500 of them, fresh from France, full of enthusiasm, able-bodied. With their help, the community could soon get on its feet. . . .

Meanwhile, in France, a revolution had taken place—only three weeks after the departure of the first Icarians. The Second Republic, established on February 24th, was in fact a bourgeois government as inimical to truly radical action as its predecessor; but at the time its promises raised great hopes among the working class. If there was a possiblity of progress at home—visible, tangible progress—why risk one's future on a completely unpredictable adventure 5,000 miles away? Better to be certain of a few extra sous in France than to lose everything in what might be a wild-goose chase. Cabet was urged, by the Home Party, to build his Icaria in France; he was even nominated, with Cavaignac and Lamartine, as candidate for the Presidency. But he refused to be diverted from the American experiment, and the Home Party withdrew from the ranks of the Icarians.

For this reason, volunteers for Texas were not forthcoming. Only nineteen could be found for the second advance party. Of these, nine fell sick between New Orleans and Texas; and only ten weary men joined their compatriots, who had expected 1,500. It was obviously hopeless to continue. Deciding to retreat, they split up into small groups, each man receiving an allowance of $6, which was all they could afford. Half a dozen died *en route*; the rest reached New Orleans in the winter of 1848.

Cabet, alarmed by the stories of these appalling hardships, left his wife and daughter in Paris without means of support and, at the age of sixty, took ship for America. He arrived at New Orleans with about 450 followers in January 1849. Between them the Icarians had $17,000—a sum of money that would have dwindled to nothing if they had attempted to make a fresh start in Texas. They therefore decided to stay in New Orleans until they could find a new site for their experiment. Two hundred withdrew from the company, either to return to France or to seek their individual fortunes in America. The remainder, numbering about 280, established themselves at Nauvoo, Illinois, in March 1849.

The great Mormon *hegira* had taken place in 1847, and Nauvoo, until then the largest and most prosperous town in the State,[1] was almost abandoned. The Icarians rented about 1,500 acres, bought a mill, a few houses, and a distillery, and settled down to six years of deserved prosperity.

A forty-room communal dwelling-house, numerous smaller houses, a large common dining-hall and meeting room, a school, mills, workshops—such were the chief buildings taken over by the Icarians from the Mormon agent in the town. United in aim and

---

[1] In 1845 the population of Nauvoo was about 15,000; of Chicago, about 8,000.

by nationality, many having the advantage of previous acquaintance with one another, and led by a man for whom they had long
had a devotion and respect, they made better use of their
opportunities than the Owenites who had taken over the Rappite
town.

Most of them were French artisans with a native intelligence
eager for new knowledge and cultural amenties, but sufficiently
shrewd, industrious, and disciplined to ensure an economic success
to the community. They published a quantity of propaganda in
English and German as well as French, acquired a library of 5,000
volumes, and provided frequent musical and theatrical entertainments. Their schools were liberal; their sexual relations orthodox;
their daily lives conventional. They might well have endured,
with gradually increasing prosperity, as long as any German
community. They might well have come to own the whole of
Nauvoo. . . .

Their affairs were administered by a *Comité de Gérance*—a
board of six directors, one of whom was President of the community. The other five were heads of the departments of Finance
and Provisions; Clothing and Lodging; Education, Health and
Amusement; Industry and Agriculture; and Publicity. The work
of the *Comité* was subject to the approval of a General Assembly
consisting of all adult males. On the face of it, the arrangement
seemed to safeguard all democratic rights; in practice, it led to
the creation of two opposed parties. The *Comité*, appointing foremen and other officers, built up an administration that was prepared to endorse every decree made by Cabet, who was annually
elected President. Cabet, however, growing old and crotchety,
became gradually more intolerant. He prohibited the use of
tobacco and whisky, interfered in the private lives of members,
and encouraged spying; nor did he realise the possibilities of
agriculture and industry, and made miserly allowances for their
development. An opposition arose and dominated the General
Assembly; and the Cabet faction drew closer round its leader.
Tempers became so strained that an open clash was inevitable. It
occurred in August 1856 at the half-yearly election of directors.

The three men chosen by the Assembly were anti-Cabet, and the Cabet faction refused to recognise them. This was the signal for the beginning of the most bitter struggle in the history of community disputes.

It began with vigorous speeches, an occasional private brawl, many printed polemics. It worked up to tirades of denunciation, constant physical violence in the streets, and floods of libellous and hysterical propaganda. Eventually the civil authorities arrived to restore order, installing the new directors by force. Not, however, without determined resistance from the Cabet faction. Cabet himself, leaning out of his study window, incited his supporters to capture the assembly hall. In the rough-house that followed, there were many casualties, crockery was smashed, and the Cabetiste schoolmistress was 'seized by the hair, knocked over by a blow in the back ... and dragged outside, while the girls in the school cried and sobbed'.

With the installation of the anti-Cabet directors, the Cabet faction rented a separate building, ceased work, and petitioned the State Legislature to revoke the Icarian charter. It was all in vain. The opposition was justifiably incensed at Cabet's refusal to accept the result of a democratic election, and in October Cabet was formally expelled. At the beginning of November he left, with 180 followers, and went to St. Louis, where, on November 8th, he was seized by an apoplectic fit and died, 5,000 miles from the country in which he had raised such optimistic expectations.

The Cabet party, stranded in St. Louis, decided to stay there and obtain work. This was not difficult, since most of them were skilled artisans. They lived comfortably in the city, publishing *La Revue Icarienne*, which gives an indication of their daily lives. Their children attended the public school; their adults formed evening classes for the study of the English language and met on Sundays for Christian instruction. They owned a large meeting hall, in which they organised musical and theatrical entertainments, and took in French, German, and American newspapers and periodicals. They gave up smoking.

Having rested at St. Louis for eighteen months, the majority moved to Cheltenham to set up a new community. About thirty stayed in St. Louis. They were the wise ones, for Cheltenham—about six miles away—was riddled with fever and heavily mortgaged. These incredible colonists, who seemed to pursue hardship, thrived none the less. Recognised as the only true Icarian community, they received much financial aid from France, which, together with their own industry, soon made them prosperous. With prosperity, however, came dissension. The older members believed in a dictatorial leader; the younger in democracy. The older members won, and forty younger members withdrew. Among them were the most intelligent and the most skilled craftsmen, without whom Cheltenham could not survive. Most of the remaining members withdrew—some joining the Federal Army to get money. In 1864 there were only fifteen men and women left, without funds and with foreclosure of the mortgage threatening. And this was the end of the third Icarian community.

Nauvoo had been severely shaken up by the disturbances which ended with the expulsion of Cabet and his followers. Although the total number of Icarians had doubled during the brief period of prosperity at Nauvoo, the loss of 180 threw their industrial system out of gear, and debts began to accumulate. They determined to move as soon as possible in order to avoid further disintegration. They had always intended to move, anyway; and had bought 3,000 acres of land in Iowa in 1852, hoping to set up a communistic society on a really grandiose scale.

Their Iowa land, near Corning, was heavily mortgaged; it was sixty miles from the Missouri River and in the midst of a wilderness. Nevertheless, they determined to concentrate their efforts at Corning, and in 1857 placed the Nauvoo property in the hands of trustees for the benefit of their creditors. The slow transfer to Iowa was completed in 1860; but three years later, scores of members had withdrawn from the apparently hopeless conditions of the new site. Only thirty-five men, women, and children were left on the immense estate, with a debt of $15,000. It looked as though the end had come at last.

It hadn't. The Civil War broke out just in time to save them. Supplies were short, prices rose, and the Icarians made money. They even made enough to pay off their mortgage, although they had to give up two-thirds of their land to help them do so. Living in primitive huts, short of food and clothing, they worked like slaves. The utopian mirage kept them going—kept them going until it seemed that it might not be a mirage after all. They built a dining-hall and assembly room, mills and workshops; they bought more land, imported Percheron horses, and were soon supplying livestock to the neighbourhood. The number of members almost doubled; and further accommodation was provided. When a nearby railroad was completed, their prosperity was assured, and for the first time in ten years they were able to relax a little and enjoy themselves. Hinds, who visited this community in 1876, described it in a letter to *The American Socialist*:

A dozen small white cottages arranged on the sides of a parallelogram; a larger central building, containing a unitary kitchen and a common dining-hall, which is also used as an assembly-room and for community amusements, including an occasional dance or theatrical presentation; a unitary bake-room and laundry near at hand; numerous log-cabins, also within easy reach of the central building—forcible reminders of the early poverty and hardships of this people; a small dairy-house near the thatched stable to the south; barns for the horses and sheep to the north; all these buildings on the bluff rising from the valley of the Nodaway river, and surrounded by the community domain of over two thousand acres of fertile land, of which seven hundred have been cultivated, and including, with some timber-land, extensive meadows and pastures, over which range 600 sheep and 140 head of cattle—the cultivated part having the present season 5 acres of potatoes, 5 acres of sorghum, 100 of wheat, 250 of corn, $1\frac{1}{2}$ of strawberries, besides vineyards, orchards, etc.; behold the present external aspects of Icaria.

At the sound of the bell all direct their footsteps to the central building; and should you enter at mealtime you would see the entire Community, now numbering seventy-five, seated at the oblong and

circular tables, as lively and sociable as French people know how to be.
Over the entrance-door you would notice in large letters the word
'Equality', and directly opposite the word 'Liberty', and at one end of
the room the suggestive '1776–1876'. You would notice also that upon
the table there is a great abundance of substantial food, but that
everything is plain.

Should you enter the same building at evening you might find most
of the members assembled, some to dance, some to converse, some
to sing their songs of equality and fraternity. Or should your call be
on a Sunday afternoon, as was my good fortune, you might hear
selections from the writings of their great apostle, Etienne Cabet, or
recitals by the young, or songs, perchance, which would stir your
socialistic enthusiasm.

When music, theatrical performances, and public readings
reappeared, so also did long debating sessions. Discussion, in fact,
of one sort and another, occupied every spare moment of their
lives, and soon resolved itself into dissension between two parties,
roughly divided between the young and the old. The pattern of
events at Nauvoo was beginning to repeat itself. The older members who had weathered all the storms of the past ten, fifteen, or
twenty years had learnt a hard lesson. They had learnt to focus
their attention on solid, tangible possessions. The mirage was forgotten, or, if remembered, remembered as a sober warning.
What they had managed to save through their trials, and what
they had acquired by sheer hard labour, they were determined
to hold. They thought—and who can blame them?—that they
deserved to be able to indulge a few private whims and fancies.

Not so the younger generation. They either did not know or
did not care about the former hardships of their fathers. Many of
them were new members who were deeply moved by the theories
of Karl Marx and his International. Several had actually belonged
to this organisation, and others had fought at the Parisian barri-
cades in 1871. These earnest young men were scandalised by the
apostasy of the older generation. They demanded that all private
possessions, valuable or worthless, should be given up to the community. The existence of private gardens and vineyards was a disgrace, encouraging vanity, enviousness (as was self-evident), and

ÉTIENNE CABET.

greed. Why were women not given equal political rights? Why was there no propaganda for communism outside the community? And why were new young members not admitted—as many as possible?

The older members refused to yield an inch. The younger party, in September 1877, demanded a formal separation. The older members refused to consider the proposal. The younger party then made application to the civil courts for the dissolution of the community. The Icarian Community, they declared, had been incorporated as a joint-stock agricultural association; in adopting communism it had plainly exceeded its chartered powers.

Judgement was given in the Adams County Court on 17th August 1878. The charter of the community was declared forfeit, on the grounds of Icaria having engaged in manufacture while registered merely as an agricultural concern. Three trustees were appointed to wind up its affairs. The younger party had won, and was jubilant—but its victory was costly; it brought neither happiness nor success to either party.

The young party made an agreement to stay on at Corning, reincorporating itself as 'The Icarian Community'. The older party (of thirty-nine members) reorganised itself under the pleasantly misleading title of 'The New Icarian Community', and, with the wisdom of years, moved to an adjacent site in order to secure an indemnity from the younger party, and to avoid paying it themselves. The Icarians failed to prosper; several of their members withdrew, and in 1883 moved to Bluxome Ranch, near Cloverdale, in California. This was a horticultural farm, which they renamed 'Icaria Speranza'. It lasted until 1887, when it was dissolved by a court decree after the prosperous members had divided their valuable land into private plots.

The New Icarians, under the presidency of M. Marchand, were content to resume their old life. Settled on the eastern part of the old Icarian estate, with an indemnity of $1,500 and eight frame houses which they removed to the new site, they had only to build a new assembly hall and start working the soil to be as comfortable as they had ever been. They made no effort to acquire new members, and although they attempted, in a desultory manner, to revive music and study-classes, the atmosphere was too apathetic to sustain any interest in such activities. The younger men drifted away. The oldest members died. By 1898 only twenty-one were left, and could not carry on. E. F. Bettannier, the last President, was appointed receiver, and each member was given a fair share of the 1,000-acre domain.

Thus, after fifty years and six changes of scene, did Cabet's dream fizzle out. For sheer perseverance against every conceivable form of disadvantage, the Icarian adventure is unrivalled in community history. It was not unique in any other important respect. It is incorrect to call the Icarian community non-religious. Theirs was simply a more radical interpretation of Christ's teaching than had usually been made. Christ was regarded as the First Communist, a mortal being like other men; supernatural phenomena were not admitted; but the conception of the Deity was retained. 'We like to think of God as the father of the human race, humanity as His family, men as His children and brothers held together by brotherly love'; and although some Icarians regarded themselves as agnostics, their publications proclaimed that they should love God above all—God being taken to represent *'Justice, Bonté, l'Amour, la Vie'*.

Apart from its example of human fortitude, the Icarian community has little to recommend it. Indeed, it is doubtful if the ability to endure virtual slavery in the name of freedom is commendable in the first place. It is certainly a dangerous example to follow in these days of mass movements. On the small scale, as in Icaria, it is harmless enough to all but the immediate sufferers; and it can call forth either pity or impatience, according to the temperament of the observer. The Icarians—the last considerable community of the century—remind one, in their continually renewed agony, of the men of the *Woman in the Wilderness,* who took their misery more philosophically, but not for very different reasons. Both groups were in pursuit of an illusion —an impossible heaven, an unattainable paradise, a reluctant

Millennium. Neither of them enjoyed much happiness *en route*. Some of the communities that existed in the intervening years, did; and that is their greatest virtue. They rode on the crest of a kindly wave—but when that wave broke against the hard bulwark of industrialisation, the golden age of communities was over. None would ever again have the insouciance of Brook Farm, the innocence of Fruitlands, the fervour of the Shaker Societies, the enthusiasm of the Phalanxes, or the moral courage of Oneida. In the late nineteenth century Utopia passed into a decline.

CHAPTER TWELVE

UTOPIA IN DECLINE

And many false prophets shall rise, and shall deceive many. . . . But
he that shall endure unto the end, the same shall be saved.

Matt. xxiv.

UTOPIAN socialism and utopian communities on a large scale
could continue to exist only so long as the economic condition
of America was favourable to them. As the population increased
and the price of land rose, it became more and more difficult for
new societies to establish themselves.

A few figures will illustrate the changes that took place in the
second half of the century. In 1850 the population of the United
States was 23 million; by 1900 it had trebled. In 1850 the wealth
of the nation was about $7,000 million; in 1890 it was $65,000
million; and whereas the wealth had formerly been fairly evenly
distributed, in 1890 more than half of it was in the hands of less
than 1 per cent. of the population. In 1850 half the wealth had
been represented by land-holdings; in 1890 less than a quarter of
it came from that source.

The poor could no longer afford the initial expenses of buying
land for large settlements. They were driven into the new manufacturing centres, where, owing to the rapid growth of industry,
they at first fared well. In the last quarter of the century, however,
the supply of labour became greater than the demand for it.
Following the European pattern, a vast industrial poor was
created, with a standing unemployed population of over 1,000,000
in 1900. To meet these new conditions, many industrial labour
organisations had been evolved, based almost exclusively upon
the doctrines of Marx and other 'scientific' socialists. Between
1881 and 1894 over 14,000 labour contests had been fought,
whereas strikes and lockouts had been almost unknown in 1870.[1]

[1] *See* Hillquit's *History of Socialism in the United States* (1903).

The days of the Owens, the Saint-Simons, the Fouriers, and the Cabets were numbered. In Europe and America alike, the class war had begun in earnest, and there was no place for dreamers in the bitter struggles of a hard-pressed proletariat. Utopian communities of socialist or communist origin were no longer attempted. At the end of the century co-operative and anarchist colonies began to take their place.

Religious or quasi-religious communities continued to flourish and to be founded. They are still being founded at the present time. Yet they too, as regards the native American sects, bear the unmistakable imprint of prevailing economic conditions. Only the Hutterian Brethren, whose roots are in the Anabaptist movement of the sixteenth century, share the simple faith and integrity of the early nineteenth-century groups. The main body of the Hutterites emigrated to Canada, but some came to the United States in the same year, 1874. They now have four communities in South Dakota and one in Minnesota, with a total membership of about 500. They are remarkable for the preservation, absolutely intact, of the same communistic principles and the same primitive faith that were held by the Separatists, the Inspirationists, and other early religious communists. Unlike their closely related brethren in the Shropshire and Paraguayan Brüderhöfe, they shut themselves off completely from the outside world. They live frugal and ascetic lives, dress plainly, do not indulge in amusements, give women little or no power in their societies, do not teach history (in order to avoid mention of war and violence), and live under a patriarchal government. Although their societies co-operate to mutual advantage, each one is autonomous in temporal affairs. Spiritually, they form a single Church whose Elders meet in counçil from time to time. Monogamy is the rule, and families live in apartments in communal buildings. Common dining-halls, bakeries, and laundries lighten the housework of the women; and children are separated from their parents while attending the state-approved schools. At the age of seventeen they become full members of the community.

So far the Hutterites have hardly lost a member, while they

have gained a considerable number. Large-scale agriculture, in which they do not scorn to use the most modern machinery, ensures their financial prosperity; daily attendance at church, and the traditional customs handed down through 400 years, bind them together socially. Together with the Russian Doukhobors, who emigrated to Canada in 1899, they are an amazing anachronism; no other sects have maintained both their religious and their communistic faiths in such an unaltered form. The significance of the Hutterite way of life, preserved through centuries of persecution in Europe, becomes obvious when the late nineteenth-century and early twentieth-century religious groups of American origin are considered.

Most of these sects had weak and shallow roots. Too often—especially in this century—they were flashy, catchpenny organisations which, in spite of wishing to escape from the hectic industrialised world that nourished them, were unwilling to make a complete break with it. Many were undoubtedly sincere, though misguided: they lacked the primitive simplicity of faith, the unconquerable pioneering spirit, and the rigid moral purpose of the early settlers. Others were virtually, if not obviously, insincere: the manufacture of patent religions became as prominent an industry as the manufacture of patent medicines. Financial backing came to them only too easily from those who had made fortunes in the great industrial expansion. Modern techniques of pressure publicity and large holdings in the rising stock markets enabled some of them to grow into international organisations with churches and temples all over the world. They became part and parcel of capitalist enterprise, and were completely divorced from, if not actually opposed to, the revolutionary ideals of the earlier sects. Consequently, most of them had no use for communities; they were more interested in a large and gullible public; but a few smaller organisations of this type attempted to gather the following they needed in order to challenge the larger ones by establishing hire-purchase heavens of doubtful quality. Other religious communities—numerous, small, and short-lived—were the work of those honest eccentrics and deluded prophets who, thank heavens, have not yet disappeared from an increasingly stereotyped world.

The close-knit development of the early nineteenth-century communities is not evident in the second half of the century. Taking the communities founded after 1850 in chronological order, only three bear any relation to the earlier movement. These are the Brotherhood of the New Life, founded in 1861; the Mormon experiment at Orderville in 1874; and Albert Owen's grandiose but hopeless scheme at Topolobampo in 1886.

The Brotherhood of the New Life, founded by Thomas Lake Harris, was a spiritualist community. As such it was a late crystallisation of those elements—the Rochester rappings of the Fox sisters and the Shaker manifestations—that were rooted in early nineteenth-century revivalism; but by 1861 these rough elements had been changed. Instead of forming an accompaniment to primitive pioneering life, spiritualism was now suffused with a vague, sophisticated, mystical, semi-scientific aura of culture and refinement. It was no accident that Harris was a follower of Swedenborg, the great scientist and the equally great mystic of the eighteenth century. Mystical and esoteric doctrines, such as Theosophy and Anthroposophism, were to keep pace with the rapid development, in the late nineteenth-century, of practical science in industry.

Harris, after a brief partnership with Andrew Jackson Davis, which he broke off after the latter's exposure, started his first community as early as 1851 with the Rev. J. L. Scott. The Mountain Cove Community of Spiritualists, in Virginia, claimed to be situated in the very Garden of Eden from which Adam and Eve had been expelled. No one, it was said, had set foot in it since the Fall; angels lived there; and Scott saw words 'printed in space' informing him that he and his friends would escape death. Yet the inhabitants of the community were curiously un-angelic—it took them only two years to quarrel and part from one another. . . .

Ten years later, after some success as a poet and lecturer, Harris founded his Brotherhood at Brocton on Lake Erie, N.Y. He was joined by about sixty followers, including five clergymen, some Japanese, some American ladies of position, and Laurence Oliphant with his wife and mother. Harris began by making wine—not ordinary wine, he was careful to explain to teetotallers but wine filled with the divine breath, which rendered it innocuous. He taught that God was bisexual, and advocated celibacy in marriage, while actually holding views that were quite incompatible with celibacy; he taught a new method of respiration which would ensure immortality; and he fastened upon the considerable fortune of the Oliphants like a leech. Under the guise of a patriarchal socialism, he exacted absolute servitude from his followers, and wrote to Hinds, with a suave complacency that cannot be mistaken for mere ingenuousness, that 'in serving me these tender hearts believe they are also serving God, working for a kingdom of universal righteousness. They do not think . . . that I rule them, except as aiding to lift and direct them into a larger freedom, wisdom and purity.'

'They do not think that I rule them . . .'—the words might serve as a motto for all the latter-day 'Masters' who, with fluent speech, occult practices, and self-confident exploitation of their followers, have acquired reputations and fortunes that seldom come to the genuine religious leader. How Harris, having squeezed Oliphant nearly dry, killed the goose that laid the golden egg, Oliphant recovering some thousands of pounds on a lawsuit; how his personal magnetism even then retained the allegiance of followers who would have been shocked by his sexual views and practices; and how, when he died in 1906, they waited three months for his resurrection, is well-known. The Brotherhood of the New Life was a community devoted to the personal welfare of Harris, and merits no further consideration here.

The Mormons, those rowdy children of revivalism, had attempted a United Order (of communal living) as early as 1832, in accordance with a revelation received by Joseph Smith. But at that time individualism was too strong, and the tentative communism was replaced, within eighteen months, by the Mormon system of tithing. In 1874, however, a second United Order

created the semi-communistic settlement of Orderville. Starting
with twenty-five families, the community had a membership of
over 500 individuals within a few years. The entire property of
the members, including their clothing, was valued, and stock was
issued upon it. Thereafter personal property ceased, each member
drawing upon a common fund for all necessities. Debts and sur-
pluses were cancelled at the end of each year. The system worked
well, and se-eral smaller Mormon communities were established
—none, however, after 1885; by that time the younger members,
envious of the competitive spirit of the outside world, had
become dissatisfied. Dissension was aggravated by the high
authorities of the Mormon Church disclaiming the United Order.
The community was soon divided into individual lots, and was
finally wound up altogether at the end of the century.

Topolobampo ('Hidden Water') was conceived by Albert K.
Owen, an American engineer, who discovered on an ocean inlet
in Mexico what he thought was an ideal site for a co-operative
land colony on an enormous scale. After ten years of negotiation,
stock was issued in 1886 to about 5,000 subscribers all over the
United States and Canada. Schemes were drawn up for a city
as large as New York and for canals, railways, and other public
services. Some stockholders travelled thousands of miles to join
the 400 who toiled on the scheme for several years. Shortage of
drinking water, lack of funds, and the unsuitability of many
members for a hard pioneering life resulted in dissension and
withdrawals. Finally, the Mexican Government changed its
original concession, and the co-operative experiment could no
longer be continued. Topolobampo—as a conception—would
have appealed to Owen's namesake, or to Fourier; it was the last
project of the century on a grand scale.

There were many smaller projects. Among co-operative associations, some half-dozen founded in the 'nineties are listed by
Hinds. With the exception of *Fairhope*, Alabama (1894), and
Ruskin Commonwealth (1894-9), which for a time showed anarchist tendencies, their influence was slight. Fairhope and Ruskin

became models for the large number of co-operative ventures that were begun in the present century.

The main activity was still in the religious field. Martha McWhirter's *Woman's Commonwealth* (1876), a community of celibate women known as the Sanctified Sisters, was located first in Texas and later in Washington, D.C., where it ran a successful boarding-house. It continued into the present century. *Shalam* (1882–96), in New Mexico, was a colony for orphaned children, based upon a Bible called Oahspee, typed out by Dr. Newborough from spiritual dictation. The children were to be reared as vegetarians, total abstainers, non-swearers, and spiritualists, and were to be supported by a projected colony of adults, subject to Shalam. Why did it last as long as it did? And what has become of Jacob Beilhart's *Spirit Fruit Society*, that genuine if ingenuous little Christian Communist group founded in 1896? Or of the more suspect *Straight-Edgers* (1899),[1] whose colony grew out of 'A School of Methods for the Application of the Teachings of Jesus to Business and Society'? Where now are the survivors of *Adonai-Shomo* (1861–96), which at one time recognised as Christ's Viceregent a gentleman who was subsequently indicted by a grand jury for 'revolting practices'? No doubt the *Universal Brotherhood* (1898), with palatial buildings at Point Loma, California, still persists in one form or another, representing the William Q. Judge faction of the Theosophical Movement. So also, I suspect, does the *House of David* (1900), founded by Benjamin and Mary, inheritors of the messages delivered by Joanna Southcott, John Wroe, and James Jezreel. But—to step an inch over the threshold of this century—what has become of the *Koreshans* (1902), founded by Cyrus ('Koresh') Teed, who believed that we live on the inside of a hollow sphere which also contains, the sun, moon, planets and heavens complete? . . .

The bold, the incredible, the mad, the bad, the plausible, the mercenary—and the childishly genuine—they still exist, they still invent new variations on old themes; but they form few communities, and find greater scope in occultism and adaptations of eastern

[1] Christ was the son of a carpenter, who used a straight-edge.

mysticism than in the strict observance of primitive Christianity. Meanwhile, what has happened to the survivors from early days?

Ephrata was dissolved in 1934, but the Old Saal, built without nail or screw in 1741, still stands as a monument to Beissel. Economy was taken over by the State in 1906; but the Working Men's Institute and Library at New Harmony is still in use—a fitting memorial to Father Rapp, Robert Owen, and William Maclure. Brook Farm is an orphanage, and Fruitlands a Transcendentalist museum. Oneida is a thriving manufacturing corporation, famed for its products and noted for its interest in the welfare of its employees, but no longer a scene of bold Perfectionist experiment.

The Shakers and the Inspirationists alone survive, but the former cannot survive much longer. They began to decline in number in the second half of the last century. From a total membership of 5,000 at peak they were reduced to half that number in 1875, and the loss was accompanied by relaxation of discipline and gradual abandonment of traditional customs. Wealth, mainly vested in land and out-farms on which the Shakers employed hired labour, may also have contributed to the introduction of more liberal ideas and conventions, and to a weakening of the spiritual authority of the Church. Whatever the causes, the effects were evident: hired labour was employed more and more, even on home farms; small luxuries began to appear; and extreme religious fervour became rare. The characteristic dance rituals were slowly modified, and eventually were altogether abandoned. Instrumental music and worldly songs began to displace the earlier chants and spirituals; worldly books were allowed; pictures appeared on the walls; flowers were cultivated for their beauty and fragrance, and were used for decorative purposes; superfluous ornamentation, derived from contemporary models, began to appear in some of the Shaker furniture. Celibacy, lack of revivalism during the latter part of the nineteenth century, and the fact that about 80 per cent. of the children brought into Shaker societies were only too eager to leave them once they had learnt a trade, were the chief causes of numerical decline. By 1900 the Shakers had no more than 1,000 members; in 1940 there were less than 100 left in the four families that still survived. These good people had evidently become more of a curiosity than a living body of the faithful, although they still retained an air of inner contentment and reflected the tranquility of a past age and a secluded life.

The population of Amana, however, remains constant at about 1,400. Until 1932 it retained its original communistic form; it then became a joint-stock co-operative society, in which individual ownership is all the more successful because it is combined with a system of mutual assistance that has grown naturally and spontaneously from a traditional communism. In this $1,000,000 corporation each stockholding member makes a daily report to head office, and work is organised in such a manner as to combine the maximum of efficiency and free choice with the minimum of redundancy. Modern agricultural machinery and electric power have been adopted, but the old houses and furnishings, the old mills with their original millstones, symbolise the stability that has persisted through all constitutional and technical changes. Women and girls are now permitted to work in the mills, and children may attend the high school built in 1933. Lessons in all schools are in English five days a week, and in German on the sixth—the younger pupils are still taught old German game-songs —and in the summer vacation there is instruction in the German language. These schools are part of a social service that includes free medical attention and burial; but young men may now also attend college if they wish—at their own expense.

Agriculture is still their main activity. Besides canning fruit and exporting Westphalian-type smoked hams and German sausages all over the States, they keep large herds of Shropshire sheep on the rolling pastures between Amana and East Amana. But their woollen industry is so successful that they also buy quantities of wool from outside sources. On Sundays all work ceases, and everyone goes to church, the older women wearing the traditional bonnet and shawl, the men dressed in homespun cloth. Religion still binds the Inspirationists together; and since it does not now regard marriage as undesirable, it also ensures the continuity of the society, which will not die of celibacy, like that of the Shakers. But whether religion will continue to attract the younger generation in the face of modern progress both within and outside the society, is another matter. Many of the young men own cars and communicate freely with the outside world; and Amana is one of the star attractions in the State for thousands of tourists and sightseers, who come not only out of curiosity, but also to buy the beautifully made replicas of old German furniture and to seek out collector's treasures in the form of antique china and pewter. It would not be surprising if the community were to suffer from this form of commerce. So far, however, the peace and quiet of a departed age, and the graciousness of the inhabitants, are strongly in evidence.

The seven villages, situated only a few miles from a busy arterial highway, form an island of tranquility and represent an integrated culture in the midst of the warring individualism and the clamorous division of purpose that chacterise modern civilisation. The old two-story gabled houses with espaliers on which vines grow almost to the eaves; the simple, but beautifully furnished interiors; the gardens bright with phlox, marigolds, hollyhocks, and zinnias; the unpretentious offices, shops, and schools, almost indistinguishable from dwelling-houses; the seven-mile mill race overhung with willows and bordered with grape vines; the gently flowing river winding through meadows of hepatica and marsh-marigold; and the carefully-tended fields and pastures —all these features, now so mellow, are a living proof of what may be achieved by strong faith, simple living, unremitting industry, and communal effort.

Whether the sacrifice of individuality, amusement, and free thought was desirable or necessary is another matter, and a problem worth considering in the wider context of the successes and failures of the nineteenth-century community movement as a whole.

CHAPTER THIRTEEN

WAS IT WORTH WHILE?

Do I censure their want of foresight? Do I regret this trial?
(*See p.* 147.)

A N Y attempt to estimate the successes and failures of nineteenth-century communities must begin by asking two questions. Did these experiments prove that communism on a limited scale was a feasible proposition? Whether it was feasible or not, were the conditions of life in the average community superior to those in contemporary American society?

The answer to the first question will depend upon the reader's interpretation of communism. If he is satisfied by a social owner-ship of production, at least a partial social ownership of all pro-perty, an equitable system of distribution, and equal opportunity for all, then communism, without any doubt, flourished peace-fully and harmoniously in a number of societies for a sufficient number of years to prove its feasibility. But the reader who is particular about the social machinery, the motives, and the ulti-mate basis of communism may refuse to acknowledge that it ever proved itself in these community experiments.

The Ephratans, the Shakers, and the Inspirationists have lasted longer than 100 years; the Rappite community lasted almost 100 years; the Zoarites and Icarians, fifty or more; Bethel, Aurora, and Oneida, more than twenty-five years. With the exception of the Icarians, these were all religious groups, for whom com-munism was not an end in itself, but a means of perpetuating a religious way of life. When they became prosperous, when a leader died or went into exile, when their faith weakened, they abandoned communism and either became industrial corpora-tions or broke up their communities. All of them—Oneida in particular—employed hired labour and could not have existed without it; nor could they have existed without trading with 'the world', for none of these societies was entirely self-sufficient. In addition, their governments were not strictly democratic, being based upon a complete surrender of the individual will to that of a commonly accepted religious ideal embodied in a patriarchal leader or leaders; but since these leaders were usually obliged to obtain the general consent of the members before making any decisions, democracy existed in theory and could be applied whenever the members might choose to apply it. That they were usually content to accept leadership cannot be held as evidence against the constitutions of the communities. But even when this allowance has been made, some of the facts already enumerated are inconsistent with ideal communism.

Ideal democratic communism, as attempted at New Harmony and among the Icarians, was a disastrous failure in the one case and less satisfactory in the other than the communism of the religious communities. The Icarians were proud of the fact that their president 'could not sell a bushel of corn without instructions from the meeting of the people';[1] but this was communism carried to absurd lengths of formalism; and the uncommunistic behaviour of the older members was a feature unknown in the religious groups. Their leaders lived very simply and austerely, without privileges, and were often indistinguishable from ordinary members. Absolute, ideal communism was a failure. The expedient communism of the religious groups was successful.

Of the answer to the second question there can be no possible doubt. Every observer agrees that life in the successful communities was far superior to industrial or agricultural life in 'the world'. The labourers and artisans were freed from poverty and insecure dependence upon the whims and caprices of employers and stock markets. Associative effort prevented wasted energy, produced many labour-saving devices, and resulted in a higher standard of living than that of the isolated working-man. 'Their barns and

[1] Nordhoff, p. 393.

other farm buildings', wrote Nordhoff, 'are usually models for convenience, labour-saving contrivances, and arrangements for the comfort of animals. Their tillage is clean and deep; and in their orchards one always finds the best varieties of fruits. In their houses they enjoy all the comforts to which they are accustomed or which they desire, and this to a greater degree than their neighbours on the same plane of life.' They lived well, on abundant and well-cooked food—'much more wholesomely than the average farmer among their neighbours'. They were healthy, and had a remarkable record of longevity, octogenarians being common and nonagenarians by no means exceptional. They worked industriously, but not hard—partly, it must be admitted, owing to the existence of hired labour. They bought wholesale, and cut out the middleman; and often sold retail with the same effect. Their children were usually well-instructed in all that it was necessary for them to know, growing up in a stable and assured society with at least one trade to support them should they wish to leave. Women, in most cases, enjoyed equal rights with men and led lives that were ideal compared with those of their contemporaries in city or farm. Their daily chores were reduced to a minimum by group effort; they were often relieved of the individual preparation of food and, in at least one case, of the individual care of children. Their husbands were never drunk, always led regular lives, and had no wages to dissipate. Nor was the communal life dull. The variety of employment, personal interest in every aspect of the community, and the opportunity for group amusements were features unknown to, and envied by, the isolated farmer. So much so that the hotels kept at Amana, Zoar, and some of the Shaker societies were frequently used by neighbours for their pleasure as well as for business purposes. When Iowa farmers brought wool for sale to Amana, they often brought their wives and children with them for a holiday; Oregon farmers praised the opportunities for amusement that existed at Aurora; and the Icarians welcomed many visitors to their exhibitions and dances.

The advantages of living near a community were widely

recognised, and very often resulted in the increased value of adjacent land. Communities provided excellent markets, invariably honest in their dealings, scrupulous in their care of livestock, and famed for the excellence of their produce and manufactured articles. They were eagerly sought out as employers. The labourers who worked for the Shakers, the Inspirationists, and the Rappites were envied by their neighbours; and the 'outsiders' who worked for the Oneida Perfectionists were so well satisfied that they spoke highly of their employers even when public opinion was roused to denunciation of their social system. The Kentucky Shakers always had first choice of the best Negroes because they treated them well, liberating them from slavery and setting up those who became Shakers in a special community of their own.

The utilitarian outlook that brought efficiency and material success to these communities was also responsible for certain disadvantages. 'You will look in vain', says Nordhoff, 'for highly educated, refined, cultivated, or elegant men or women. They profess no exalted views of humanity or destiny; . . . they do not speak much of the Beautiful with a big B. They are utilitarians. Some do not even like flowers; some reject instrumental music. . . . Art is not known among them; mere beauty and grace are undervalued, even despised.' Solitude, either physical or mental, was also unobtainable. The safeguards of celibacy, which obliged Shakers to go about in pairs of the same sex, the system of keeping a check on the whereabouts of each person, the constant communal activities of every kind, and the practices of criticism and confession ensured, even if they were not specifically designed to encourage, lack of individual thought and action. Such disadvantages, however, did not trouble the stolid peasants and unintellectual working men who, partly on account of this very capacity for simplicity and austerity, were the most successful communists. If they had no Art with a capital A, they were excellent craftsmen; if they rejected Beauty with a big B, they were nevertheless surrounded by the beauty of the countryside, and no doubt found a spiritual beauty in their peculiar forms of worship. Intellectuals, on the other hand, found the austerity that was forced upon them by economic conditions a trial hard to bear; and if they attempted to place culture and amusement before hard work and financial security, they were almost invariably faced with disaster. This was the experience of New Harmony and of many Fourierist Phalanxes. Only Brook Farm and Oneida managed to combine work, culture, and pleasure in an harmonious manner; but life at the Farm, as Hawthorne discovered, was no picnic, and there is no telling how the experiment would have ended if it had not been cut short.

Allowing for such limitations, the success of the nine societies already mentioned cannot be denied. What were the reasons for their success? That eight of them were religious communities is an important but not a necessary condition of successful communal living. Owing final allegiance to God, implicitly obeying His representatives—who were often credited with supernatural powers—and using communism as a means to an end, it was natural that the sectarians should submit easily to order and discipline. The non-religious did not submit so easily. Many of them, such as the younger Icarians, had been rebels against civil authority before joining communities, and they were only too inclined to remain rebels against all discipline. For them communism was an end in itself, and they would not tolerate the strict moral government exercised by the religious groups. They were impatient for change; but the abolition of evil by a mere change of environment, as predicted by Owen and Fourier, never came; instead, dissension usually proved that human waywardness dies hard. The Icarians were exceptional. They alone succeeded in substituting communism for religion—but at tremendous cost in hardship and misadventure. However, they prove the truth of Nordhoff's assertion that 'a commune, to exist harmoniously, must be composed of persons who are of one mind upon some question which to them shall appear so important as to take the place of a religion, if it is not essentially religious; though it need not be fanatically held'.

If religion was not an essential condition of success, nor was the abolition of the family. The Inspirationists, the Zoarites, and the Bethel-Aurorans permitted, even if they did not encourage, marriage; and the Icarians almost enforced it. In these communities separate households were also the general rule.

One of the most important ingredients of success was frequent meetings, in which the religious or communist morale was kept at as high a pitch as possible, aided by such devices as confession and mutual criticism. Among the Shakers, the Inspirationists, and the Perfectionists such meetings were held daily, and no communities were more successful than these three. Yet the Zoarites and Bethel-Aurorans had no such system of moral discipline. . . .

In short, there is no complete recipe for success. What applies in one case, does not apply in another. Safeguards that protect one community fail to prevent disaster elsewhere, while a society with hardly any safeguards at all survives unscathed. It is a matter partly of racial temperament, partly of prudence, partly of trust, partly of strong faith; but in communities, no less than in other societies, success or failure depends ultimately upon chance or a complex concatenation of events.

It is certain, however, that there must be some fundamental belief to which all members subscribe—a belief capable of sustaining them in all crises and uniting them in spite of minor dissensions; and that this belief, if it is not already so embedded in the personalities of each individual as to need no evocation or encouragement, must be ritualised until it provides a sanction for all conduct. To ensure that this solidarity shall be maintained, a very careful system of admission must be devised; and to ensure that there shall be solidarity to maintain, previous acquaintance of the founder-members is essential. Nothing could provoke disruption more speedily than the foolhardy calling together of a heterogeneous collection of individuals with little in common but a vague desire for community life—as Owen proved at New Harmony and many of the Phalanxes substantiated.

The idlers and ne'er-do-wells of New Harmony have no place in a community knit together by the morality implicit in a common belief. Public opinion forces them out of the society; and therein lies the final justification and safeguard of all communities. Those who do not wish to subscribe to the rules and regulations are free to leave at any time. If they do not choose to leave, they may find themselves expelled; and it must be laid to the credit of all communities, that no member was ever sent into the world without money to give him a new start in life.

The community experiment was certainly worth while. The lowest possible estimate must admit that it was harmless, alike to the nation, the State, and the individual. This cannot be said of violent revolutions, or even of the militant working class organisations. If they achieved better conditions for the working-class, they did so at the cost of bloodshed—which brought violent reaction—or of the independence of the worker. Whatever benefits it may have brought with it, the trade union movement has taught the worker to expect a master. It has not taught him to take control into his own hands, or to co-operate independently of the central government. By perpetuating a traditional slave-mentality, it is in danger of producing a body of negative and irresponsible men, in whom true self-reliance is supplanted by allegiance to a machine for inflating those very desires and appetites which the working man finds obnoxious in the rich. This acquisition of a whole set of false values and material follies is very natural and very understandable after the centuries of deprivation and oppression; but it is not admirable. It perpetuates the existing lack of interest in work, and accentuates the exclusive interest in hours and money.

Communities, on the other hand, produced a high standard of living and workmanship, were pioneers in Negro and feminine emancipation, in democratic government, in eugenics, in the primitive psycho-analysis of mutual criticism, and in education and social reform. They were a benefit to their neighbours and also to the nation; and they showed by example that associative effort of this type can be highly satisfactory. It is well for us that these examples exist, with all their faults and follies; for whether we like the idea or not, it is always possible that necessity may force such a life upon us. If so, we should be grateful for this fund of experience. It may prove to be invaluable.

'I do not even consider it unlikely', concludes Professor Gide,[1] 'that either this century or next these communitarian associations —or integral co-operative societies, if you like—may occupy as large a place in the world as the religious communities did in the Middle Ages.'

Certainly, if centralisation were to break down or become intolerable, or if a devastating war were to destroy national organisation, some such movement might well be expected.

Meanwhile communities still exist, and are still in process of formation.

[1] At the end of his book, *Communist and Co-operative Colonies*.

THE IDEA PERSISTS

Not in Utopia—subterranean fields—
Or some secreted island, Heaven knows where!
But in the very world, which is the world
Of all of us. . . .

Wordsworth

IDEAL communities have always been formed by minority movements. When socialism and communism became the orthodox churches of the working-class, idealism of the community-founding type ran underground. It reappeared in the undenominational movement of co-operation and in the heresy of anarchism.

The anarchist phase in the history of communities was more or less confined to the years between 1880 and 1915, although some of the colonies founded at that time persisted beyond the latter date. Usually, the more extreme the anarchist principles, the shorter the life of the community. Such groups included *Clousden Hill* (1891–98) and *Whiteway* (founded 1898) in England; and the *Free Society of Vaux* (1903–06) and *Aiglemont* (1903–07) in France. There were also anarchist colonies elsewhere, such as *Cecilia* in Brazil; but the promise of anarchism was brighter in this respect than its ability to endure.

Co-operative schemes include both the independent and the sponsored varieties. Following the pioneer efforts of Fairhope and Ruskin Commonwealth, *New Llano* (1914–35) and *Sunrise* (1933–36) were formed, and since then many schemes have been organised both individually and under the Farm Security Administration of the United States. In Mexico the Government-sponsored *Ejido* collectives, and in Israel the *kibbutzim*—both embracing numerous communities and hundreds of members—are other examples of the enormous expansion of co-operative methods applied to resettlement of the land.

Of these organisations, the *kibbutzim* are the most vital and the most enterprising. Some of them have flourished for more than fifty years and are still thriving; others have been formed recently. It is interesting to note that these communities have been made by men and women who returned to the land of those ancient communists, the Essenes. To this satisfying completion of a historical circle may be added a similar detail which will interest those who like to follow the interweaving of personal threads in the community fabric: Laurence Oliphant, on leaving Harris's Brotherhood, went to Palestine to help found the pioneer Zionist colonies; he also married, as his second wife, the daughter of Robert Dale Owen.

The most interesting series of communities outside Israel is situated in France. These are the Communities of Work, of which there are a score or more, which were started in the first instance by Marcel Barbu in 1941. These communities include communists, socialists, anarchists, Catholics and men and women of other faiths, all of whom work together harmoniously. The first community in Valence, like its successors, was grouped about the place of work, in this case a factory. The work-place is also used as a communal centre for recreation and assemblies of all kinds. Members live in their own houses anywhere in the town; and the family, rather than the individual, is the basic unit. Several families are grouped under a district leader, and the district groups form a community. Communities, Barbu suggests, might form a community city, and the hierarchy might be extended to embrace the whole State. The fundamental principle involved in this arrangement is delegation of power from the smaller units to the larger ones, so that the State—if Barbu's system were adopted on a national scale—would possess only those powers that its members cared to give it. In this respect, the system has much in common with anarcho-syndicalism. In other respects it makes a sound modern adaptation of certain features found in earlier communities. The factory, farm, quarry, pit, or other economic enterprise about which the community is grouped serves all the purposes of the Phalanstery apart from residence. It provides a cinema, a library, a canteen, and a day-nursery; it organises lectures and theatricals; it provides sporting and educational facilities.

Obligatory change of employment for at least one week in twelve is also reminiscent of earlier community practice. What is quite new, however, is the extension of meaning given to the word 'work'. Work includes all activities that benefit the community, and payment is made for a week of about forty-seven hours, of which eight are devoted to 'obligatory sport, education, and philosophic enquiry'. Payment is based upon a points system, assessed for each individual by his associates, and rated according to his social value as well as his productive capacity. In this way, the development of the individual in every aspect is encouraged, as it is also by the frequent debates between those holding dissimilar faiths and political opinions. Diversity of faith and ideology are encouraged, since they stimulate the growth of understanding and ensure the vitality of a community that might otherwise die —like so many in the past—of self-complacency and inanition. All members, however, undertake to observe a minimum code of morality—usually generalised and fundamental—based upon those early Christian tenets which have been adopted to a greater or a lesser extent by almost all communities from the earliest times to the present day.

Strictly speaking, these communities are not of the type with which this book has been concerned. They are not entirely self-supporting and separated from 'the world'. This, however, is a pattern of living which is unlikely to persist without modification, except in special situations such as that in Israel, and even there perhaps not for very much longer. Barring special situations, which include the breakdown of communications due to war, any future that communities may have will be likely to stem from some such viable adaptation as has already been made in France— partly syndicalist, partly socialist, with an absolute respect for the individual conscience, for minorities, and for the self-development of all.

BIBLIOGRAPHY

ONE of the earliest general surveys of American communities was made by A. J. Macdonald. A Scotsman by birth and a printer by trade, he followed Owen to New Harmony, but arrived too late to participate in that short-lived enterprise. During the next two decades he compiled first-hand reports of dozens of community experiments. Macdonald died of cholera in New York about 1856. His unpublished MSS (now in the Library at Yale) were obtained by John Humphrey Noyes, who used them as the basis of his *History of American Socialisms*, published in Philadelphia in 1870 (to be reprinted by Dover in 1966). This is the most interesting survey that exists. Noyes realised the true significance of the movement, and placed it fittingly in its context of the economic and spiritual development of the nation. His judgements are always sound and most of this theories and conclusions hold good. His outlook is wide, his sympathies are generous, and his style vigorous. His book is given shape and form by his theory of national development; mere information never blurs this outline. Meanwhile, William Hepworth Dixon, the English author and traveller and Editor of the *Athenæum*, published two books which contain interesting material relating to the Shakers, Perfectionists, and other societies. These were *New America* (1867) and *Spiritual Wives* (1868), both published in London by Hurst and Blackett. Dixon's writing is discursive and his information is not always reliable; but his perception of the historical antecedents of the movements he describes is valuable.

Noyes's survey was followed five years later by Charles Nordhoff's *Communistic Societies of the United States* (New York, 1875; to be reprinted by Dover in 1966). This book includes only those communities that existed at the time it was written. Nordhoff, who had been Editor of *Harper's* and of the *New York Evening Post*, visited all the societies he describes. He conveys straightforward information, mostly reliable, though sometimes repetitive and ill-arranged. He deals in great detail with the larger religious societies. He has an appetising interest in their social life, carefully and vividly describing their songs, dances, meetings, clothes, buildings, and amusements. His book is illustrated with characteristic nineteenth-century cuts and engravings.

The Rev. Alexander Kent, in the *Bulletin* of the U.S. Department of Labour (1901), and F. A. Bushee, in *Political Science Quarterly*, Vol. XX (1905), published brief surveys, largely statistical; and Morris Hillquit's *History of Socialism in the United States* (New York and London, Funk and Wagnalls Co., 1903) devotes 125 pages to a concise description of the most important communities; but the most comprehensive of all surveys is that of William Alfred Hinds, of the Oneida Community. The second revision (1908) of his *American Communities* (Chicago, Charles H. Kerr Co.) contains detailed accounts of societies from the end of the eighteenth century to the date of publication. Most of the material is compiled from former histories and from information supplied by the communities themselves; but it is supplemented by personal impressions of communities that Hinds visited. He has little space for speculation, theory, or appreciation of the community movement in its national context. His 600 pages are devoted to fact, but have less human interest than the accounts of Noyes and Nordhoff.

The works of Noyes, Nordhoff, and Hinds were outstanding among less adequate surveys and have not really been superseded in overall inclusiveness. None of these authors was scholarly, however, and during the first half of the present century, when specialist research was done on individual communities, various errors of fact, interpretation, or unavoidable omission were revealed in the early surveys. Results of specialist scholarship were brought together in those sections of Alice Felt Tyler's *Freedom's Ferment* (Minneapolis, 1944) which deal with the communitarian movement.

This book was succeeded by *Backwoods Utopias*, by Professor A. E. Bestor, Jr. (Philadelphia, 1950). This book is likely to be definitive on the Owenite phase of communitarianism, and has set a standard in scholarship and research which will be hard to excel. The bibliography (21 pages) covers general surveys, Ephrata, Harmony, Zoar, Shakers, Owenism and New Harmony in considerable detail.

Another indispensable general work is *Socialism and American Life*, D. D. Egbert and Stow Persons, eds. (Princeton, 1952) in two substantial volumes, one of which is a detailed bibliography by T. D. Seymour Bassett. Professor Charles Gide's *Communist and Co-operative Colonies*, translated by Ernest F. Row (London, 1930) provides an engagingly sympathetic introduction to communities in general and is useful for some of the communities which come at the end of or after the period covered by this book. Professor Henrik Infield's *Co-operative Communities at Work* (New York, 1945) covers the same period more fully.

The books listed below are recommended as being the most practical or interesting. In the majority of cases they contain useful or extensive bibliographies which will enable the enquiring reader to explore further. To save space, I have given the shortest possible titles and descriptions.

INTRODUCTION

Massingham, H. J.: *The Golden Age*, London, 1927. Hose, Charles: *Natural Man, A Record from Borneo*, London, 1926. Baldry, H. C.: *Ancient Utopias*, Southampton, 1956. Diodorus Siculus: Book II, 55–60. Herodotus: Book IV, 23–27. Plutarch: *Lycurgus*. Plato: *Republic*, esp. III, 416, and V, 449–66; *Timaeus*; *Critias*. Diogenes Laërtius, Book VII, xxviii.

ESSENES. Philo Judaeus: *Quòd omnis probus liber* (§ 12–13). Josephus: *Bellum judaicum*, Book II, viii, 2. Pliny: *Historia naturalis*, Book V, 17. Burrows, Millar: *The Dead Sea Scrolls*, 1956; *More Light on the Dead Sea Scrolls*, 1958.

CATHARS, ALBIGENSES. Madaule, Jacques: *Le Drame Albigeois et le Destin Francais*, Paris, 1962. Nelli, René: *Ecritures cathares*, Paris, 1959. Oldenbourg, Zoë: *Le Bûcher de Montségur*, Paris, 1959.

WALDENSES. Jalla, Jean: *Histoire des Vaudois des Alpes*, Pignerol, 1926. Watts, George B.: *The Waldenses in the New World*, Durham, N.C., 1941.

ANABAPTISTS. Smithson, R. J.: *The Anabaptists*, London, 1935. See also the *Studies in Anabaptist and Mennonite History* of the Mennonite Historical Society, Goshen College, Goshen, Indiana.

CHAPTER ONE

LABADISTS. Birch, U. C.: *Anna van Schurman*, London, 1909. James, B. B.: *The Labadist Colony in Maryland*, Baltimore, 1899.

WOMAN IN THE WILDERNESS. Learned, Marion: *Life of Francis Daniel Pastorius*, Philadelphia, 1908. Sachse, J. F.: *The German Pietists of Provincial Pennsylvania, 1694–1708*, Philadelphia, 1895.

EPHRATA. Ernst, J. E.: *Ephrata, A History* (Penn. German Folklore Soc.), Penn. Hist. & Museum Commission, Harrisburg, 1963. Brothers Lamech and Agrippa: *Chronicon Ephratense*, Lancaster, Pa., 1889. Klein, Walter C.: *Johann Conrad Beissel*, Philadelphia, 1942. Sachse, J. F.: *The German Pietists* (as above); *The German Sectarians of Provincial Pennsylvania*, Vol. 1, *1708–1742*, and Vol. 2, *1742–1800*, Philadelphia, 1899 and 1900.

CHAPTERS TWO AND THREE

SHAKERS. Noyes. Nordhoff. Hinds. Bestor (bibliography, pp. 255–58). And note especially: MacLean, J. P.: *Bibliography of Shaker Literature*, Columbus, Ohio, 1905. Melcher, M. F.: *The Shaker Adventure*, Princeton, 1941. Andrews, E. D.: *The People Called Shakers*, New York, 1953 (Dover reprint, 1963); *The Gift to be Simple* (*Shaker songs, dances, rituals*), New York, 1940 (Dover reprint, 1962); (with Faith Andrews) *Shaker Furniture*, New Haven, 1937 (Dover reprint, 1950).

JERUSALEM. Hudson, David: *History of Jemima Wilkinson*, Geneva, N.Y., 1821. St. John, Robert P.: 'Jemima Wilkinson' in *N.Y. State Historical Association Proceedings*, Vol. xxviii, pp. 158–175 (April, 1930).

CHAPTER FOUR

JONATHAN EDWARDS, REVIVALISM, ETC. Bates, E. S.: *American Faith*, New York, 1940. Miller, Perry: *Jonathan Edwards*, New York, 1949. McNemar, R.: *The Kentucky Revival*, Cincinnati, 1807.

PANTISOCRACY. Sister Eugenia: 'Coleridge's Scheme of Pantisocracy,' in *Publications of the Modern Language Association of America*, Vol. XLV, pp. 1069–84 (December, 1930). Kelley, Maurice W.: 'Thomas Cooper and Pantisocracy,' in *Modern Language Notes*, Vol. XLV, pp. 218–20 (April, 1930). MacGillivray, J. R.: 'The Pantisocracy Scheme and its Immediate Background,' in *Studies in English by Members of University College, Toronto*, Malcolm W. Wallace, ed., Toronto, 1931.

CHAPTER FIVE

RAPPITES. Noyes. Nordhoff. Hinds. Bestor. Williams, Aaron: *The Harmony Society*, Pittsburgh, 1866. Duss, John A.: *The Harmonists, A Personal History*, Harrisburg, 1943. Knoedler, C. F.: *The Harmony Society*, New York, 1954. Arndt, Karl J. R.: *George Rapp's Harmony Society*, *1785–1847*, Philadelphia, 1965.

ZOARITES. Noyes. Nordhoff. Hinds. Bestor. Landis, George B.: 'The Society of Separatists of Zoar, Ohio,' in *American Historical Association Annual Report, 1898*, pp. 163–220. Randall, E. O.: *History of the Zoar Society*, Columbus, Ohio, 1904.

CHAPTER SIX

ST.-SIMON. Gray, Alexander: *The Socialist Tradition*, London, 1946. Manuel, F. E.: *The New World of Henri St.-Simon*, Cambridge, Mass., 1956.

FOURIER. See Chapter Eight, below.

NEW HARMONY MOVEMENT. The amount of material is voluminous, much in MS or ephemeral publications. Books dealing with the multifarious aspects of the communities and with or by the leading participants are numerous. It seems better to mention none rather than some, and to refer the reader straight to Bestor, pp. 259–68.

CHAPTER SEVEN

WARREN. Bailie, William: *Josiah Warren*, Boston, 1906. Bernard, L. L., and J.: *Origins of American Sociology*, New York, 1943. Warren, Josiah: *Equitable Commerce*, New Harmony, 1846; *True Civilization*, Boston, 1863.

HOPEDALE. Ballou, Adin: *Practical Christian Socialism*, 1854; *Autobiography*, 1896; *History of Hopedale Community*, 1897.

SKANEATELES. Noyes. Hinds. *The Social Pioneer*, Boston, 1844. *The Communitist*, Skaneateles, N.Y. (No. 1, January 1, 1844).

NORTHAMPTON ASSOCIATION. McBee, A. E.: *From Utopia to Florence*, (Smith College Studies in History, Vol. xxxii), Northampton, Mass., 1947.

BROOK FARM. There are a large number of references, but there is nothing better to start with than Swift, Lindsay: *Brook Farm*, New York, 1900, which has an extensive bibliography.

FRUITLANDS. Shepard, O.: *Pedlar's Progress: The Life of Bronson Alcott*, Boston, 1937.

CHAPTER EIGHT

Fourier, F. M. C.: *Oeuvres complètes*, Paris, 1841–48. Considérant, V. P.: *Destinée Social*, Paris, 1834–35. Brisbane, Albert: *Social Destiny of Man*, Philadelphia, 1840. Sotheran, C.: *Horace Greeley and Other*

Pioneers of American Socialism, New York, 1915. Greeley, H.: *Recollections of a Busy Life*, New York, 1868. Bestor, A. E.: 'Albert Brisbane,' in *New York History*, Vol. XXVIII, pp. 128–58 (April, 1947). Pinloche, A.: *Fourier et le socialisme*, Paris, 1933.

CHAPTER NINE

BETHEL, AURORA. Hendricks, R. J.: *Bethel and Aurora*, New York, 1933.

BISHOP HILL. Mikkelson, M. A.: *The Bishop Hill Colony*, Baltimore, 1892.

AMANA, Shambaugh, B. H. M.: *Amana*, Iowa City, 1908; *Amana That Was and Amana That Is*, Iowa City, 1932.

CHAPTER TEN

Noyes, John Humphrey: *A Treatise on the Second Coming of Christ*, Putney, Vt., 1840; *Doctrine of Salvation from Sin*, Putney, Vt., 1843; *Confessions*, Oneida, N.Y., 1849; *Male Continence*, Oneida, N.Y., 1872; *Essay on Scientific Propagation*, Oneida, N.Y., 1875. Parker, Robert A.: *A Yankee Saint*, New York, 1935. Noyes, P. B.: *My Father's House*, New York, 1937; *A Goodly Heritage*, New York, 1958. Estlake, Allan: *The Oneida Community*, New York, 1900.

CHAPTER ELEVEN

Cabet, Étienne: *Voyage en Icarie*, Paris, 1840; *Colonie Icarienne aux Etats-Unis d'Amérique, 1856*. Prudhommeaux, Jules: *Icarie et son Fondateur*, Paris, 1907. Shaw, Albert: *Icaria, A Chapter in the History of Communism*, New York, 1884. Hine, R. V.: *California's Utopian Colonies*, San Marino, Calif., 1953.

CHAPTER TWELVE

HUTTERITES. Deets, L. E.: 'Data from Utopia,' in *Sociolog*, Vol. III, No. 3, New York (Hunter College), Dec., 1940; *The Hutterites*, Gettysburg, Pa., 1939.

DOUKHOBORS. Maude, Aylmer: *A Peculiar People, The Doukhobors*, London, 1905. Wright, J. F. C.: *Slava Bohu*, New York, Toronto, 1940. Holt, Simma: *Terror in the Name of God*, Toronto, 1964.

HARRIS. Schneider, H. W., and Lawton, G.: *A Prophet and a Pilgrim*, New York, 1942.

BIBLIOGRAPHY

ORDERVILLE. Allen, E. J.: *The Second United Order among the Mormons*, New York, 1936. Hamilton, G.: 'Communism among the Mormons,' in *Quarterly J. of Economics*, Vol. XXXVII, pp. 134–74 (1922–23). McNiff, W. J.: *Heaven on Earth*, Oxford, Ohio, 1940.

TOPOLOBAMPO. Bernard, L. L., and J.: *Origins of American Sociology*, New York, 1943. Owen,.Albert K.: *Integral Co-operation*, New York, 1884.

FAIRHOPE. Gide. Bennett, H. C.: 'Fairhope—a Single-Tax Colony,' in *Collier's*, Vol. XLIX, p. 24 (Sept. 14, 1912).

RUSKIN. Broome, Isaac: *Last Days of the Ruskin Co-operative Association*, Chicago, 1902. Wayland, Julius A.: *Leaves of Life*, Girard, Kansas, 1912.

COMMUNITIES ON PAGE 218. Elucidation of some of the rhetorical questions on this page can be found in Hinds and in the following: Clark, Elmer T.: *The Small Sects in America*, Nashville, Tenn., 1937. Webber, Everett: *Escape to Utopia*, New York, 1959.

EPILOGUE

NEW LLANO. Gide. Infield. Hine, R. V.: *California's Utopian Colonies*, San Marino, Calif., 1953. Brown, R. C.: *Can We Co-operate?*, Pleasant Plains, N.Y., 1940. Young, Sid: *The Crisis in Llano Colony 1935–36*, Los Angeles, 1936.

SUNRISE. Infield.

FARM SECURITY ADMINISTRATION. Infield.

EJIDOS. Infield, *op. cit.*; and *People in Ejidos*, New York, 1954.

KIBBUTZIM. Infield, Henrik F.: *Co-operative Living in Palestine*, London, 1946. Spiro, M. E.: *Kibbutz, Venture in Utopia*, Cambridge, Mass., 1956. Darin, H.: *The Other Society*, New York, 1963.

CLOUSDEN HILL. Gide. *Labour Annual, 1896*. Armytage, W. H. G.: *Heavens Below*, London, 1961.

WHITEWAY. Armytage, *op. cit.* Shaw, Nellie: *Whiteway*, London, 1935.

CECILIA. Nettlau, Max: *Bibliographie de l'anarchie*, Brussels, 1897.

FREE SOCIETY OF VAUX. Gide. Descaves, L., and Donnay, M.: *La Clairière*, Paris, 1900.

AIGLEMONT. Gide. Henry, Fortuné: *Lettres de pioupious*, Aiglemont, 1906. Monnier, A.: *En communisme*, Aiglemont, 1905. *Le Temps* (June 11 & 13, 1905).

COMMUNITIES OF WORK. Bishop, Claire Huchet: *All Things Common*, New York, 1950. Fromm, Erich: *The Sane Society*, London, 1956.

INDEX

241

A CATALOG OF SELECTED
DOVER BOOKS
IN ALL FIELDS OF INTEREST

A CATALOG OF SELECTED DOVER
BOOKS IN ALL FIELDS OF INTEREST

100 BEST-LOVED POEMS, Edited by Philip Smith. "The Passionate Shepherd to His Love," "Shall I compare thee to a summer's day?" "Death, be not proud," "The Raven," "The Road Not Taken," plus works by Blake, Wordsworth, Byron, Shelley, Keats, many others. 96pp. 5³⁄₁₆ x 8¼.　　　　　　　　　　0-486-28553-7

100 SMALL HOUSES OF THE THIRTIES, Brown-Blodgett Company. Exterior photographs and floor plans for 100 charming structures. Illustrations of models accompanied by descriptions of interiors, color schemes, closet space, and other amenities. 200 illustrations. 112pp. 8⅜ x 11.　　　　　　　　0-486-44131-8

1000 TURN-OF-THE-CENTURY HOUSES: With Illustrations and Floor Plans, Herbert C. Chivers. Reproduced from a rare edition, this showcase of homes ranges from cottages and bungalows to sprawling mansions. Each house is meticulously illustrated and accompanied by complete floor plans. 256pp. 9⅜ x 12¼.

0-486-45596-3

101 GREAT AMERICAN POEMS, Edited by The American Poetry & Literacy Project. Rich treasury of verse from the 19th and 20th centuries includes works by Edgar Allan Poe, Robert Frost, Walt Whitman, Langston Hughes, Emily Dickinson, T. S. Eliot, other notables. 96pp. 5³⁄₁₆ x 8¼.　　　　　　0-486-40158-8

101 GREAT SAMURAI PRINTS, Utagawa Kuniyoshi. Kuniyoshi was a master of the warrior woodblock print — and these 18th-century illustrations represent the pinnacle of his craft. Full-color portraits of renowned Japanese samurais pulse with movement, passion, and remarkably fine detail. 112pp. 8⅜ x 11.　　0-486-46523-3

ABC OF BALLET, Janet Grosser. Clearly worded, abundantly illustrated little guide defines basic ballet-related terms: arabesque, battement, pas de chat, relevé, sissonne, many others. Pronunciation guide included. Excellent primer. 48pp. 4³⁄₁₆ x 5¾.

0-486-40871-X

ACCESSORIES OF DRESS: An Illustrated Encyclopedia, Katherine Lester and Bess Viola Oerke. Illustrations of hats, veils, wigs, cravats, shawls, shoes, gloves, and other accessories enhance an engaging commentary that reveals the humor and charm of the many-sided story of accessorized apparel. 644 figures and 59 plates. 608pp. 6⅛ x 9¼.

0-486-43378-1

ADVENTURES OF HUCKLEBERRY FINN, Mark Twain. Join Huck and Jim as their boyhood adventures along the Mississippi River lead them into a world of excitement, danger, and self-discovery. Humorous narrative, lyrical descriptions of the Mississippi valley, and memorable characters. 224pp. 5³⁄₁₆ x 8¼.　　0-486-28061-6

ALICE STARMORE'S BOOK OF FAIR ISLE KNITTING, Alice Starmore. A noted designer from the region of Scotland's Fair Isle explores the history and techniques of this distinctive, stranded-color knitting style and provides copious illustrated instructions for 14 original knitwear designs. 208pp. 8⅜ x 10⅞.　　0-486-47218-3

Browse over 9,000 books at www.doverpublications.com

CATALOG OF DOVER BOOKS

ALICE'S ADVENTURES IN WONDERLAND, Lewis Carroll. Beloved classic about a little girl lost in a topsy-turvy land and her encounters with the White Rabbit, March Hare, Mad Hatter, Cheshire Cat, and other delightfully improbable characters. 42 illustrations by Sir John Tenniel. 96pp. 5³⁄₁₆ x 8¼. 0-486-27543-4

AMERICA'S LIGHTHOUSES: An Illustrated History, Francis Ross Holland. Profusely illustrated fact-filled survey of American lighthouses since 1716. Over 200 stations — East, Gulf, and West coasts, Great Lakes, Hawaii, Alaska, Puerto Rico, the Virgin Islands, and the Mississippi and St. Lawrence Rivers. 240pp. 8 x 10¾. 0-486-25576-X

AN ENCYCLOPEDIA OF THE VIOLIN, Alberto Bachmann. Translated by Frederick H. Martens. Introduction by Eugene Ysaye. First published in 1925, this renowned reference remains unsurpassed as a source of essential information, from construction and evolution to repertoire and technique. Includes a glossary and 73 illustrations. 496pp. 6⅛ x 9¼. 0-486-46618-3

ANIMALS: 1,419 Copyright-Free Illustrations of Mammals, Birds, Fish, Insects, etc., Selected by Jim Harter. Selected for its visual impact and ease of use, this outstanding collection of wood engravings presents over 1,000 species of animals in extremely lifelike poses. Includes mammals, birds, reptiles, amphibians, fish, insects, and other invertebrates. 284pp. 9 x 12. 0-486-23766-4

THE ANNALS, Tacitus. Translated by Alfred John Church and William Jackson Brodribb. This vital chronicle of Imperial Rome, written by the era's great historian, spans A.D. 14-68 and paints incisive psychological portraits of major figures, from Tiberius to Nero. 416pp. 5³⁄₁₆ x 8¼. 0-486-45236-0

ANTIGONE, Sophocles. Filled with passionate speeches and sensitive probing of moral and philosophical issues, this powerful and often-performed Greek drama reveals the grim fate that befalls the children of Oedipus. Footnotes. 64pp. 5³⁄₁₆ x 8 ¼. 0-486-27804-2

ART DECO DECORATIVE PATTERNS IN FULL COLOR, Christian Stoll. Reprinted from a rare 1910 portfolio, 160 sensuous and exotic images depict a breathtaking array of florals, geometrics, and abstracts — all elegant in their stark simplicity. 64pp. 8⅜ x 11. 0-486-44862-2

THE ARTHUR RACKHAM TREASURY: 86 Full-Color Illustrations, Arthur Rackham. Selected and Edited by Jeff A. Menges. A stunning treasury of 86 full-page plates span the famed English artist's career, from *Rip Van Winkle* (1905) to masterworks such as *Undine, A Midsummer Night's Dream,* and *Wind in the Willows* (1939). 96pp. 8⅜ x 11. 0-486-44685-9

THE AUTHENTIC GILBERT & SULLIVAN SONGBOOK, W. S. Gilbert and A. S. Sullivan. The most comprehensive collection available, this songbook includes selections from every one of Gilbert and Sullivan's light operas. Ninety-two numbers are presented uncut and unedited, and in their original keys. 410pp. 9 x 12. 0-486-23482-7

THE AWAKENING, Kate Chopin. First published in 1899, this controversial novel of a New Orleans wife's search for love outside a stifling marriage shocked readers. Today, it remains a first-rate narrative with superb characterization. New introductory Note. 128pp. 5³⁄₁₆ x 8¼. 0-486-27786-0

BASIC DRAWING, Louis Priscilla. Beginning with perspective, this commonsense manual progresses to the figure in movement, light and shade, anatomy, drapery, composition, trees and landscape, and outdoor sketching. Black-and-white illustrations throughout. 128pp. 8⅜ x 11. 0-486-45815-6

Browse over 9,000 books at www.doverpublications.com

THE BATTLES THAT CHANGED HISTORY, Fletcher Pratt. Historian profiles 16 crucial conflicts, ancient to modern, that changed the course of Western civilization. Gripping accounts of battles led by Alexander the Great, Joan of Arc, Ulysses S. Grant, other commanders. 27 maps. 352pp. 5⅜ x 8½. 0-486-41129-X

BEETHOVEN'S LETTERS, Ludwig van Beethoven. Edited by Dr. A. C. Kalischer. Features 457 letters to fellow musicians, friends, greats, patrons, and literary men. Reveals musical thoughts, quirks of personality, insights, and daily events. Includes 15 plates. 410pp. 5⅜ x 8½. 0-486-22769-3

BERNICE BOBS HER HAIR AND OTHER STORIES, F. Scott Fitzgerald. This brilliant anthology includes 6 of Fitzgerald's most popular stories: "The Diamond as Big as the Ritz," the title tale, "The Offshore Pirate," "The Ice Palace," "The Jelly Bean," and "May Day." 176pp. 5⅜ x 8½. 0-486-47049-0

BESLER'S BOOK OF FLOWERS AND PLANTS: 73 Full-Color Plates from Hortus Eystettensis, 1613, Basilius Besler. Here is a selection of magnificent plates from the *Hortus Eystettensis*, which vividly illustrated and identified the plants, flowers, and trees that thrived in the legendary German garden at Eichstätt. 80pp. 8⅜ x 11. 0-486-46005-3

THE BOOK OF KELLS, Edited by Blanche Cirker. Painstakingly reproduced from a rare facsimile edition, this volume contains full-page decorations, portraits, illustrations, plus a sampling of textual leaves with exquisite calligraphy and ornamentation. 32 full-color illustrations. 32pp. 9⅜ x 12¼. 0-486-24345-1

THE BOOK OF THE CROSSBOW: With an Additional Section on Catapults and Other Siege Engines, Ralph Payne-Gallwey. Fascinating study traces history and use of crossbow as military and sporting weapon, from Middle Ages to modern times. Also covers related weapons: balistas, catapults, Turkish bows, more. Over 240 illustrations. 400pp. 7¼ x 10⅛. 0-486-28720-3

THE BUNGALOW BOOK: Floor Plans and Photos of 112 Houses, 1910, Henry L. Wilson. Here are 112 of the most popular and economic blueprints of the early 20th century — plus an illustration or photograph of each completed house. A wonderful time capsule that still offers a wealth of valuable insights. 160pp. 8⅜ x 11. 0-486-45104-6

THE CALL OF THE WILD, Jack London. A classic novel of adventure, drawn from London's own experiences as a Klondike adventurer, relating the story of a heroic dog caught in the brutal life of the Alaska Gold Rush. Note. 64pp. 5³⁄₁₆ x 8¼. 0-486-26472-6

CANDIDE, Voltaire. Edited by Francois-Marie Arouet. One of the world's great satires since its first publication in 1759. Witty, caustic skewering of romance, science, philosophy, religion, government — nearly all human ideals and institutions. 112pp. 5³⁄₁₆ x 8¼. 0-486-26689-3

CELEBRATED IN THEIR TIME: Photographic Portraits from the George Grantham Bain Collection, Edited by Amy Pastan. With an Introduction by Michael Carlebach. Remarkable portrait gallery features 112 rare images of Albert Einstein, Charlie Chaplin, the Wright Brothers, Henry Ford, and other luminaries from the worlds of politics, art, entertainment, and industry. 128pp. 8⅜ x 11. 0-486-46754-6

CHARIOTS FOR APOLLO: The NASA History of Manned Lunar Spacecraft to 1969, Courtney G. Brooks, James M. Grimwood, and Loyd S. Swenson, Jr. This illustrated history by a trio of experts is the definitive reference on the Apollo spacecraft and lunar modules. It traces the vehicles' design, development, and operation in space. More than 100 photographs and illustrations. 576pp. 6¾ x 9¼. 0-486-46756-2

Browse over 9,000 books at www.doverpublications.com

A CHRISTMAS CAROL, Charles Dickens. This engrossing tale relates Ebenezer Scrooge's ghostly journeys through Christmases past, present, and future and his ultimate transformation from a harsh and grasping old miser to a charitable and compassionate human being. 80pp. 5³⁄₁₆ x 8¼. 0-486-26865-9

COMMON SENSE, Thomas Paine. First published in January of 1776, this highly influential landmark document clearly and persuasively argued for American separation from Great Britain and paved the way for the Declaration of Independence. 64pp. 5³⁄₁₆ x 8¼. 0-486-29602-4

THE COMPLETE SHORT STORIES OF OSCAR WILDE, Oscar Wilde. Complete texts of "The Happy Prince and Other Tales," "A House of Pomegranates," "Lord Arthur Savile's Crime and Other Stories," "Poems in Prose," and "The Portrait of Mr. W. H." 208pp. 5³⁄₁₆ x 8¼. 0-486-45216-6

COMPLETE SONNETS, William Shakespeare. Over 150 exquisite poems deal with love, friendship, the tyranny of time, beauty's evanescence, death, and other themes in language of remarkable power, precision, and beauty. Glossary of archaic terms. 80pp. 5³⁄₁₆ x 8¼. 0-486-26686-9

THE COUNT OF MONTE CRISTO: Abridged Edition, Alexandre Dumas. Falsely accused of treason, Edmond Dantès is imprisoned in the bleak Chateau d'If. After a hair-raising escape, he launches an elaborate plot to extract a bitter revenge against those who betrayed him. 448pp. 5³⁄₁₆ x 8¼. 0-486-45643-9

CRAFTSMAN BUNGALOWS: Designs from the Pacific Northwest, Yoho & Merritt. This reprint of a rare catalog, showcasing the charming simplicity and cozy style of Craftsman bungalows, is filled with photos of completed homes, plus floor plans and estimated costs. An indispensable resource for architects, historians, and illustrators. 112pp. 10 x 7. 0-486-46875-5

CRAFTSMAN BUNGALOWS: 59 Homes from "The Craftsman," Edited by Gustav Stickley. Best and most attractive designs from Arts and Crafts Movement publication — 1903–1916 — includes sketches, photographs of homes, floor plans, descriptive text. 128pp. 8¼ x 11. 0-486-25829-7

CRIME AND PUNISHMENT, Fyodor Dostoyevsky. Translated by Constance Garnett. Supreme masterpiece tells the story of Raskolnikov, a student tormented by his own thoughts after he murders an old woman. Overwhelmed by guilt and terror, he confesses and goes to prison. 480pp. 5³⁄₁₆ x 8¼. 0-486-41587-2

THE DECLARATION OF INDEPENDENCE AND OTHER GREAT DOCUMENTS OF AMERICAN HISTORY: 1775-1865, Edited by John Grafton. Thirteen compelling and influential documents: Henry's "Give Me Liberty or Give Me Death," Declaration of Independence, The Constitution, Washington's First Inaugural Address, The Monroe Doctrine, The Emancipation Proclamation, Gettysburg Address, more. 64pp. 5³⁄₁₆ x 8¼. 0-486-41124-9

THE DESERT AND THE SOWN: Travels in Palestine and Syria, Gertrude Bell. "The female Lawrence of Arabia," Gertrude Bell wrote captivating, perceptive accounts of her travels in the Middle East. This intriguing narrative, accompanied by 160 photos, traces her 1905 sojourn in Lebanon, Syria, and Palestine. 368pp. 5⅜ x 8½. 0-486-46876-3

A DOLL'S HOUSE, Henrik Ibsen. Ibsen's best-known play displays his genius for realistic prose drama. An expression of women's rights, the play climaxes when the central character, Nora, rejects a smothering marriage and life in "a doll's house." 80pp. 5³⁄₁₆ x 8¼. 0-486-27062-9

Browse over 9,000 books at www.doverpublications.com

DOOMED SHIPS: Great Ocean Liner Disasters, William H. Miller, Jr. Nearly 200 photographs, many from private collections, highlight tales of some of the vessels whose pleasure cruises ended in catastrophe: the *Morro Castle, Normandie, Andrea Doria, Europa,* and many others. 128pp. 8⅞ x 11¾.   0-486-45366-9

THE DORÉ BIBLE ILLUSTRATIONS, Gustave Doré. Detailed plates from the Bible: the Creation scenes, Adam and Eve, horrifying visions of the Flood, the battle sequences with their monumental crowds, depictions of the life of Jesus, 241 plates in all. 241pp. 9 x 12.   0-486-23004-X

DRAWING DRAPERY FROM HEAD TO TOE, Cliff Young. Expert guidance on how to draw shirts, pants, skirts, gloves, hats, and coats on the human figure, including folds in relation to the body, pull and crush, action folds, creases, more. Over 200 drawings. 48pp. 8¼ x 11.   0-486-45591-2

DUBLINERS, James Joyce. A fine and accessible introduction to the work of one of the 20th century's most influential writers, this collection features 15 tales, including a masterpiece of the short-story genre, "The Dead." 160pp. 5³⁄₁₆ x 8¼.
0-486-26870-5

EASY-TO-MAKE POP-UPS, Joan Irvine. Illustrated by Barbara Reid. Dozens of wonderful ideas for three-dimensional paper fun — from holiday greeting cards with moving parts to a pop-up menagerie. Easy-to-follow, illustrated instructions for more than 30 projects. 299 black-and-white illustrations. 96pp. 8⅜ x 11.
0-486-44622-0

EASY-TO-MAKE STORYBOOK DOLLS: A "Novel" Approach to Cloth Dollmaking, Sherralyn St. Clair. Favorite fictional characters come alive in this unique beginner's dollmaking guide. Includes patterns for Pollyanna, Dorothy from *The Wonderful Wizard of Oz,* Mary of *The Secret Garden,* plus easy-to-follow instructions, 263 black-and-white illustrations, and an 8-page color insert. 112pp. 8¼ x 11.   0-486-47360-0

EINSTEIN'S ESSAYS IN SCIENCE, Albert Einstein. Speeches and essays in accessible, everyday language profile influential physicists such as Niels Bohr and Isaac Newton. They also explore areas of physics to which the author made major contributions. 128pp. 5 x 8.   0-486-47011-3

EL DORADO: Further Adventures of the Scarlet Pimpernel, Baroness Orczy. A popular sequel to *The Scarlet Pimpernel,* this suspenseful story recounts the Pimpernel's attempts to rescue the Dauphin from imprisonment during the French Revolution. An irresistible blend of intrigue, period detail, and vibrant characterizations. 352pp. 5³⁄₁₆ x 8¼.   0-486-44026-5

ELEGANT SMALL HOMES OF THE TWENTIES: 99 Designs from a Competition, Chicago Tribune. Nearly 100 designs for five- and six-room houses feature New England and Southern colonials, Normandy cottages, stately Italianate dwellings, and other fascinating snapshots of American domestic architecture of the 1920s. 112pp. 9 x 12.   0-486-46910-7

THE ELEMENTS OF STYLE: The Original Edition, William Strunk, Jr. This is the book that generations of writers have relied upon for timeless advice on grammar, diction, syntax, and other essentials. In concise terms, it identifies the principal requirements of proper style and common errors. 64pp. 5⅜ x 8½.   0-486-44798-7

THE ELUSIVE PIMPERNEL, Baroness Orczy. Robespierre's revolutionaries find their wicked schemes thwarted by the heroic Pimpernel — Sir Percival Blakeney. In this thrilling sequel, Chauvelin devises a plot to eliminate the Pimpernel and his wife. 272pp. 5³⁄₁₆ x 8¼.   0-486-45464-9

AN ENCYCLOPEDIA OF BATTLES: Accounts of Over 1,560 Battles from 1479 B.C. to the Present, David Eggenberger. Essential details of every major battle in recorded history from the first battle of Megiddo in 1479 B.C. to Grenada in 1984. List of battle maps. 99 illustrations. 544pp. 6½ x 9¼. 0-486-24913-1

ENCYCLOPEDIA OF EMBROIDERY STITCHES, INCLUDING CREWEL, Marion Nichols. Precise explanations and instructions, clearly illustrated, on how to work chain, back, cross, knotted, woven stitches, and many more — 178 in all, including Cable Outline, Whipped Satin, and Eyelet Buttonhole. Over 1400 illustrations. 219pp. 8⅜ x 11¼. 0-486-22929-7

ENTER JEEVES: 15 Early Stories, P. G. Wodehouse. Splendid collection contains first 8 stories featuring Bertie Wooster, the deliciously dim aristocrat and Jeeves, his brainy, imperturbable manservant. Also, the complete Reggie Pepper (Bertie's prototype) series. 288pp. 5⅜ x 8½. 0-486-29717-9

ERIC SLOANE'S AMERICA: Paintings in Oil, Michael Wigley. With a Foreword by Mimi Sloane. Eric Sloane's evocative oils of America's landscape and material culture shimmer with immense historical and nostalgic appeal. This original hardcover collection gathers nearly a hundred of his finest paintings, with subjects ranging from New England to the American Southwest. 128pp. 10⅝ x 9.
0-486-46525-X

ETHAN FROME, Edith Wharton. Classic story of wasted lives, set against a bleak New England background. Superbly delineated characters in a hauntingly grim tale of thwarted love. Considered by many to be Wharton's masterpiece. 96pp. 5¾₆ x 8 ¼.
0-486-26690-7

THE EVERLASTING MAN, G. K. Chesterton. Chesterton's view of Christianity — as a blend of philosophy and mythology, satisfying intellect and spirit — applies to his brilliant book, which appeals to readers' heads as well as their hearts. 288pp. 5⅜ x 8½.
0-486-46036-3

THE FIELD AND FOREST HANDY BOOK, Daniel Beard. Written by a co-founder of the Boy Scouts, this appealing guide offers illustrated instructions for building kites, birdhouses, boats, igloos, and other fun projects, plus numerous helpful tips for campers. 448pp. 5¾₆ x 8¼. 0-486-46191-2

FINDING YOUR WAY WITHOUT MAP OR COMPASS, Harold Gatty. Useful, instructive manual shows would-be explorers, hikers, bikers, scouts, sailors, and survivalists how to find their way outdoors by observing animals, weather patterns, shifting sands, and other elements of nature. 288pp. 5⅜ x 8½. 0-486-40613-X

FIRST FRENCH READER: A Beginner's Dual-Language Book, Edited and Translated by Stanley Appelbaum. This anthology introduces 50 legendary writers — Voltaire, Balzac, Baudelaire, Proust, more — through passages from *The Red and the Black, Les Misérables, Madame Bovary,* and other classics. Original French text plus English translation on facing pages. 240pp. 5⅜ x 8½. 0-486-46178-5

FIRST GERMAN READER: A Beginner's Dual-Language Book, Edited by Harry Steinhauer. Specially chosen for their power to evoke German life and culture, these short, simple readings include poems, stories, essays, and anecdotes by Goethe, Hesse, Heine, Schiller, and others. 224pp. 5⅜ x 8½. 0-486-46179-3

FIRST SPANISH READER: A Beginner's Dual-Language Book, Angel Flores. Delightful stories, other material based on works of Don Juan Manuel, Luis Taboada, Ricardo Palma, other noted writers. Complete faithful English translations on facing pages. Exercises. 176pp. 5⅜ x 8½. 0-486-25810-6

Browse over 9,000 books at www.doverpublications.com

FIVE ACRES AND INDEPENDENCE, Maurice G. Kains. Great back-to-the-land classic explains basics of self-sufficient farming. The one book to get. 95 illustrations. 397pp. 5⅜ x 8½. 0-486-20974-1

FLAGG'S SMALL HOUSES: Their Economic Design and Construction, 1922, Ernest Flagg. Although most famous for his skyscrapers, Flagg was also a proponent of the well-designed single-family dwelling. His classic treatise features innovations that save space, materials, and cost. 526 illustrations. 160pp. 9⅜ x 12¼. 0-486-45197-6

FLATLAND: A Romance of Many Dimensions, Edwin A. Abbott. Classic of science (and mathematical) fiction — charmingly illustrated by the author — describes the adventures of A. Square, a resident of Flatland, in Spaceland (three dimensions), Lineland (one dimension), and Pointland (no dimensions). 96pp. 5$\frac{3}{16}$ x 8¼. 0-486-27263-X

FRANKENSTEIN, Mary Shelley. The story of Victor Frankenstein's monstrous creation and the havoc it caused has enthralled generations of readers and inspired countless writers of horror and suspense. With the author's own 1831 introduction. 176pp. 5$\frac{3}{16}$ x 8¼. 0-486-28211-2

THE GARGOYLE BOOK: 572 Examples from Gothic Architecture, Lester Burbank Bridaham. Dispelling the conventional wisdom that French Gothic architectural flourishes were born of despair or gloom, Bridaham reveals the whimsical nature of these creations and the ingenious artisans who made them. 572 illustrations. 224pp. 8⅜ x 11. 0-486-44754-5

THE GIFT OF THE MAGI AND OTHER SHORT STORIES, O. Henry. Sixteen captivating stories by one of America's most popular storytellers. Included are such classics as "The Gift of the Magi," "The Last Leaf," and "The Ransom of Red Chief." Publisher's Note. 96pp. 5$\frac{3}{16}$ x 8¼. 0-486-27061-0

THE GOETHE TREASURY: Selected Prose and Poetry, Johann Wolfgang von Goethe. Edited, Selected, and with an Introduction by Thomas Mann. In addition to his lyric poetry, Goethe wrote travel sketches, autobiographical studies, essays, letters, and proverbs in rhyme and prose. This collection presents outstanding examples from each genre. 368pp. 5⅜ x 8½. 0-486-44780-4

GREAT EXPECTATIONS, Charles Dickens. Orphaned Pip is apprenticed to the dirty work of the forge but dreams of becoming a gentleman — and one day finds himself in possession of "great expectations." Dickens' finest novel. 400pp. 5$\frac{3}{16}$ x 8¼. 0-486-41586-4

GREAT WRITERS ON THE ART OF FICTION: From Mark Twain to Joyce Carol Oates, Edited by James Daley. An indispensable source of advice and inspiration, this anthology features essays by Henry James, Kate Chopin, Willa Cather, Sinclair Lewis, Jack London, Raymond Chandler, Raymond Carver, Eudora Welty, and Kurt Vonnegut, Jr. 192pp. 5⅜ x 8½. 0-486-45128-3

HAMLET, William Shakespeare. The quintessential Shakespearean tragedy, whose highly charged confrontations and anguished soliloquies probe depths of human feeling rarely sounded in any art. Reprinted from an authoritative British edition complete with illuminating footnotes. 128pp. 5$\frac{3}{16}$ x 8¼. 0-486-27278-8

THE HAUNTED HOUSE, Charles Dickens. A Yuletide gathering in an eerie country retreat provides the backdrop for Dickens and his friends — including Elizabeth Gaskell and Wilkie Collins — who take turns spinning supernatural yarns. 144pp. 5⅜ x 8½. 0-486-46309-5

Browse over 9,000 books at www.doverpublications.com

HEART OF DARKNESS, Joseph Conrad. Dark allegory of a journey up the Congo River and the narrator's encounter with the mysterious Mr. Kurtz. Masterly blend of adventure, character study, psychological penetration. For many, Conrad's finest, most enigmatic story. 80pp. $5\frac{3}{16}$ x $8\frac{1}{4}$. 0-486-26464-5

HENSON AT THE NORTH POLE, Matthew A. Henson. This thrilling memoir by the heroic African-American who was Peary's companion through two decades of Arctic exploration recounts a tale of danger, courage, and determination. "Fascinating and exciting." — *Commonweal.* 128pp. $5\frac{3}{8}$ x $8\frac{1}{2}$. 0-486-45472-X

HISTORIC COSTUMES AND HOW TO MAKE THEM, Mary Fernald and E. Shenton. Practical, informative guidebook shows how to create everything from short tunics worn by Saxon men in the fifth century to a lady's bustle dress of the late 1800s. 81 illustrations. 176pp. $5\frac{3}{8}$ x $8\frac{1}{2}$. 0-486-44906-8

THE HOUND OF THE BASKERVILLES, Arthur Conan Doyle. A deadly curse in the form of a legendary ferocious beast continues to claim its victims from the Baskerville family until Holmes and Watson intervene. Often called the best detective story ever written. 128pp. $5\frac{3}{16}$ x $8\frac{1}{4}$. 0-486-28214-7

THE HOUSE BEHIND THE CEDARS, Charles W. Chesnutt. Originally published in 1900, this groundbreaking novel by a distinguished African-American author recounts the drama of a brother and sister who "pass for white" during the dangerous days of Reconstruction. 208pp. $5\frac{3}{8}$ x $8\frac{1}{2}$. 0-486-46144-0

THE HUMAN FIGURE IN MOTION, Eadweard Muybridge. The 4,789 photographs in this definitive selection show the human figure — models almost all undraped — engaged in over 160 different types of action: running, climbing stairs, etc. 390pp. $7\frac{7}{8}$ x $10\frac{5}{8}$. 0-486-20204-6

THE IMPORTANCE OF BEING EARNEST, Oscar Wilde. Wilde's witty and buoyant comedy of manners, filled with some of literature's most famous epigrams, reprinted from an authoritative British edition. Considered Wilde's most perfect work. 64pp. $5\frac{3}{16}$ x $8\frac{1}{4}$. 0-486-26478-5

THE INFERNO, Dante Alighieri. Translated and with notes by Henry Wadsworth Longfellow. The first stop on Dante's famous journey from Hell to Purgatory to Paradise, this 14th-century allegorical poem blends vivid and shocking imagery with graceful lyricism. Translated by the beloved 19th-century poet, Henry Wadsworth Longfellow. 256pp. $5\frac{3}{16}$ x $8\frac{1}{4}$. 0-486-44288-8

JANE EYRE, Charlotte Brontë. Written in 1847, *Jane Eyre* tells the tale of an orphan girl's progress from the custody of cruel relatives to an oppressive boarding school and its culmination in a troubled career as a governess. 448pp. $5\frac{3}{16}$ x $8\frac{1}{4}$. 0-486-42449-9

JAPANESE WOODBLOCK FLOWER PRINTS, Tanigami Kônan. Extraordinary collection of Japanese woodblock prints by a well-known artist features 120 plates in brilliant color. Realistic images from a rare edition include daffodils, tulips, and other familiar and unusual flowers. 128pp. 11 x $8\frac{1}{4}$. 0-486-46442-3

JEWELRY MAKING AND DESIGN, Augustus F. Rose and Antonio Cirino. Professional secrets of jewelry making are revealed in a thorough, practical guide. Over 200 illustrations. 306pp. $5\frac{3}{8}$ x $8\frac{1}{2}$. 0-486-21750-7

JULIUS CAESAR, William Shakespeare. Great tragedy based on Plutarch's account of the lives of Brutus, Julius Caesar and Mark Antony. Evil plotting, ringing oratory, high tragedy with Shakespeare's incomparable insight, dramatic power. Explanatory footnotes. 96pp. $5\frac{3}{16}$ x $8\frac{1}{4}$. 0-486-26876-4

THE JUNGLE, Upton Sinclair. 1906 bestseller shockingly reveals intolerable labor practices and working conditions in the Chicago stockyards as it tells the grim story of a Slavic family that emigrates to America full of optimism but soon faces despair. 320pp. 5³⁄₁₆ x 8¼. 0-486-41923-1

THE KINGDOM OF GOD IS WITHIN YOU, Leo Tolstoy. The soul-searching book that inspired Gandhi to embrace the concept of passive resistance, Tolstoy's 1894 polemic clearly outlines a radical, well-reasoned revision of traditional Christian thinking. 352pp. 5³⁄₁₆ x 8¼. 0-486-45138-0

THE LADY OR THE TIGER?: and Other Logic Puzzles, Raymond M. Smullyan. Created by a renowned puzzle master, these whimsically themed challenges involve paradoxes about probability, time, and change; metapuzzles; and self-referentiality. Nineteen chapters advance in difficulty from relatively simple to highly complex. 1982 edition. 240pp. 5⅜ x 8½. 0-486-47027-X

LEAVES OF GRASS: The Original 1855 Edition, Walt Whitman. Whitman's immortal collection includes some of the greatest poems of modern times, including his masterpiece, "Song of Myself." Shattering standard conventions, it stands as an unabashed celebration of body and nature. 128pp. 5³⁄₁₆ x 8¼. 0-486-45676-5

LES MISÉRABLES, Victor Hugo. Translated by Charles E. Wilbour. Abridged by James K. Robinson. A convict's heroic struggle for justice and redemption plays out against a fiery backdrop of the Napoleonic wars. This edition features the excellent original translation and a sensitive abridgment. 304pp. 6⅛ x 9¼. 0-486-45789-3

LILITH: A Romance, George MacDonald. In this novel by the father of fantasy literature, a man travels through time to meet Adam and Eve and to explore humanity's fall from grace and ultimate redemption. 240pp. 5⅜ x 8½. 0-486-46818-6

THE LOST LANGUAGE OF SYMBOLISM, Harold Bayley. This remarkable book reveals the hidden meaning behind familiar images and words, from the origins of Santa Claus to the fleur-de-lys, drawing from mythology, folklore, religious texts, and fairy tales. 1,418 illustrations. 784pp. 5⅜ x 8½. 0-486-44787-1

MACBETH, William Shakespeare. A Scottish nobleman murders the king in order to succeed to the throne. Tortured by his conscience and fearful of discovery, he becomes tangled in a web of treachery and deceit that ultimately spells his doom. 96pp. 5³⁄₁₆ x 8¼. 0-486-27802-6

MAKING AUTHENTIC CRAFTSMAN FURNITURE: Instructions and Plans for 62 Projects, Gustav Stickley. Make authentic reproductions of handsome, functional, durable furniture: tables, chairs, wall cabinets, desks, a hall tree, and more. Construction plans with drawings, schematics, dimensions, and lumber specs reprinted from 1900s *The Craftsman* magazine. 128pp. 8⅛ x 11. 0-486-25000-8

MATHEMATICS FOR THE NONMATHEMATICIAN, Morris Kline. Erudite and entertaining overview follows development of mathematics from ancient Greeks to present. Topics include logic and mathematics, the fundamental concept, differential calculus, probability theory, much more. Exercises and problems. 641pp. 5⅜ x 8½. 0-486-24823-2

MEMOIRS OF AN ARABIAN PRINCESS FROM ZANZIBAR, Emily Ruete. This 19th-century autobiography offers a rare inside look at the society surrounding a sultan's palace. A real-life princess in exile recalls her vanished world of harems, slave trading, and court intrigues. 288pp. 5⅜ x 8½. 0-486-47121-7

THE METAMORPHOSIS AND OTHER STORIES, Franz Kafka. Excellent new English translations of title story (considered by many critics Kafka's most perfect work), plus "The Judgment," "In the Penal Colony," "A Country Doctor," and "A Report to an Academy." Note. 96pp. 5³⁄₁₆ x 8¼.   0-486-29030-1

MICROSCOPIC ART FORMS FROM THE PLANT WORLD, R. Anheisser. From undulating curves to complex geometrics, a world of fascinating images abound in this classic, illustrated survey of microscopic plants. Features 400 detailed illustrations of nature's minute but magnificent handiwork. The accompanying CD-ROM includes all of the images in the book. 128pp. 9 x 9.   0-486-46013-4

A MIDSUMMER NIGHT'S DREAM, William Shakespeare. Among the most popular of Shakespeare's comedies, this enchanting play humorously celebrates the vagaries of love as it focuses upon the intertwined romances of several pairs of lovers. Explanatory footnotes. 80pp. 5³⁄₁₆ x 8¼.   0-486-27067-X

THE MONEY CHANGERS, Upton Sinclair. Originally published in 1908, this cautionary novel from the author of *The Jungle* explores corruption within the American system as a group of power brokers joins forces for personal gain, triggering a crash on Wall Street. 192pp. 5⅜ x 8½.   0-486-46917-4

THE MOST POPULAR HOMES OF THE TWENTIES, William A. Radford. With a New Introduction by Daniel D. Reiff. Based on a rare 1925 catalog, this architectural showcase features floor plans, construction details, and photos of 26 homes, plus articles on entrances, porches, garages, and more. 250 illustrations, 21 color plates. 176pp. 8⅜ x 11.   0-486-47028-8

MY 66 YEARS IN THE BIG LEAGUES, Connie Mack. With a New Introduction by Rich Westcott. A Founding Father of modern baseball, Mack holds the record for most wins — and losses — by a major league manager. Enhanced by 70 photographs, his warmhearted autobiography is populated by many legends of the game. 288pp. 5⅜ x 8½.   0-486-47184-5

NARRATIVE OF THE LIFE OF FREDERICK DOUGLASS, Frederick Douglass. Douglass's graphic depictions of slavery, harrowing escape to freedom, and life as a newspaper editor, eloquent orator, and impassioned abolitionist. 96pp. 5³⁄₁₆ x 8¼.
                         0-486-28499-9

THE NIGHTLESS CITY: Geisha and Courtesan Life in Old Tokyo, J. E. de Becker. This unsurpassed study from 100 years ago ventured into Tokyo's red-light district to survey geisha and courtesan life and offer meticulous descriptions of training, dress, social hierarchy, and erotic practices. 49 black-and-white illustrations; 2 maps. 496pp. 5⅜ x 8½.   0-486-45563-7

THE ODYSSEY, Homer. Excellent prose translation of ancient epic recounts adventures of the homeward-bound Odysseus. Fantastic cast of gods, giants, cannibals, sirens, other supernatural creatures — true classic of Western literature. 256pp. 5³⁄₁₆ x 8¼.
                         0-486-40654-7

OEDIPUS REX, Sophocles. Landmark of Western drama concerns the catastrophe that ensues when King Oedipus discovers he has inadvertently killed his father and married his mother. Masterly construction, dramatic irony. Explanatory footnotes. 64pp. 5³⁄₁₆ x 8¼.   0-486-26877-2

ONCE UPON A TIME: The Way America Was, Eric Sloane. Nostalgic text and drawings brim with gentle philosophies and descriptions of how we used to live — self-sufficiently — on the land, in homes, and among the things built by hand. 44 line illustrations. 64pp. 8⅜ x 11.   0-486-44411-2

ONE OF OURS, Willa Cather. The Pulitzer Prize–winning novel about a young Nebraskan looking for something to believe in. Alienated from his parents, rejected by his wife, he finds his destiny on the bloody battlefields of World War I. 352pp. 5³⁄₁₆ x 8¼.   0-486-45599-8

ORIGAMI YOU CAN USE: 27 Practical Projects, Rick Beech. Origami models can be more than decorative, and this unique volume shows how! The 27 practical projects include a CD case, frame, napkin ring, and dish. Easy instructions feature 400 two-color illustrations. 96pp. 8¼ x 11.   0-486-47057-1

OTHELLO, William Shakespeare. Towering tragedy tells the story of a Moorish general who earns the enmity of his ensign Iago when he passes him over for a promotion. Masterly portrait of an archvillain. Explanatory footnotes. 112pp. 5³⁄₁₆ x 8¼.
0-486-29097-2

PARADISE LOST, John Milton. Notes by John A. Himes. First published in 1667, *Paradise Lost* ranks among the greatest of English literature's epic poems. It's a sublime retelling of Adam and Eve's fall from grace and expulsion from Eden. Notes by John A. Himes. 480pp. 5³⁄₁₆ x 8¼.   0-486-44287-X

PASSING, Nella Larsen. Married to a successful physician and prominently ensconced in society, Irene Redfield leads a charmed existence — until a chance encounter with a childhood friend who has been "passing for white." 112pp. 5⅜ x 8½. 0-486-43713-2

PERSPECTIVE DRAWING FOR BEGINNERS, Len A. Doust. Doust carefully explains the roles of lines, boxes, and circles, and shows how visualizing shapes and forms can be used in accurate depictions of perspective. One of the most concise introductions available. 33 illustrations. 64pp. 5⅜ x 8½.   0-486-45149-6

PERSPECTIVE MADE EASY, Ernest R. Norling. Perspective is easy; yet, surprisingly few artists know the simple rules that make it so. Remedy that situation with this simple, step-by-step book, the first devoted entirely to the topic. 256 illustrations. 224pp. 5⅜ x 8½.   0-486-40473-0

THE PICTURE OF DORIAN GRAY, Oscar Wilde. Celebrated novel involves a handsome young Londoner who sinks into a life of depravity. His body retains perfect youth and vigor while his recent portrait reflects the ravages of his crime and sensuality. 176pp. 5³⁄₁₆ x 8¼.   0-486-27807-7

PRIDE AND PREJUDICE, Jane Austen. One of the most universally loved and admired English novels, an effervescent tale of rural romance transformed by Jane Austen's art into a witty, shrewdly observed satire of English country life. 272pp. 5³⁄₁₆ x 8¼.
0-486-28473-5

THE PRINCE, Niccolò Machiavelli. Classic, Renaissance-era guide to acquiring and maintaining political power. Today, nearly 500 years after it was written, this calculating prescription for autocratic rule continues to be much read and studied. 80pp. 5³⁄₁₆ x 8¼.   0-486-27274-5

QUICK SKETCHING, Carl Cheek. A perfect introduction to the technique of "quick sketching." Drawing upon an artist's immediate emotional responses, this is an extremely effective means of capturing the essential form and features of a subject. More than 100 black-and-white illustrations throughout. 48pp. 11 x 8¼.
0-486-46608-6

RANCH LIFE AND THE HUNTING TRAIL, Theodore Roosevelt. Illustrated by Frederic Remington. Beautifully illustrated by Remington, Roosevelt's celebration of the Old West recounts his adventures in the Dakota Badlands of the 1880s, from round-ups to Indian encounters to hunting bighorn sheep. 208pp. 6¼ x 9¼.   0-486-47340-6

Browse over 9,000 books at www.doverpublications.com

THE RED BADGE OF COURAGE, Stephen Crane. Amid the nightmarish chaos of a Civil War battle, a young soldier discovers courage, humility, and, perhaps, wisdom. Uncanny re-creation of actual combat. Enduring landmark of American fiction. 112pp. 5³⁄₁₆ x 8¼.   0-486-26465-3

RELATIVITY SIMPLY EXPLAINED, Martin Gardner. One of the subject's clearest, most entertaining introductions offers lucid explanations of special and general theories of relativity, gravity, and spacetime, models of the universe, and more. 100 illustrations. 224pp. 5⅜ x 8½.   0-486-29315-7

REMBRANDT DRAWINGS: 116 Masterpieces in Original Color, Rembrandt van Rijn. This deluxe hardcover edition features drawings from throughout the Dutch master's prolific career. Informative captions accompany these beautifully reproduced landscapes, biblical vignettes, figure studies, animal sketches, and portraits. 128pp. 8⅜ x 11.   0-486-46149-1

THE ROAD NOT TAKEN AND OTHER POEMS, Robert Frost. A treasury of Frost's most expressive verse. In addition to the title poem: "An Old Man's Winter Night," "In the Home Stretch," "Meeting and Passing," "Putting in the Seed," many more. All complete and unabridged. 64pp. 5³⁄₁₆ x 8¼.   0-486-27550-7

ROMEO AND JULIET, William Shakespeare. Tragic tale of star-crossed lovers, feuding families and timeless passion contains some of Shakespeare's most beautiful and lyrical love poetry. Complete, unabridged text with explanatory footnotes. 96pp. 5³⁄₁₆ x 8¼.   0-486-27557-4

SANDITON AND THE WATSONS: Austen's Unfinished Novels, Jane Austen. Two tantalizing incomplete stories revisit Austen's customary milieu of courtship and venture into new territory, amid guests at a seaside resort. Both are worth reading for pleasure and study. 112pp. 5⅜ x 8½.   0-486-45793-1

THE SCARLET LETTER, Nathaniel Hawthorne. With stark power and emotional depth, Hawthorne's masterpiece explores sin, guilt, and redemption in a story of adultery in the early days of the Massachusetts Colony. 192pp. 5³⁄₁₆ x 8¼.
                                                                0-486-28048-9

THE SEASONS OF AMERICA PAST, Eric Sloane. Seventy-five illustrations depict cider mills and presses, sleds, pumps, stump-pulling equipment, plows, and other elements of America's rural heritage. A section of old recipes and household hints adds additional color. 160pp. 8⅜ x 11.   0-486-44220-9

SELECTED CANTERBURY TALES, Geoffrey Chaucer. Delightful collection includes the General Prologue plus three of the most popular tales: "The Knight's Tale," "The Miller's Prologue and Tale," and "The Wife of Bath's Prologue and Tale." In modern English. 144pp. 5³⁄₁₆ x 8¼.   0-486-28241-4

SELECTED POEMS, Emily Dickinson. Over 100 best-known, best-loved poems by one of America's foremost poets, reprinted from authoritative early editions. No comparable edition at this price. Index of first lines. 64pp. 5³⁄₁₆ x 8¼. 0-486-26466-1

SIDDHARTHA, Hermann Hesse. Classic novel that has inspired generations of seekers. Blending Eastern mysticism and psychoanalysis, Hesse presents a strikingly original view of man and culture and the arduous process of self-discovery, reconciliation, harmony, and peace. 112pp. 5³⁄₁₆ x 8¼.   0-486-40653-9

SKETCHING OUTDOORS, Leonard Richmond. This guide offers beginners step-by-step demonstrations of how to depict clouds, trees, buildings, and other outdoor sights. Explanations of a variety of techniques include shading and constructional drawing. 48pp. 11 x 8¼.   0-486-46922-0

Browse over 9,000 books at www.doverpublications.com

SMALL HOUSES OF THE FORTIES: With Illustrations and Floor Plans, Harold E. Group. 56 floor plans and elevations of houses that originally cost less than $15,000 to build. Recommended by financial institutions of the era, they range from Colonials to Cape Cods. 144pp. 8⅜ x 11. 0-486-45598-X

SOME CHINESE GHOSTS, Lafcadio Hearn. Rooted in ancient Chinese legends, these richly atmospheric supernatural tales are recounted by an expert in Oriental lore. Their originality, power, and literary charm will captivate readers of all ages. 96pp. 5⅜ x 8½. 0-486-46306-0

SONGS FOR THE OPEN ROAD: Poems of Travel and Adventure, Edited by The American Poetry & Literacy Project. More than 80 poems by 50 American and British masters celebrate real and metaphorical journeys. Poems by Whitman, Byron, Millay, Sandburg, Langston Hughes, Emily Dickinson, Robert Frost, Shelley, Tennyson, Yeats, many others. Note. 80pp. 5³⁄₁₆ x 8¼. 0-486-40646-6

SPOON RIVER ANTHOLOGY, Edgar Lee Masters. An American poetry classic, in which former citizens of a mythical midwestern town speak touchingly from the grave of the thwarted hopes and dreams of their lives. 144pp. 5³⁄₁₆ x 8¼. 0-486-27275-3

STAR LORE: Myths, Legends, and Facts, William Tyler Olcott. Captivating retellings of the origins and histories of ancient star groups include Pegasus, Ursa Major, Pleiades, signs of the zodiac, and other constellations. "Classic." — *Sky & Telescope.* 58 illustrations. 544pp. 5⅜ x 8½. 0-486-43581-4

THE STRANGE CASE OF DR. JEKYLL AND MR. HYDE, Robert Louis Stevenson. This intriguing novel, both fantasy thriller and moral allegory, depicts the struggle of two opposing personalities — one essentially good, the other evil — for the soul of one man. 64pp. 5³⁄₁₆ x 8¼. 0-486-26688-5

SURVIVAL HANDBOOK: The Official U.S. Army Guide, Department of the Army. This special edition of the Army field manual is geared toward civilians. An essential companion for campers and all lovers of the outdoors, it constitutes the most authoritative wilderness guide. 288pp. 5³⁄₁₆ x 8¼. 0-486-46184-X

A TALE OF TWO CITIES, Charles Dickens. Against the backdrop of the French Revolution, Dickens unfolds his masterpiece of drama, adventure, and romance about a man falsely accused of treason. Excitement and derring-do in the shadow of the guillotine. 304pp. 5³⁄₁₆ x 8¼. 0-486-40651-2

TEN PLAYS, Anton Chekhov. *The Sea Gull, Uncle Vanya, The Three Sisters, The Cherry Orchard,* and *Ivanov,* plus 5 one-act comedies: *The Anniversary, An Unwilling Martyr, The Wedding, The Bear,* and *The Proposal.* 336pp. 5³⁄₁₆ x 8¼. 0-486-46560-8

THE FLYING INN, G. K. Chesterton. Hilarious romp in which pub owner Humphrey Hump and friend take to the road in a donkey cart filled with rum and cheese, inveighing against Prohibition and other "oppressive forms of modernity." 320pp. 5⅜ x 8½. 0-486-41910-X

THIRTY YEARS THAT SHOOK PHYSICS: The Story of Quantum Theory, George Gamow. Lucid, accessible introduction to the influential theory of energy and matter features careful explanations of Dirac's anti-particles, Bohr's model of the atom, and much more. Numerous drawings. 1966 edition. 240pp. 5⅜ x 8½. 0-486-24895-X

TREASURE ISLAND, Robert Louis Stevenson. Classic adventure story of a perilous sea journey, a mutiny led by the infamous Long John Silver, and a lethal scramble for buried treasure — seen through the eyes of cabin boy Jim Hawkins. 160pp. 5³⁄₁₆ x 8¼. 0-486-27559-0

CATALOG OF DOVER BOOKS

THE TRIAL, Franz Kafka. Translated by David Wyllie. From its gripping first sentence onward, this novel exemplifies the term "Kafkaesque." Its darkly humorous narrative recounts a bank clerk's entrapment in a bureaucratic maze, based on an undisclosed charge. 176pp. 5³⁄₁₆ x 8¼. 0-486-47061-X

THE TURN OF THE SCREW, Henry James. Gripping ghost story by great novelist depicts the sinister transformation of 2 innocent children into flagrant liars and hypocrites. An elegantly told tale of unspoken horror and psychological terror. 96pp. 5³⁄₁₆ x 8¼. 0-486-26684-2

UP FROM SLAVERY, Booker T. Washington. Washington (1856-1915) rose to become the most influential spokesman for African-Americans of his day. In this eloquently written book, he describes events in a remarkable life that began in bondage and culminated in worldwide recognition. 160pp. 5³⁄₁₆ x 8¼. 0-486-28738-6

VICTORIAN HOUSE DESIGNS IN AUTHENTIC FULL COLOR: 75 Plates from the "Scientific American – Architects and Builders Edition," 1885-1894, Edited by Blanche Cirker. Exquisitely detailed, exceptionally handsome designs for an enormous variety of attractive city dwellings, spacious suburban and country homes, charming "cottages" and other structures — all accompanied by perspective views and floor plans. 80pp. 9¼ x 12¼. 0-486-29438-2

VILLETTE, Charlotte Brontë. Acclaimed by Virginia Woolf as "Brontë's finest novel," this moving psychological study features a remarkably modern heroine who abandons her native England for a new life as a schoolteacher in Belgium. 480pp. 5³⁄₁₆ x 8¼. 0-486-45557-2

THE VOYAGE OUT, Virginia Woolf. A moving depiction of the thrills and confusion of youth, Woolf's acclaimed first novel traces a shipboard journey to South America for a captivating exploration of a woman's growing self-awareness. 288pp. 5³⁄₁₆ x 8¼. 0-486-45005-8

WALDEN; OR, LIFE IN THE WOODS, Henry David Thoreau. Accounts of Thoreau's daily life on the shores of Walden Pond outside Concord, Massachusetts, are interwoven with musings on the virtues of self-reliance and individual freedom, on society, government, and other topics. 224pp. 5³⁄₁₆ x 8¼. 0-486-28495-6

WILD PILGRIMAGE: A Novel in Woodcuts, Lynd Ward. Through startling engravings shaded in black and red, Ward wordlessly tells the story of a man trapped in an industrial world, struggling between the grim reality around him and the fantasies his imagination creates. 112pp. 6⅛ x 9¼. 0-486-46583-7

WILLY POGÁNY REDISCOVERED, Willy Pogány. Selected and Edited by Jeff A. Menges. More than 100 color and black-and-white Art Nouveau–style illustrations from fairy tales and adventure stories include scenes from Wagner's "Ring" cycle, The Rime of the Ancient Mariner, Gulliver's Travels, and Faust. 144pp. 8⅜ x 11. 0-486-47046-6

WOOLLY THOUGHTS: Unlock Your Creative Genius with Modular Knitting, Pat Ashforth and Steve Plummer. Here's the revolutionary way to knit — easy, fun, and foolproof! Beginners and experienced knitters need only master a single stitch to create their own designs with patchwork squares. More than 100 illustrations. 128pp. 6½ x 9¼. 0-486-46084-3

WUTHERING HEIGHTS, Emily Brontë. Somber tale of consuming passions and vengeance — played out amid the lonely English moors — recounts the turbulent and tempestuous love story of Cathy and Heathcliff. Poignant and compelling. 256pp. 5³⁄₁₆ x 8¼. 0-486-29256-8

Browse over 9,000 books at www.doverpublications.com